JACOPO SANNAZARO

A detail of Jacopo Sannazaro contained in Raphael's
Parnassus fresco from the Stanza della Segnatura, Vatican
Palace, Rome, dated 1510-1511.

WILLIAM J. KENNEDY

JACOPO SANNAZARO AND THE USES OF PASTORAL

 UNIVERSITY PRESS OF NEW ENGLAND
HANOVER AND LONDON, 1983

This book has been published with the aid of a grant from the Hull Memorial Publication Fund of Cornell University.

LIBRARY OF CONGRESS CATALOGING IN PUBLICATION DATA

Kennedy, William J. (William John), 1942–
  Jacopo Sannazaro and the uses of pastoral.

  Bibliography: p.
  Includes index.
    1. Sannazaro, Jacopo, 1458–1530—Criticism and interpretation.   2. Pastoral poetry, Italian—History and criticism.   3. Pastoral poetry, Latin (Medieval and modern)—History and criticism.   I. Title.
P Q4633. Z5 K4   1983   851'.2   83-40011
ISBN   0-87451-268-9

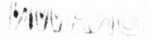

CONTENTS

PREFACE

This book is the first in English to narrate Sannazaro's life and to treat each of his works in critical fashion. Aside from books in Italian by Torraca (1879), Pèrcopo (1931), and Altamura (1951), no others attempt such an assessment. The situation is odd. On the one hand Sannazaro's Italian and Latin texts represent a high achievement in Renaissance literature; their breadth, depth, and variety deserve their own share of critical notice. On the other hand they exerted a powerful influence on the work of others for two centuries and more afterwards: Tasso, Guarini, Montemayor, Cervantes, Lope, Sidney, Spenser, Shakespeare, Belleau, Marino, d'Urfé, Milton, and countless others all profited from the alternately pastoral and epic modes of *Arcadia*, the *Piscatoriae*, and *De Partu Virginis*. For the modern student the best critical access to these works appears in ad hoc commentary supplementing studies on those other authors. This book attempts to pay Sannazaro's work its own due regard.

Naturally I come to it from a certain perspective. In my *Rhetorical Norms in Renaissance Literature* (New Haven: Yale University Press, 1978), I asserted the usefulness of understanding literary works through their strategies of voice and address. This approach can aid our comprehension of how modes, styles, and genres develop and interact in the course of literary history. Here I apply that approach to the texts of a single author. The voice of their speaker emerges quietly but persistently from the early Italian poems to the later Latin ones. The audiences that they address, moreover, are varied both internally as fictive ones within the texts and externally as historical ones in Renaissance culture; an awareness of their functions can illumi-

nate both the texts themselves and the culture that produced
them. Since I have intended this book to survey Sannazaro's
work comprehensively, however, I will not allow this approach
to overwhelm the topic. The focus is on Sannazaro's lifelong
development as an artist.

I would like to express my deepest thanks to several people
who have read, listened to, and encouraged my work on Sannazaro: first, Robert Hall, Anthony Oldcorn, and Patricia Wil-
liams; then Mario Di Cesare, Andrew Fichter, Pilar Green-
wood, James Mirollo, Ralph Nash, David Quint, Thomas P.
Roche, Jr., Peter Rudnitsky, Irma Garlick. Each has helped me
a great deal, though the errors, inconsistencies, and misinter-
pretations that remain are mine entirely.

I am also grateful to the committee of the Hull Memorial
Publication Fund of Cornell University for its generosity. The
support of my family has been finally indispensable. Since their
own names are beginning to appear in print to designate them
as writers and performing artists of some distinction, it may
be supererogatory to cite them. For the record they are Mary,
Liam, and Maura.

JACOPO SANNAZARO

INTRODUCTION

If Jacopo Sannazaro (1458-1530) did not quite rediscover the classical pastoral eclogue at the beginning of the High Renaissance in Italy, he at least put it to new and influential uses. With a few important exceptions the pastoral eclogue had lain dormant since antiquity. Sannazaro was one of the first to adapt it to the medium of vernacular poetry. In *Arcadia* (1504), moreover, he connected twelve examples of the genre with passages of prose narrative that confer a semblance of unity upon the whole text. When he later turned to the production of Latin verse, he enriched many of his epigrams, odes, and elegies with pastoral conventions. In 1526 he published his *Piscatoriae*, a series of five Latin eclogues that transpose the pastoral motifs of Arcadian shepherds to the seascape of Naples and the lives of its fishermen. That year he also published his short Latin epic, *De Partu Virginis* (On the Virgin Birth). At every turn pastoral motifs unify that epic about Christ's birth among the shepherds in Bethlehem. From first to last, therefore, Sannazaro's career may be seen as a progressive development of the possibilities of pastoral.

To Sannazaro the pastoral mode was valuable for three reasons. Firstly, because it is a hybrid mode that incorporates elements of monologue, dialogue, narrative action, philosophical reflection, satiric commentary, and a host of other forms, it integrates several varieties of genre, style, and mode. It therefore allows the young poet to test all these varieties. In this regard it has an experimental importance. Secondly, it has an archaeological importance. Because pastoral displays a long ancient history, its rediscovery led to a new understanding of antiquity. For a humanist like Sannazaro, this aspect of pastoral was at least as important as its practical literary aspect. Finally, pastoral has a philological importance. Because its language and rhetorical conventions lay embedded in ancient roots, any attempt to appropriate them entails a study of the syntax and semantics of the ancient language. It therefore invites a closer logocentric exploration of its context and allusions as a means towards understanding them more fully. Sannazaro exploited each of these experimental, archaeological, and philological aspects of pastoral by putting them to varied uses. This book studies those uses.

Sannazaro's uses of pastoral evolved over the span of a long career, and sometimes they emerge in texts whose modes were prima facie other than pastoral. Even Sannazaro's nonpastoral texts, however, would illustrate the claims of pastoral on his literary production. His Italian *Rime* provide a case in point. When they were reprinted at Venice in 1561, their celebrated editor Francesco Sansovino appended a biographical introduction that suggests how closely they reflect the experimental, archaeological, and logocentric concerns of pastoral.[1] Sansovino explained that Sannazaro wrote these poems well before the turn of the century, but that he chose not to publish them even after the success of *Arcadia*. The editor attributed his motives to sensitivity about writing in the Neapolitan dialect after the greatest authors of Italian literature—Dante, Petrarch, and Boccaccio—had elevated the Tuscan dialect to premier status for vernacular expression. Sansovino speculated that the poet had composed *Arcadia* in Italian to avoid invidious comparisons with Virgil's Latin eclogues, "il quale si può più tosto invidiar che agguagliare" (p. 322; "which he was sooner able to envy than equal"), but that afterwards he renounced Italian altogether. According to Sansovino the reason was that Cardinal Bembo in his *Prose della volgar lingua* (1525, but written and circulated much earlier) had placed too many strictures on vernacular writers by urging Tuscan as the norm of good Italian style: "ma poi che 'l Bembo con le prose cavò dalla tenebre il Petrarca, e il Boccaccio, s'avvide il Sanazzaro [*sic*] che le cose volgari non erano secondo il suo desiderio; ed egli si sdegnava di dover imparar la lingua volgare secondo il parer del Bembo" (p. 323; "but after Bembo in his *Prose* drew from the shadows both Petrarch and Boccaccio, Sannazaro realized that ordinary things did not accord with his desire; and he was irritated with being obliged to learn the vernacular language according to the judgment of Bembo). Sannazaro simply did not want to conform to Bembo's newly established rules, and thus he turned exclusively to Latin composition.

Sansovino's hypothesis is intriguing but not accurate. Indeed, Sannazaro had followed Bembo's suggestions almost to the letter when he revised his Italian texts for publication. The ultimate reasons for Sannazaro's defection from Italian to Latin may lie yet deeper. They concern not just the status of the vernacular in Sannazaro's day, but the status of Latin and the pastoral as well, which in turn depended upon certain developments in the history of the humanist movement. At a time when it had seemed to some humanists almost possible to reclaim Classical Latin as a living language, its vitality became more fugitive than ever. Sannazaro's deliberate turn to Latin may reflect less his anxieties about measuring up to a Tuscan norm in the vernacular than his ambition to capture the elusive qualities of Latin itself. Pastoral would be Sannazaro's chief vehicle to capture those qualities, and its recovery would be ultimately connected with the development of the humanist movement.

The origins of the humanist movement in the fourteenth century were fraught with optimism. Its early proponents—Petrarch (1304–74), Coluccio Salutati (1331–1406), and Leonardo Bruni (1370–1444)—felt a heady sense of being able to reassemble parts of ancient culture, piece together its fragments, and reconstitute its original language. By the mid-fifteenth century, however, their profound discoveries about that language paradoxically alerted their followers to inexorable semantic differences that separated them from antiquity. Humanist philology had come to cast deep doubts on long-accepted ideas about classical words and phrases, and even on whole texts. Moreover, increasing evidence of their haphazard transmission during the ages now called into question everything the earlier humanists had assumed about them, so that soon the most advanced sectors of the humanist movement faced the challenge of rampant skepticism. In some ways the pastoral longing for retreat may reflect the tensions generated by that skepticism.

The new skepticism manifested itself on several levels. Lorenzo Valla (1405–57) in the Prefaces to his *De Linguae Latinae Elegantia* (1444) complained that time and human history mediate our approach to antiquity so that they thwart its absolute recovery. One hears Valla's anxiety when he reflects that each generation until now has departed further from the sources and that our real knowledge of antiquity is scant: "Furthermore, many authors do not even remain in our memory. . . . One must realize . . . that no text is complete in every respect and that we are not in possession of everything."[2] Leon Battista Alberti (1404–72) had articulated a similar line of reasoning in his *Tre libri della famiglia* (1433–34); there he staunchly defended the growth of the vernacular because the ancient language had become so hopelessly contaminated that "from day to day it grew wild and corrupt."[3] Nearly half a century later Cristoforo Landino (1424–98) in his *Disputationes Camaldulenses* (1473) would cast Alberti in a role as expositor of the contemplative life and as a mouthpiece for his own thoughts about the difficulty of interpreting the ancient language. As Landino's Alberti points out, according to the etymology of the title noun, disputation characterizes all quests for an originary source. It is the art of using language in a purified way: "For *putare* (to think, estimate, clear up) is related to *purgare* (to cleanse, clean), . . . whence *disputare* (to discuss, debate), when to avoid obscurity and confusion we apply a form of reasoning whereby pure, clear, lucid language is established."[4] And yet the establishment of that language is scholarship's most difficult task. Sannazaro saw the diverse, heterogeneous textuality of pastoral as a means of achieving that language.

By the end of the fifteenth century the best minds of the Renaissance seemed to despair of appropriating the thought, words, and expressions of the ancients in their pristine state. They recognized how wrong the old language seemed on the lips of the moderns. Angelo Poliziano (1454–94), for example, argued against the slavish imitation of classical styles urged by Paolo Cortese (1469–1510): "Those who compose by imitating seem to me like parrots or magpies, uttering words that they don't understand. What they write lacks forcefulness and life; it lacks energy, emotion, and character; it lies sleeping and snoring. There's nothing true, solid, or effective about it."[5] Desiderius Erasmus (1466–1536) later made the same point in his *Ciceronianus* (1527), because "there are as many kinds of mind as there are forms of voices and the mirror will be straightway deceptive unless it give back the real image of the mind."[6] The sixteenth century fostered the continuance and exacerbation of these ideas in works by Rabelais, Vives, Melanchthon, Giordano Bruno, Montaigne, and others, far beyond pastoral.

Heightening these skeptical attitudes was the widespread dissemination of printed books that the invention of the printing press had made possible. Access to a greater number of texts led to the need for more elaborate forms of cross-referencing as well as for new ways of combining, recombining, copying, and revising.[7] At the same time successive editions of old texts with new emendations laid bare the discrepancies between different versions, motivating scholars to devise more refined techniques for editing manuscripts, collating variants, and determining their authenticity. The task of reconstituting antiquity came to seem endless, with conclusions nowhere in sight. Ironically the very advances in philology that had sharpened the humanists' awareness of language produced this result.

In this context the decline of Latin and the rise of the vernacular acquired new meaning. The humanists saw Latin not so much as a dead or dying language but as an elusive one. The growing cult of Virgilianism in poetry and Ciceronianism in prose represented strained attempts to confer stability first on

Virgil's and Cicero's texts, and then on the language as a whole. In the end these cults killed its natural growth, as Poliziano, Ermolao Barbaro, Erasmus, and others understood when they decried them as lifeless distortions of an originally vital language. At the same time the endorsement of the vernacular with its varied dialects gave rise to new problems. Bembo's endeavor to standardize the Italian literary language according to Tuscan norms paralleled developments in Latin. Although Sannazaro followed Bembo's prescriptions when he revised *Arcadia*, they must have seemed to him to encourage a myopic constriction of linguistic resources.

Sannazaro wrote in an age that, in its critical and theoretical outlook, resembled our own in many ways. Several decades before his time the science of philology had set about unravelling the mysteries of ancient texts. By the end of the century the masters of philology began to question their own assumptions. In our own century we have seen the birth and development of modern scientific linguistics. Its paradigms for the structural study of language have proved so flexible that by mid-century they became privileged models for the study of other *sciences humaines*. Since then, however, a "deconstructive" reaction has set in, whereby the task of critical method becomes a skeptical opening of questions, a departure from the closure of self-evidence, the putting into doubt of any explanatory system of differences inherent in language. It is a condition of radical skepticism that the late Renaissance knew well. If that skepticism found some thematic outlet in the topos of pastoral retreat, it found a still more powerful linguistic outlet in the heterogeneous eclecticism of pastoral style. The language of pastoral is a hybrid drawn from diverse genres, styles, and modes. It is a wholly artificial literary language as expansive as the many resources that it draws upon.

For his own time Sannazaro may have been exploring the possibilities of pastoral as a reaction against a type of "deconstructionism" in the loosest sense of the word. Quietly he explored the literary production of earlier ages in hopes of recov-

ering its pure arcadian textuality. The longer he worked with
the allusive qualities of the pastoral mode, the more he came to
feel their power to communicate intertextually. Fully to comprehend their possibilities he tried to sense how the ancients
might have perceived each word and grammatical construction
with experiences and expectations different from his own. No
modern audience can pretend to know those experiences and
expectations exactly as the ancients did, but, by examining the
repository of classical texts to which pastoral refers, one can cir-
cumscribe a fuller understanding of them in their many contexts. The coherence of these contexts is important in pastoral.
It must be understood as a coherence of meaning that wholly
transcends the individual audience's horizon of experience,
while yet permitting the audience a subjective awareness of its
significance.

With its evocation of ancient forms, pastoral is a literature of
allusion where allusion enables the author and the audience to
share their awareness of a common source.[8] It encourages modern audiences to recollect something of older authors' attitudes
towards purely linguistic signs when they appear in new contexts. In *Arcadia*, though Sannazaro wrote his text in the vernacular, the author set out to exploit this condition. There he
created a text whose levels of meaning depend upon his audience's recognition of earlier texts and traditions. Later, in the
Latin poetry of his *Piscatoriae* and *De Partu Virginis*, Sannazaro
extended this endeavor and once more he found that pastoral is
the most apt of all literary modes to gain insight into the nature
of classical antiquity. The reason for the simultaneously experimental, archaeological, and philological values of pastoral lies
in the mode's very origin.

Historically the first pastorals of Theocritus were allusive
amalgams of earlier literary achievements. Within their lyric
form they incorporated the qualities of dramatic dialogue, epic
and epyllionic narrative, epigrammatic terseness, hymnic awe,
folksong simplicity, and even philosophical rumination. When
Sannazaro began his own composition in the 1480s, he had

only an imperfect knowledge of Theocritus. The latter's *Idylls* were just then beginning to appear in Latin translation, and their complete Greek text was not published until 1495. But Sannazaro did know the work of Virgil and other Roman poets who had direct contact with Theocritus's mode and who had invested it with a capacity for self-reflexivity and topical referentiality. Sannazaro viewed his own life's work as a continuous exploration of the possibilities of pastoral—first in the poetry and prose of *Arcadia*, then in the eclogues of the *Piscatoriae*, and finally in the epic of Christ's birth among the shepherds, *De Partu Virginis*. Even in his shorter nonpastoral works—the Italian *Rime*, the "*farse*," and the Latin epigrams, odes, and elegies—he leaned heavily on the literary and topical resources of pastoral.

From one perspective Sannazaro's compositon of *Arcadia* in Italian seemed an attempt to prove that the classical tradition is alive and well and can translate into a living speech—that it can flourish in and through the vernacular, not despite it. From another perspective it seemed an attempt to prove that the vernacular itself can be enriched by contact with Latin. Sannazaro sought to enforce his point by drawing copiously upon Latinate diction and syntactical constructions. At the same time he sought to avert the threat of equating Latin only with the forms of Virgil and Cicero. When he turned from Italian to Latin in the *Piscatoriae* and *De Partu Virginis* he would acknowledge as models such diverse writers as Ovid, Calpurnius, Martial, Nemesianus, Propertius, Columella, Claudian, and Ausonius. His style in both Italian and Latin is nothing if not ample.

Sannazaro's eventual preference for Latin over Italian seemed to show that it is not hopeless to communicate in the older language, that one can revive the classical language here and now. Even in his Italian compositions he sought to achieve a fusion of the vernacular with Latin. The style of *Arcadia* proves that the vernacular can absorb the classical language. The style of the *Piscatoriae* proves a more difficult point—that classical Latin is not dead despite the rise of the vernacular, the growing negativity of classical scholarship, and the distancing effects of printing. Above all, the exquisite style of *De Partu Virginis* manifests that Latin remains a vital poetic language.

This book traces the history of these endeavors and it attempts to evaluate their merits. Chapter 1 explores Sannazaro's early career as a young humanist and the consequences of how he understood pastoral and other ancient literature for his shorter lyric poetry in Italian and Latin. Chapter 2 focuses on the Italian pastoral masterpiece of his youth, *Arcadia*. Chapter 3 studies the two Neo-Latin pastoral masterpieces of Sannazaro's maturity, the *Piscatoriae* and *De Partu Virginis*. In all these texts the experimental, archaeological, and philological values that Sannazaro perceived in pastoral emerge as constant principles guiding his art. Not only do they do this, but they also elevate it to a high level of perfection. Such are Sannazaro's uses of pastoral that they acquire for the mode a prestige lost since antiquity.

1 SANNAZARO'S HUMANISM AND HIS SHORTER POETRY

The experimental, archaeological, and philological thrust of pastoral impelled Sannazaro throughout his career both as a humanist scholar and as a powerfully creative writer in Italian and Latin. Because of his tireless experiment with the variety of genres, modes, and styles embedded in pastoral, because of his unflagging effort to recover through pastoral the archaeological remains of antiquity as the Greeks and Romans had experienced it, and because of his concern to enrich both the modern vernacular and his understanding of the ancient languages, Sannazaro represents the apex of southern Italian Renaissance humanism. In other ways he was atypical of his time and place. By the early sixteenth century in Italy, the tendency was to move away from the proving ground of Latin to the cultivation of the vernacular. Sannazaro, however, moved counter to the mainstream by dedicating himself exclusively to the composition of Latin verse after having wrought so many innovations in his native Italian.

To a large extent Sannazaro's choices reflected the particular concerns of the humanist circle at Naples. That circle had nourished him socially and intellectually since his earliest years, and in his later years he became its unrivaled leader. In the prime of his life, political turmoil interrupted the course of his work. He published his *Arcadia* in 1504 during his exile in France, though he had written most of it fifteen years earlier. At the same time he brought his *Piscatoriae* to completion and laid plans for his *De Partu Virginis*. Amidst this activity his production of shorter Italian and Latin lyrics—chiefly his Petrarchan sonnets and *canzoni* and his Neo-Latin epigrams, odes, and elegies—continued unabated.

The pastoral impulses that shaped his longer texts also inflected his shorter ones. Because pastoral entails the hybridization of diverse genres, modes, and styles, its mastery implies mastery of shorter component forms as well. Likewise the cultivation of those forms seriatim also enhances the development of pastoral. With a mind to what pastoral had taught him about shorter forms and to what these forms could teach him about pastoral, Sannazaro applied himself assiduously to his lyric production. The Petrarchan sonnet, for example, provided the perfect rhetorical frame for the pastoral language of love, and Sannazaro quickly incorporated it into his pastoral texts, even transposing its rhetorical conventions into Latin for his *Piscatoriae* and *De Partu Virginis*. The epigram, with its traditional penchant towards satiric wit, complemented pastoral's similar inclination towards satire and helped Sannazaro to sharpen his own pointed style. The fixity of the formal ode helped Sannazaro to master the stanzaic patterns of *Arcadia* and the disciplined hexameter of his Latin pastorals. The elegies offered a range of topics—autobiographical, amatory, encomiastic, political, mythological—that pastoral also treats, and they greatly expanded Sannazaro's competence in handling them.

In his shorter lyrics, therefore, Sannazaro explored the very issues of forms and content that he developed more amply in his longer pastoral eclogues and narratives. His experience with the latter contributed to his excellence in the former, and that excellence likewise honed his craft for the masterpieces of his maturity. Sannazaro's masterpieces represent a lifelong preoccupation with the pastoral, and their development illustrates both the achievement and the risk of his vocation. Sannazaro's vocation in turn typifies the aims of mid-Renaissance humanism.

THE YOUNG HUMANIST

Early in the 1480s, some time before Sannazaro's twenty-fifth birthday, the learned members of Naples's foremost literary academy admitted him to their august society.[1] No one was surprised. Ever since he could remember, Jacopo (or Iacobo) Sannazaro had enjoyed the life of letters, learning, scholarship, and poetic composition. Introduced to Latin literature by his mother, Masella di Santomango, and trained formally in it by the best teachers of Naples, he had already composed a good deal of short Latin poetry in his adolescence. He had also experimented with some composition in the vernacular dialect of his Neapolitan homeland.

The ceremony at his induction required that he adopt a new Latinate name to signal his devotion to the study of classical "humanities." Sannazaro chose "Actius Syncerus," though no one knows precisely why. Some say that "Actius" refers to the Latin *acta*, "seashore," reflecting his love for the Neapolitan seascape that he would celebrate two decades later in his *Eclogae Piscatoriae*. Others say that it derives from the Latin diminutive *-accius* sometimes affixed to his Christian name "Jacopo," implying its bearer's warm endearing qualities. Certainly "Syncerus," "sincere," seems to point to these qualities. Throughout his long life everyone agreed that that name was appropriate.

If Sannazaro's reception into the academy presaged a brilliant future, it also climaxed a period of exceptional growth. He had been born in the Kingdom of Naples on 28 July 1458, or possibly 1457, at the end of the reign of Alfonso I.[2] By happy coincidence the day itself was the feast of St. Nazarius, his family's titular patron and the poet's own favorite saint. The family received a major income from sulfur mines at Agnano and had been in the service of the Neapolitan kings since 1381. The fall of Jacopo's grandfather from favor with the last Angevin queen, Joan II, only increased the family's prestige with Alfonso I, the Aragonese king who supplanted the Angevin rulers.

In 1456 Jacopo's father, Cola, had married [Tom] Masella, the well-educated daughter of a petty nobleman from Portanova in the province of Salerno. Within two years Jacopo was born. Cola died shortly after the birth of his second son, Marcantonio, in 1462. A few years later Masella commissioned two of Naples's leading humanist scholars, Lucio Crasso and Giuniano Maio, to begin her sons' education, but by 1469 she decided to move with them back to her family's estate in Salernitano. Even at so tender an age Jacopo must have impressed his teachers, for in 1473 Giuniano Maio persuaded Masella to return to Naples to assure Jacopo a better education. She herself was fated to an early death, as Jacopo lamented in Chapter VII of his *Arcadia*. According to one account, she died on the poet's own seventeenth birthday, 1475.

Well before his mother's death, Sannazaro had come to regard the members of Naples's learned academy, the Accademia Antoniana, as more than a foster family. Its name derived from a meeting place near the Porticus Antoniana, where its founder, Antonio Beccadelli (1394–1471), directed the group's activities.[3] Born in Palermo, whence his assumed name "il Panormita" (from *Panormus*, the Latin name of the city), Beccadelli came to Naples from Pavia upon the invitation of Alfonso I to enrich its cultural life. He served the king as ambassador, secretary, and historian, and he composed a series of anecdotes, *De Dictis et Factis Alphonsi Regis Aragonum*, that supplemented his widely read collection of licentious epigrams dedicated to Cosimo de' Medici.

More importantly Beccadelli attracted to the kingdom some of the greatest minds of the era: Lorenzo Valla (1405–57) spent time there when the king himself ordered the publication of his remarkable *De Falso Credita et Ementita Constantini Donatione Declamatio* (1440), which proved through philological analysis that old papal claims to temporal power were illegitimate. Another visitor between 1452 and 1455 was the distinguished Greek émigré George Trebizond (1395–1472), who in his *Rhetoricorum Libri* V (1434) had enriched the Latin rhetorical tradition of Cicero with the long-forgotten one of Hermogenes, and who later would translate Aristotle's *Rhetoric* into Latin. Still another visitor was Giovanni Pontano.

Giovanni Pontano (1429–1503) came to Naples from his native Umbria in 1448, and he remained there for the rest of his life. Not only did he succeed Beccadelli as the acknowledged leader of the academy in 1471, but he also enjoyed the prestige of having the academy itself become known as the Accademia Pontaniana. He moreover played the role of Sannazaro's influential teacher, trusted friend, and virtual father figure. Throughout the 1480s and 90s he served as secretary to two kings, Ferrante I and Alfonso II, but he died in disgrace after having welcomed French invaders into Naples in 1495. Until the end, however, Sannazaro retained a deep affection for him.

Pontano's own literary production was enormous.[4] Proud of his acquired Neapolitan citizenship, he entitled his collection of youthful Latin poems the *Parthenopeus* (The Neapolitan), after the earliest name of the city, derived from that of its mythic foundress, the siren Parthenope. His most enduring Latin poetry records his love for his wife, Adriana, in *De Amore Coniugale* (Conjugal Love); his sorrow at the death of loved ones in *De tumulis* (Burial Mounds); a love affair with a young girl in *Eridanus*; an epic about the creation of the starry sphere, *Urania*; and a didactic poem about the cultivation of lemon trees, *De Hortu Hesperidum* (Garden of the Hesperides).

Like Beccadelli, moreover, he attracted to Naples a host of learned people. One was Michael Marullus Tarcaniota (1453–1500), a talented Byzantine poet, author of the widely admired *Epigrammata* and *Hymni Naturales*, who eventually moved in 1489 to the Medici court at Florence, but who maintained contact with Sannazaro and his other Neapolitan friends long afterwards. Still others were the Italian vernacular poets, Serafino de' Ciminelli and Benedetto Gareth. The former, born in Aquila in 1466 (whence the name by which he is more commonly known, Serafino Aquilano) was regarded at the time of his premature death in 1500 as the greatest Petrarchist of his day; he had visited Naples on many occasions under the patronage of his uncle, Guevara, Count of Potenza. Benedetto Gareth, called "il Cariteo" by his humanist friends, had been born in Barcellona in 1450, but he spent most of his life in Naples, and he accompanied Sannazaro and their king, Federigo II, into exile in France in 1501–05. In Naples he published his collection of songs and sonnets, the *Endimione*, in 1506, and he died there in 1514.

Besides these towering figures, Sannazaro's closest friends at the academy included his teachers, Lucio Crasso (ca. 1430–90), professor of poetry at the University of Naples, and Giuniano Maio (1430–93), professor of rhetoric at the university.[5] Another tutor was Pietro Compatre (1431–1501), a scholar who rose to the rank of Lieutenant of the Grand Chamberlain during the reign of Alfonso I. An elder statesman whom Sannazaro particularly respected was Tristano Caracciolo (1434–1528), historian of Ferdinand I; in *Arcadia*'s tenth eclogue he would play an important role as commentator on the political misfortunes of Naples. Still another was Gabriele Altilio (1440–1501), bishop of Policastro, who composed a brief "Life of Sannazaro" before the poet went into exile. Closer to Sannazaro in age were two brothers, Bellisario Acquaviva (1456–1528), author of a treatise on hunting, and Andrea Matteo Acquaviva (1458–1529), lieutenant general of the Neapolitan army, learned translator of Plutarch, and patron of the humanists. A close contemporary, Pietro Summonte (1463–1526), served as editor and publisher of *Arcadia* and *De Partu Virginis* as well as of Pontano's complete works (1505–12). A younger acquaintance, Antonio Garlon, Prince of Alife, served as literary executor of Sannazaro's shorter poetry after his death. The intellectual energy and personal affection binding this group of scholars left their marks on Sannazaro's own poetic development.

The quality of their influence survives in Pontano's dialogues based on conversations among the academy's members. These dialogues explore topics ranging from ethics and politics to art and aesthetics, and, because Sannazaro plays a prominent role in several of them, they usefully illuminate cultural, social, literary, and linguistic ideas sometimes attributed to him. Beneath the lively surface of their represented speech one finds the incipient skepticism that would drive Sannazaro into his pastoral refuge. The early humanist confidence in grasping classical civilization on its own terms through the nuances of its own language comes to seem less feasible as the dialogues advance. Sannazaro and other members of Pontano's circle emerge as poignant victims of the conflict between what as humanists they optimistically construed classical civilization to mean and what as men bounded by history they were sadly unable to understand.

The bases of that conflict emerge fugaciously from Pontano's dialogues amidst their celebration of the humanists' delight in making their own discoveries. Pontano composed all these texts long before their publication in 1507.[6] The titular hero of *Antonius* is Antonio Beccadelli, il Panormita, and that dialogue evokes the merriment and festivity that he conferred on gatherings at the academy until his death in 1471. The titular hero of *Actius* is Sannazaro himself, and that dialogue evokes the seriousness and sobriety of gatherings at the academy before the poet's exile in 1501. *Aegidius*, dedicated to the young Aegidius da Viterbo (1469–1532), however, takes place during Sannazaro's exile. Its tone is heavy with nostalgia and regret not only for the absence of Sannazaro and other members of the royal court but also for the recent deaths of Compatre, Altilio, and Calenzio. The accretion of somber emotional tones in the later dialogues limns the participants' crisis of faith about their ability to master the logocentric codes of antiquity.

A sense of this abatement issues with clarity from a comparison between *Antonius* and *Aegidius*. In the early dialogue Compatre recalls with fondness il Panormita's undaunted confidence in his powers to understand the greatness of Virgil's poetry: "Hoc loco rei indignitate commotum exclamare Antonium memini improbos, facinorosos, detestabiles eos dicentem Iovemque ausos regnis detrudere, quippe qui Romanae poeticae principem et quasi Deum quendam suo e regno, suo e solio pellere ac deturbare conarentur" ("Here I remember how Antonio, shaken with indignation, called them perverse, criminal, abominable, summoning Jove to dislodge from power those audacious critics who attempted to topple and eject Virgil from his power and dominion as the foremost Roman poet, quasi-divine").[7] This confidence bolsters the confidence of il Panormita's own students. At the end of the dialogue, for example, after the impressive performance of a Neo-Latin pastoral eclogue by an unnamed poet, another interlocutor, Herricus, praises the anonymous poet for having restored to the present age the pristine honor and excellence ("pristinam dignitatem excellentiamque," p. 100) of antiquity, and for leaving a standard to be imitated in the future: "Plenos voluptatis nos relinquis ac bonae spei, suavissime homo; nam quanquam multum tibi aetas debet nostra, qui ex agresti illa musica sic emerseris, debituri tamen plura multo sunt posteri, si qui te volent imitari" (pp. 99–100; "You leave us full of joy and good hope, most pleasant man, for although our age owes much to you for causing music to emerge from the pastoral mode, still those in the future will be even more indebted if they chose to imitate you"). The poet may indeed have been the young Sannazaro, and Pontano's speaker may well have been forecasting his future success. In any case, Herricus's forward-looking optimism typifies the spirit of the early Renaissance.

In the later dialogue, however, the sense of confidence in having recognized a single standard of excellence and in having laid the foundations for a sweeping restoration of antiquity is notably lacking. Puccio praises Pontano's own elegant Latin style, but he remarks that classical eloquence barely escaped oblivion and that careful stylists are still laboring to sharpen our understanding of its potentials:

Sed eloquentiae studium post Romani imperii declinationem prorsus interiit vixque grammaticae ipsius perstitere vestigia. . . . Qua quidem de causa haud ita mirum videri debet eloquentiae si defuere studia. Tamen et spes est brevi futurum ut eloquentia cum doctrina tum naturali tum divina in gratiam redeat. (p. 259)

> But after the decline of the Roman Empire, the pursuit of eloquence utterly perished and vestiges of grammar barely survived. . . . For these reasons it hardly ought to seem a wonder if studies of eloquence declined. Nevertheless our

hope is that eloquence will shortly return in the natural as well as theological sciences.

Beneath the standard topos of humanist restoration lurks the uneasy awareness that the texts of the past are not yet fully comprehended and that partial gains in knowing them have been offset by the humanists' practical inability to understand them entirely. At the end of the dialogue, Pontano himself, now more than seventy years old, expresses the wish that his successors may achieve the refinement in using Latin that eluded him, but his expression is notably more tempered, more restrained than that of Herricus in the earlier dialogue:

Itaque quanquam senem me annisque gravatum, spes tamen cepit fore ut, antequam a vobis emigrem, Latinam videam philosophiam et cultu maiore verborum et elegantia res suas explicantem utque, relicta litigatrice hac disputandi ratione, quietiorem ipsa formam accipiat et dicendi et sermocinandi ac verbis item suis utendi propriis maximeque Romanis. (p. 280)

> Thus, although I should be old and heavy in years, still I hope that before I leave you I will see Latin philosophy explicating its doctrines both with a greater refinement of words and with greater eloquence, and that having put aside this contentious manner of argument it will assume a quieter form of speech and discourse, using its own proper Roman diction for greatest effect.

The closer humanists like Pontano approached the secret of the past, the farther they realized they were from disclosing it fully.

Actius, Pontano's dialogue dedicated to Sannazaro, apparently echoes conversations at the academy in the 1490s, when Sannazaro had completed his first version of *Arcadia* and was starting to compose his own Latin elegies, odes, and epigrams. Less melancholy than *Aegidius*, it records a tranquil discussion by Sannazaro, Paulo, Pardo, Compatre, Puderico, Summonte, and Altilio about poetry's rank in the hierarchy of composition. Early in the dialogue Sannazaro delivers a long speech on the effects of *admiratio* that poetry achieves within its audience. The speaker expresses confidence in analyzing these effects: "ni-

hil autem nisi excellens admodum parit admirationem" (p. 146;
"for unless it is wholly excellent, nothing produces admiration"). Sannazaro's demonstration focuses on the properties of
poetic rhythm and meter, which in turn depend upon semantics and syntax, the poet's choice of diction, and his arrangement of words. For Sannazaro, the synthesis between poetry's
aural structure and its deeper units of meaning, between sound
and sense, form and content, represents the pinnacle of poetic
craft: "Numerus autem ipse cum primis et movet et delectat
et admirationem gignit. Eius autem prima illa laus est quod
varietatem parit, cuius natura ipsa videtur fuisse vel in primis
studiosa" (p. 146; "From the beginning meter itself moves and
attracts and begets admiration. Moreover its first praiseworthy
quality is that it produces *variety*, to which nature itself seems
to have been devoted"). In succeeding pages Sannazaro offers a
long, detailed examination of *admiratio* and *maraviglia* in the
rhythm and meter, syntax and semantics of Virgil's verse, and
he concludes by restating the goal of inducing *admiratio* as poetry's highest aim.

The second half of the dialogue is more provocative. In it the
various interlocutors compare poetry with historical writing
and oratorical composition. With deliberate insistence their
comparisons lay bare irresolvable problems inherent in the nature of poetic discourse. Both history and oratory, for example,
aspire to a clarity and directness that poetry avoids. History
proposes to explain the truth of events while oratory attempts
to move its audience to a specific course of action. Poetry, however, achieves its aims indirectly and obscurely and by methods
that elude precise explanation. By implication, any of the
reader's attempts to capture the poet's precise intention are
futile. Poetry is like a wild animal that cannot be tamed. One
interlocutor, Puderico, compares poetry to history by emphasizing poetry's luxuriance, lavishness, and potential lack of re-
straint: "In verbis item ac sententiis altera castigatior, altera ut
etiam in numeris sic in verbis nunc liberalior est nunc etiam
affectatior. Nam parum contenta priscis atque usitatis vocibus

exultat persaepe novandis illis aut peregre afferendis" (p. 194;
"In diction and meaning history is more restrained than poetry, just as poetry is more lavish in language and rhythm. For
too little content with old-fashioned and ordinary words, it
often delights in words invented or brought in from foreign
countries"). Another interlocutor, Altilio, emphasizes oratory's
avoidance of intricacy, obscurity, and eccentricity, and, precisely by contrast, poetry's inclination towards those qualities:
"Hoc est igitur illud genus quod paulo ante diximus assumen-
dum: fusum, lene, aequabiliter defluens, neque ieiunum neque
intumescens atque corruptum. Etenim fusa oratorio concisio-
nem longius a se repellit obscuritatis sociam sibique adversan-
tem atque contrariam" (p. 210; "Oratory is that genre that we
earlier characterized as diffuse, smooth, uniformly flowing, neither lean or swollen nor incorrect; for diffuse oratory forbids
concision as an ally of obscurity, both adverse and contrary to
itself"). The comparisons are disturbing, both for the humanist
seeking to understand ancient poetry and for the contemporary
writer seeking to compose new verse. They challenge the humanist and artist to discipline the anarchic powers of interpretation and composition and to harness them more securely
to the energies of the medium.

At this point Sannazaro recognizes that poetry's energies in-
tersect with resources that lay in the mine of classical culture.
The problem of penetrating that mine, of deconstructing its
textual resources and grasping their meaning, becomes one
with the problem of composing significant poetry. The powers
of language exceed both the scholar's and the poet's grasp, but
with patient labor both scholar and poet can acquire some measure of control over understanding and expression. Sannazaro's
concluding encomium of poetry salutes its vatic force: "Quae
princeps de Deo et disseruit et eius laudes cecinit, instituitque
sacra, unde primi poetae sacerdotes vocati, verbisque eum pla-
cavit et cantibus, docuitque habere rerum humanarum curam,
benigneque cum probis agere, excandescenter cum improbis"
(p. 239; "It first proclaimed God and sang his praises and estab-

lished sacred orders, whence the first poets were called priests; and it appeased God with words and songs; and it taught him to have care for human affairs and to act kindly towards the virtuous and angrily toward the wicked"). In this way he acknowledges the response that poetry achieves, even though he confesses that the means by which it achieves that response are largely inscrutable.

Besides illuminating some of Sannazaro's possible ideas about poetry, Pontano's dialogues show the extent to which humanist uncertainty pervades the cultural context of the poet's work. On the one hand the poet's production seems steady and assured in its finely honed stylistic precision. On the other it seems beset by doubt in an endless series of displacements and revisions. The poet's concurrent movement from the vernacular to Latin only complicates the issue of bridling the vatic force of poetic language. Beyond Pontano's circle, the growing doubt and outright pessimism about approaching classical culture on its own terms even intensify the problem. In this context Sannazaro experimented towards a solution by returning to the example of pastoral. By untangling various strands of lyric, narrative, and dramatic elements fused in the pastoral eclogue, he could penetrate the archaeological roots of classical culture buried in that composite form, and he could attempt to reunite them in his own work. In this way he would accomplish his own calling as a humanist who strove to understand the manifold variety of the past, and as a poet who sought to express its linguistic variety in a form suitable to his own age.

POLITICAL TURMOIL, EXILE, AND RETURN

The work of the academy reflects only one aspect of the comprehensive cultural, political, and economic renewal in Naples sponsored by the Aragonese royal family.[8] The founder of that line, Alfonso I, was known as "il Magnanimo" for his patronage of the arts. His son and successor, also an enthusiastic patron of the arts, Ferrante I, ruled from 1458 to 1494. The latter's eldest son, Alfonso II, succeeded him, but had ruled for less than a year when he abdicated in favor of his own son, Ferrandino, who in turn died heirless within two years, leaving the throne to Alfonso II's younger brother, Federigo, in 1496. Sannazaro had been formally attached to the court of Alfonso II since the time of his admission to the academy, but all along he enjoyed a more intimate relationship with the learned, sensitive, approachable Federigo. During Federigo's rule, however, the kingdom was lost to Spain, and when Federigo went into exile in 1501 Sannazaro accompanied him.

Sannazaro would probably not have done so much for Alfonso II. Early in his career Alfonso displayed astute military skill, but little else. In 1478–79, at the age of thirty, he had campaigned boldly against the Republic of Florence. A few years earlier Pope Sixtus IV had encouraged Naples to league with him against Florence to counter the latter's alliance with Venice against Milan. On 26 April, 1478, the Pazzi conspiracy against Medici rule in Florence resulted in the assassination of Giuliano de' Medici and left the city vulnerable to attack. Alfonso, supported by the pope, led a massive campaign. Only the personal journey of Lorenzo de' Medici to Naples in December, 1479, to enlist the aid of his friend Federigo for peace, ended the strife.

Early in 1481 Sannazaro became a member of Alfonso's court retinue. Alfonso was then at the peak of his military skill. On 10 September of that year he achieved the greatest victory of his career when he drove the Turks from Otranto. Sannazaro did not participate in that expedition, but the next year he did accompany Alfonso north to defend the latter's sister Eleonora and her husband Ercole d'Este against the Venetians besieging Ferrara. Crispo, Sannazaro's sixteenth-century biographer, reports that Sannazaro entertained the troops with his spontaneous, witty, and elegant epigrams. Along the way Alfonso attacked Rome because the pope was supporting the Venetians. The campaign allowed Sannazaro his first glimpse of the Eternal City, even though his patron had threatened to annihilate it.

Eventually in 1484 Pontano negotiated a successful peace with the pope and the Venetians.

Around this time Sannazaro had begun work on his *Arcadia*. In 1482 an Italian translation of Virgil's *Eclogues* by Bernardino Pulci had been printed in Florence along with several new Italian eclogues by Francesco Arsocchi, Jacopo Fiorino de' Bonisegni, and Girolamo Benivieni. These are reputed to have been the first Renaissance eclogues composed in the vernacular on classical models, and they may have suggested to Sannazaro the form for his own Eclogues I, II, and VI in the *Arcadia*.[9] He no doubt composed these poems separately without considering them as parts of a sequence. Later he came upon the idea of linking them with a prose narrative inspired by his youthful love for Carmosina Bonifacio, whom he had known as a child in Naples during the 1460s and who had died at the age of fourteen while he was away on his mother's estate near Salerno. The narrative that he planned for *Arcadia* would depict the grief of a speaker who wanders into self-imposed exile among the shepherds.

By 25 September 1489, Sannazaro had completed ten eclogues and ten prose chapters of *Arcadia*. On that date a scribe had finished copying them into the oldest surviving manuscript of that work. Sannazaro's composition had been sporadic. Political strife in 1485–86 almost certainly interrupted his work. The newly elected Pope Innocent VIII had fueled a revolt of the barons against the king of Naples. Alfonso again laid siege to Rome, and Sannazaro, along with Pontano, accompanied him. On 27 December 1486, Alfonso entered the city in triumph. Pontano negotiated a new peace with the pope, and for his efforts he received a crown of laurel. Sannazaro was impressed.

More serious political troubles that undermined the kingdom and eventually determined Sannazaro's fate began in 1492. The current pope, Alexander VI, Rodrigo Borgia from Valencia, Spain, had declared the aging monarch Ferrante deposed and pledged the kingdom to the French King Charles VIII.[10] Only the timely intervention of Federigo's friend, Lorenzo de' Medici, aborted those plans. Within a few months, however, Lorenzo died, and on 25 January 1494, King Ferrante himself died. Alfonso succeeded him, crowned amidst great pomp on Ascension Day, 8 May 1494. The following October Lodovico il Moro became duke of Milan. He had once promised an alliance with Naples by marrying Alfonso's daughter, Isabella, but he broke his pledge and married Beatrice d'Este; at the same time he invited King Charles VIII of France to invade his rivals, Florence and Naples.

Alfonso II meanwhile suffered from fears and superstitions. He believed that at his birth a beam of fire had portended disaster to the realm. As political conditions grew worse, Pope Alexander VI and Pontano both persuaded him to abdicate in favor of his now stronger son, Ferrandino. On 23 January 1495, Alfonso sailed to a Benedictine monastery in Sicily, where he died of an abscess the following November. Sannazaro viewed these events with trepidation.

By the end of February 1495, Charles VIII entered Naples. Pontano disloyally welcomed him with an enthusiastic oration while Sannazaro fled with Ferrandino and Federigo into hiding in Ischia. A few months later, however, Charles's former allies, the papacy and Spain, leagued against him. With this change in fortune, Ferrandino reentered Naples on 7 July, and by November he succeeded in expelling the French. His victory, however, was short-lived. Less than a year later on 7 October 1496, he died of natural causes.

Federigo succeeded him. By now Sannazaro's friendship with Federigo was quite close. The new king invited him to become the godfather of his son in 1497, and on 12 June 1499, Federigo awarded him the villa of Mergellina on the bay of Naples. Sannazaro settled there and began writing his *Piscatoriae*. The same year a woman of his acquaintance, Cassandra Marchese, married Alfonso Castriota, the Marquis of Altripolda; she was destined to play an important role in Sannazaro's later life.

Federigo's political fortune ended in disaster when the French

King Louis XII mounted a new invasion of Naples. He leagued with Ferdinand of Spain, who was himself the brother of Federigo's stepmother, the widow of Ferrante I. In response to their alliance, Federigo made overtures to the Turks for protection from the French and Spanish. Pope Alexander VI excommunicated him for treason against Christendom and invited Louis XII to take over the kingdom. On 4 August 1501, the French entered Naples.

To aid Federigo, Sannazaro sold his personal property; but the effort was useless. On 6 September 1501, Sannazaro sailed with his king into exile. They went to Ischia, Marseilles, Milan, and finally Blois, where Louis offered Federigo refuge in exchange for all of the Kingdom of Naples. The days of Louis's own victory, however, were numbered. Ferdinand of Spain challenged his right to Naples, and by 1502 France and Spain were at war over the issue. In a battle at the river Garigliano, the Spanish Captain Gonsalvo de Cordoba defeated the French troops. He entered Naples, reduced the barons to subjects, and was declared its vice-regent. Naples remained a Spanish viceroyalty until 1733.

In exile Sannazaro learned that a pirated edition of ten chapters of his *Arcadia* had been published in Venice on 14 June 1502. Other reprintings followed in Venice (22 November 1502), Naples (23 January 1503), and Milan (9 January 1504). Friends who had remained in Naples, Pietro Summonte and Cariteo, contacted him and urged him to publish his own authorized edition. Sannazaro revised his entire text, added two new chapters with two new eclogues, and sent it to the printer on 4 March 1504.

The following years were filled with grief for Sannazaro. In September 1503, Pontano had died, still enduring disgrace for his reception of the French in 1495. Next his beloved Federigo died in exile at Tours on 9 November 1504. Early the following year Sannazaro returned to Naples, which was itself a city in mourning. Federigo's son, Prince Ferrante, had been kept as prisoner of war in Spain since 1502. Federigo's widow, Queen

Isabella, lived in seclusion with her mother-in-law, Queen Giovanna, the widow of King Ferrante I; with the latter's own widowed daughter, Queen Giovanna, who had been King Ferrandino's wife; and with Queen Beatrice, the daughter of King Ferrante I and the widow of Matthias Corvinus, king of Hungary. These four women, known throughout Europe as "the four sad queens of Naples," were all that remained of the Aragonese dynasty.

Avoiding public and political contact, Sannazaro occupied himself with the composition of De Partu Virginis. By 1513 he completed a sketch of his epic. Increasing ill health, consumption, and stomach problems plagued him, and he worked at a slow pace. On 6 August 1521, Pope Leo X sent him a motu proprio urging him to finish the poem as a weapon against the German heretics like Luther who were rejecting the authority of Rome. After still another urging by the next pope, Clement VII, Sannazaro finally published it in 1526.

The only extraliterary affair that claimed his attention during these years was a controversy involving Cassandra Castriota. In 1505 her husband sought a divorce to marry Camilla Gonzaga. Cassandra refused to comply, and Sannazaro defended her objections. Litigation continued until September 1518, when Pope Leo X finally ruled in Alfonso's favor after accepting huge sums to annul the marriage. Between 27 June 1517, and 13 April 1521, Sannazaro protested the course of events in forty impassioned letters to Antonio Seripando, secretary of Cardinal Ludovico d'Aragona.[11] Cassandra eventually rewarded Sannazaro's efforts by helping to arrange for the publication of his Latin poetry.

The closing years of Sannazaro's life marked his continued retreat to a private existence. In 1524 he had commissioned the building of two chapels at Mergellina, one dedicated to St. Narzarius, the other to the Virgin. He also planned the building of a large church that would link the chapels. Early in 1527 a plague in Naples forced him to live with Angelo di Costanzo at Somma Vesuviana. Cassandra Castriota took refuge nearby at the home of Maria Dias Garlon. No doubt through her influence Sannazaro entrusted the manuscript of his unpublished Latin lyrics to Antonio Garlon for posthumous publication. Simultaneously the French king François I was renewing his predecessors' efforts to gain control in Italy. Pope Clement VII encouraged him in his designs to break Spanish hegemony, but François ultimately failed. The Spanish imprisoned the French king and took revenge on the pope by sacking Rome on 6 May 1527. In April 1528, the French armies laid siege to Naples, but Sannazaro nowhere mentions the event.

By this time the ailing poet was seventy years old. On Christmas Day 1529, he bequeathed his chapels to Dionisio Lauriero, the producer general of the Order of the Servants of Mary. In return the priests of the order said masses for him and promised to bury him in a tomb at the chapel of St. Nazarius. The following summer he spent some time at the country home of Cassandra Castriota polishing his collection of Italian sonnets that he had composed at least three decades earlier. On 6 August 1530, he died there at the age of seventy-two.

Within the next few years Sannazaro's friends planned and executed a series of monumental editions of his works. Under their care the first complete edition of all the Latin works, except for certain censored epigrams, appeared from the Aldine Press in Venice in 1535. Over the next century it received at least nineteen reprintings in Venice, Rome, and Paris. The complete Italian works appeared in 1531, with many reprintings and translations into other languages before the century's end. Major commentries on the *Arcadia* appeared in the editions of 1558 by Tommaso Porcacchi and Girolamo Ruscelli, in 1559 by Francesco Sansovino, and in 1596 by Giovambattista Massarengo. From these editions and commentaries Sannazaro's fame and influence spread across Italy and Western Europe throughout the sixteenth century. His works proved to be both symptomatic of their time and influential on it.

THE PASTORAL INHERITANCE

Sannazaro's works are both symptomatic of their time and influential on it because they draw upon pastoral's experimental, archaeological, and philogical resources in profoundly new ways. It is not sufficient simply to say that they use ancient Greek and Roman conventions to render contemporary Neapolitan realities. They do much more. On the one hand pastoral topoi supply a poetic correlative for emotions reflecting sadness and tranquility, permanence and displacement, nostalgia and withdrawal. They correspond to the intellectual tensions and skepticism of the age. On the other hand, the artifically hybrid and allusive nature of the pastoral style goes far beyond its mere thematics towards evoking a sense of what ancient literature really was like. As a humanist and as a creative poet Sannazaro used these resources to their fullest. His sense of the pastoral tradition was remarkably rich for a time when not all the pastoral texts of antiquity had been rediscovered and when the great development of the modern pastoral that he had helped to initiate had hardly begun.

Despite the temptation to thematize pastoral as a longing for peace, retreat, and resolution, Sannazaro knew that the pastoral world does not necessarily evoke an irresponsible golden age nor do its characters inhabit a sheltered pleasance or *locus amoenus*. Its shepherds constantly face social tensions, amatory conflicts, and political threats, and they exert themselves to the utmost in trying to resolve them. The pastoral's distinguishing characteristic is its simplified setting where the shepherd's emotions stand out in bold relief. It is an "other" world different from the one that its presumably literate and sophisticated audience experiences. It remains free from the restraints of modern civilized manners, yet it imposes its own code of manners distinguishing the shepherds from rude primitives.

To the sophisticated audience its leisure might afford a perfect opportunity for reassessment, vision, and prophecy, often about literature itself. It is a place where shepherds attempt to cope with their social and emotional problems. The pastoral "other" world extends thus to both an "outer" world and an "inner" world. Its outer world bears analogies with organized, institutionalized societies that the audience knows as part of its own real world. The speaker's reassessment of them leads to satirical, encomiastic, and other modes of poetry. Its inner world, on the other hand, bears analogy with the poet's own mental self-reflexive activity as a poet. Its landscape is interior. Emphasis falls on the speaker's role as a fashioner of verse, trying to develop his own personal talent in response to whatever tradition he may be aware of. His reassessment of that talent and tradition leads him to assert his own artistic greatness by promising better poetry yet to come. Pastoral's inner world thrives on its rich linguistic possibilities.

In his own day the history of pastoral was undergoing a transformation to which Sannazaro would contribute immeasurably. The texts of Theocritus (316–260 B.C.), the first pastoral poet of classical antiquity, had recently been recovered. Though the complete poems were not published in Greek until the Aldine edition of 1495, they had appeared in extracts of Latin translations during the 1480s. It is possible that Sannazaro had read them in that form while composing *Arcadia*, and probable that he did so before composing the *Piscatoriae* and *De Partu Virginis*. As rich as the Virgilian model would be for Sannazaro, the Theocritan one offered yet new insights. Its art is a composite, eclectic, hybrid one emphasizing the shepherds' inner world of poetry. Writing in the Hellenistic age after the great achievements of earlier ages, Theocritus represents the whole history of Greek literature in miniature form.[12] He incorporates myth from the Homeric hymns, narratives from the epyllia, descriptions from the epic, stanzaic refrains from folksong, witty and pithy sayings from epigrams, emotional tones from the lyric, aspects of characterization from Attic comedy and tragedy, and the flow of conversation from Socratic dialogues.

Speculations on Theocritus's models range from the idea that he collected folksongs to the notion that his poems were literary masquerades, poems à clef whose outer world depicts life amidst the author's circle of friends. Not all of Theocritus's poetry is pastoral. The name of the collection, the Idylls, derives from eidos "picture." Each poem presents a small, narrowly circumscribed scene set in an "other" world where a single person confronts himself and his passions, or where two people confront each other to resolve the tensions between them.

Theocritus wrote only one funeral dirge—Thyrsis's lament for Daphnis in Idyll I—but that form quickly became assimilated to the pastoral by two of his imitators whose texts were often published with his.[13] Bion (fl. 120 B.C.) wrote an elegant Lament for Adonis partly as an epyllionic narrative in his own voice, partly as a substantial monologue by Aphrodite (lines 49–77) expressing grief at her beloved's death. A later poet, often wrongly identified with Moschus (fl. 150 B.C.), composed a Lament for Bion modelled on Bion's song for Adonis. The poem has a concrete setting in a pastoral "other" world as the speaker recounts Bion's care of his flock, his talent for playing the reed pipe, and his conduct with other shepherds. The poem verges on literary allegory in commending Bion's poetic production; the pastoral society is ostensibly the poet's inner literary world, and the shepherd's nurturing care is a metaphor for the poet's cultivation of verse. It would be an important model for Sannazaro's own Eclogue XI in Arcadia.

In Rome Virgil made literary allegory the structural center of his ten eclogues (42–39 B.C.). The "other" world is named "Arcadia," but it is an imaginative landscape that exists only as a composite of other literary worlds from Greek and Latin texts. Their outer world is Rome in the last years of its civil wars, yet on the verge of becoming the empire. The Eclogues, however, emphasize the inner, literary world of pastoral. They concern the writing of poetry in general, and the process of their own composition in particular.

For Sannazaro, Virgil's emphasis on the pastoral's inner world would be decisive. The frequency with which Virgil's speaker addresses his muses indicates his seriousness about his craft.

These muses, sources of the speaker's inspiration, are recurrent audiences in IV.1, VI.13, VIII.1, and X.70. Other prominent members of his audience include poets and patrons, especially Pollio (III.88, VIII.8) and Varus (VI.10), who have asked him for verses about their own martial exploits. Above all, the speakers of Virgil's eclogues project highly personal concerns into their discussions, at least some of which have autobiographical relevance for Virgil. Thus in *Eclogue* I Tityrus praises the political conditions that have been propitious for his career as a poet:

> O Meliboee, deus nobis haec otia fecit.
> namque erit ille mihi semper deus, illius aram
> saepe tener nostris ab ovilibus imbuet agnus.
> ille meas errare boves, ut cernis, et ipsum
> ludere quae vellem calamo permisit agresti.
>
> (I.6–10)[14]

O Meliboeus, it is a god who wrought for us this peace—for a god he shall ever be to me; often shall a tender lamb from our folds stain his altar. Of his grace my kine roam, as you see, and I, their master, play what I will on my rustic pipe.

In *Eclogue* IX Menalcas intercedes with the state on behalf of the community:

> Certe equidem audieram, qua se subducere colles
> incipiunt mollique iugum demittere clivo,
> usque ad aquam et veteres, iam fracta cacumina, fagos
> omnia carminibus vestrum servasse Menalcan.
>
> (IX.7–10)

Yet surely I heard that, from where the hills begin to rise, then sink their ridge in a gentle slope, down to the water and the old beeches with their now shattered tops, your Menalcas had with his songs saved all.

Poetic self-consciousness marks every passage of the eclogues and lends further authority to the development of pastoral as a highly self-reflexive literary mode.

Ironically Virgil's dramatic situations often reinforce the personal and poetic liabilities of his speakers. Frequently the latters' performances emerge as curiously hollow and ineffective. In *Eclogue* I, for example, Tityrus naively defends Rome's policy of confiscating farmers' lands by referring to his own privileged prosperity as a poet. In *Eclogue* II Corydon sings unstudied complaints ("haec incondita," 1.4) taught by Pan to win the love of Alexis, but his art, which should draw him closer to his beloved, only forces him to self-doubt.

Virgil's irony would prompt Sannazaro's imitation. The Roman poet's last two eclogues would be especially important. They conclude on the verge of rejecting the pastoral altogether, or at least of implying that the poet is ready to take leave of the mode. In *Eclogue* IX Menalcas, who has often been identified with Virgil himself, is able to save his lands from confiscation by composing appropriate poetry. Another shepherd, Moeris, has lost his property, and Lycidas accompanies him to the city to plead his case. Along the way Lycidas attempts to resolve his friend's grief with song, but he soon falls short of his purpose. Another more forceful metrical voice is needed. The final poem, *Eclogue* X, overtly suggests pastoral's limitations. The love-sick poet, Gallus, laments his beloved's infidelity. Menalcas, Apollo, Sibanus, and Pan all warn him about the dangers of melancholy, but to no avail. In the concluding verses the speaker himself confesses that he cannot cure Gallus. Nor is his excuse simply that "omnia vincit Amor, et nos cedamus Amori" (69; "Love conquers all; let us, too, yield to Love"). Rather, the time has come for him to venture beyond the pastoral. His riper maturity demands other, more challenging forms of poetry, fresh woods and new pastures. The renunciation of pastoral thus becomes a convention of pastoral.

To the direct influence of Virgil's texts as Sannazaro received them, one must add the influence of Virgilian commentaries. The most important of them were the early ones of Servius and Donatus (fourth century), the newly discovered one of Probus, and ones assembled by Sannazaro's contemporaries, Cristoforo

Landino (1488), Antonius Mancinellus (1490), and Badius Ascensius (1500), for publication in the first printed editions of Virgil's *opera*. These commentaries clearly shaped Sannazaro's reception of Virgil's texts. They provided archaeological, experimental, and philological illumination about the pastoral enterprise. With the expansion of printed editions in Sannazaro's own day, moreover, they were undergoing a shift in focus from serving as narrowly supportive informational aids to serving as variously interpretive ones. They were changing the whole shape of how readers were perceiving Virgil's inner, outer, and "other" worlds.

Virgil's influence on Sannazaro, whether direct or mediated by the commentaries, was enhanced by that of later Roman pastorals rediscovered in the Renaissance. Calpurnius (fl. A.D. 55), who lived during Nero's reign and composed seven eclogues that were printed in Rome in 1471, emphasized the role of the shepherd as poet and imparted to his poems a serious concern about the inner world of the singer's craft.[15] Calpurnius moreover enriched the pastoral by representing its "other" world in more concretely visual terms than his predecessors had done. For example, one notable convention that he developed and Sannazaro appropriated is the carving of words on the barks of trees, as in I by Faunus in praise of the emperor and the renewal of the Golden Age, and in III by Iolas, who so inscribes the amatory laments of his friend Lycidas for the disdainful Phyllis.

The late Latin pastoralist Nemesianus (late third century A.D.) held a special attraction for Sannazaro. The humanist poet edited one of his manuscripts and suggested several textual emendations. More importantly for Sannazaro, Nemesianus's four eclogues manage to epitomize all the major motifs of the Greek and Roman pastoral. In Nemesianus's brief collection the funeral, amatory, and mythic motifs constitute an anthology of possibilities left to the classical pastoralist after Virgil. They include a dirge (I), a singing contest (II), a mythic narrative (III), and an amatory lament (IV).

The Renaissance recovery of the pastoral eclogue began with

an exchange of four Latin eclogues between Dante and his friend Giovanni del Virgilio, a professor of poetry at Bologna. Appropriately their topic concerns the inner world of poetry and the relative merits of Latin and the vernacular in composing it. Dante's *persona* explicitly rejects Latin as the language for his own poetic expression. In the pastoral guise of Tityrus, he not only refuses the Latin sheep urged on him by Giovanni, but he also commends native Italian ones, referring to the *Paradiso* when he claims to be tending a highly esteemed sheep: "'Est mecum quam noscis ovis gratissima' dixi / 'ubera vix que ferre potest, tam lactis abundans'" (II. 58–59; "'There is with me a highly esteemed sheep, as you know,' I said, 'with udders so full of milk that she can hardly carry them'").[16]

In using the pastoral to discuss the inner world of poetry, Dante sanctioned a mode that Petrarch, Sannazaro, and the rest of the Renaissance would cultivate even though Dante did not share their attitudes towards classical Latin. Petrarch would. His twelve Latin pastorals comprising his *Bucolicum Carmen* (1346–52, autograph manuscript 1357, Milan) afford fuller, richer poetry than Dante's eclogues, and they set a model for the form that Neo-Latin poets would use up to Sannazaro's time.[17]

Taking Virgil's example with the utmost gravity, Petrarch emulated his master's classical diction and hexameter form, and he associated the content of his own pastorals with the personal, political, and polemical allegory that the Virgilian commentaries of Servius and others had taught him to see in the *Eclogues*. Modern readers may find Petrarch's allegory obscure, but Sannazaro and his humanist audience appreciated it through Renaissance commentaries that in turn grew around Petrarch's texts. They probably appreciated even more Petrarch's recurring self-conscious references to his vocation as scholar and poet. *Carmen* I is a dialogue between Sylvius (the poet) and Monicus (his brother Gherardo, a Cistertian monk) on the values of the active scholarly life as against the contemplative monastic life. In *Carmen* III Stupeus the poet praises Daphne (Laura) and her charms and declares that she has inspired him to write his best poetry. In the climactic poem on the literary theme, X. 37–348, Sylvanus the poet names the many shepherds (classical poets) who have aided him. They include Virgil, Catullus, Homer, Alcaeus, Callimachus, Ovid, Tibullus, Propertius, Lucan, and Prudentius. The list constitutes a catalogue of Petrarchan sources and influences, the wellspring of his inspiration (though Petrarch himself knew the Greek poets he mentions only very imperfectly, and in Latin, if at all), and of Sannazaro's inspiration in the late fifteenth century. It also points once again to the nature of pastoral as a hybrid mode drawing upon the resources of many styles and genres. Pastoral appeals to a mood of literary nostalgia that evokes the past by its synthesis of forms.

Sannazaro doubtless found inspiration in many Neo-Latin pastorals written after Petrarch. In Latin the greatest of them were Boccaccio's *Bucolicum Carmen*, Boiardo's ten eclogues, Mantuan's ten eclogues, and Pontano's *Lepidina*. The last two would be especially important for his own Latin *Piscatoriae*. The chief vernacular pastorals composed according to classical models were by Fiorino, Benivieni, and Arsocchi published in Florence in 1482. The lesson of all of them is that the topics of their outer world—Church history, secular politics, private friendships, sexual love, family affairs—all engage with inner self-reflexive meditations on the artistic process, the composition of poetry, and the endeavors of art. The "other" world of their pastoral settings accommodates these concerns with grace, economy, and wit. The lesson would not be lost on Sannazaro when he wrote *Arcadia*.

One further element of the pastoral tradition needs to be mentioned. It is the pastoral romance, developed in Hellenistic antiquity in Greek prose and revived in the early Renaissance by Boccaccio in the Italian vernacular. That form of prose narrative, which Boccaccio in turn intercalated with brief poems, allows colorful, complicated events and marvelously heroic achievements to unfold against a background of seemingly pastoral simplicity. The earliest prose romances in fact emphasized their pastoral settings. Longus's *Daphnis and Chloe*, dating from the end of the Roman Empire, is the supreme example.[18] In it a shepherd and shepherdess come to discover that they are actually long-lost aristocratic offspring. At the dawn of the Renaissance, Boccaccio in his *Filocolo* (1336) and *Ameto* (1342) employed the narrative conventions of this form of romance, and in the latter, moreover, he punctuated long sections of the prose with poems that comment on the action.[19] Boccaccio's example was decisive for Sannazaro.

Sannazaro blended all the foregoing elements of the pastoral tradition into a new synthesis. In *Arcadia* he imitated the form of the classical eclogue in the Italian vernacular and to it he joined the prose romance that Boccaccio had developed in Italian. Moreover, the poetic forms that Sannazaro achieved were more self-consciously classical. They were direct descendants of the Theocritan and Virgilian eclogue mediated by the Neo-Latin eclogues of Petrarch, Boccaccio, Mantuan, and Pontano. Sannazaro finally tightened the kind of prose links that Boccaccio had situated between the poems. In the process, he gave birth to a literary type that would be imitated for centuries to come.

The history of *Arcadia*'s reception is remarkable enough, but Sannazaro went on to experiment further with the pastoral mode. While he was writing *Arcadia* and for several years afterward, Sannazaro occasionally composed vernacular sonnets and *canzoni* in the Petrarchan manner. He soon discovered a connection between the Petrarchan and pastoral modes when he perceived the usefulness of Petrarchan rhetorical conventions for amatory pastoral motifs and, mutatis mutandis, the adaptability of various pastoral motifs to the Petrarchan lyric. During those years he also turned more and more to the composition of Latin verse. In his collection of Neo-Latin epigrams, odes, and elegies, he again discovered connections between their conventional motifs and pastoral forms. By the time he wrote his *Piscatoriae* and *De Partu Virginis* in splendid Latin hexameters, he had cultivated enough expertise in Latin style to endow those pastorals with unrivalled excellence. Sannazaro's shorter poetry therefore represents no deviation from his pastoral masterpieces. Instead it constitutes an approach to them. It reveals a complex dialectical movement towards integrating diverse forms with the pastoral mode that accommodates them.

VERNACULAR *RIME*

Sannazaro's Italian sonnets and *canzoni* (or odes) include some of the best examples of pure Petrarchan verse that the Renaissance produced. Petrarch had imparted to his *Rime* the form that dominated Italian lyric poetry between the mid-fourteenth and early seventeenth centuries. The history of Petrarchism, however, evolves in a sprawling pattern from Petrarchan inspiration through various stages of exaggeration, a period of reform led by Cardinal Bembo in the early sixteenth century, and eventual dissipation into other modes afterwards. Sannazaro wrote at the end of the fifteenth century, just when the original model had undergone such changes as to be in danger of dissolving altogether. He contributed to its recall by faithfully evoking Petrarch's rhetorical strategies with some measure of their own complexity.[20] Those strategies in turn proved useful for developing amatory motifs in the pastorals. The amatory songs of *Arcadia* are full of Petrarchan topoi, while passages of Sannazaro's Latin poetry suggest the transposition of Petrarchan conventions to the ancient language. Sannazaro's undertaking entailed enormous risk.

Petrarch's rhetoric easily lent itself to misappropriation. Most of its fifteenth-century imitators saw in it a vast store of diction, tropes, figures, and other elocutionary devices derived from Petrarch's *Rime*. These include the familiar antitheses, oxymorons, and paradoxes that Petrarch echoed and reechoed: the "living death, pleasurable ill" ("O viva morte, o dilettoso male," *Rime* XXXII); the love that "reassures and frightens, burns and freezes" ("Assecura e spaventa, arde e agghiaccia," *Rime* LXXVIII); the beloved's "sweet wrath, sweet disdain" ("Dolce ire, dolci sdegni," *Rime* CCV).[21] Often, however, the fifteenth-century Petrarchist missed the more subtle rhetorical strategies of voice and address that gave Petrarch's poetry its impassioned urgency and haunting, meditative, reflective tone. It missed above all the moral valence that inflects Petrarch's representation of his beloved. Petrarch's lover experiences torment because his beloved is distant from him. That distance requires compensation. To achieve it the lover valorizes his beloved as the figure of his literary pursuit. He exists not just in order to desire her, but also in order to write about her. Precisely because she supplies him with matter to write about, she becomes a figure for his literary enterprise. Laura the woman betokens the poetic laurel. She is now distant in a double sense, both as scornful *donna* and as a yet unattained literary goal, and she precipitates a moral crisis that surrounds the speaker in his vocation as poet. She represents an irretrievable textuality, whether in the speaker's attempt to grasp the texts of others, especially those of classical antiquity, or in his attempt to create his own new texts in her honor. By focusing on these levels of meaning, Petrarch achieves a perfect dialogic synthesis of dramatic representation, literary self-reflexivity, and moral allegory. This synthesis would fall apart in the fifteenth century.

The poetry of one of Sannazaro's closest associates, Benedetto Gareth (known as il Cariteo), a Spaniard who had taken up residence in Naples and had produced a sizable volume of poetry in Italian, illustrates this disintegration of Petrarchan motifs. Cariteo's sequence of sonnets and *canzoni*, the *Endimione*, was published in 1506. Here the speaker proclaims his love for a woman named Luna in elegantly turned but often curiously strained phrases that repeat Petrarchan diction while attenuating its literary allegory and moral fervor. In "Sì come salamandra in fiamme ardenti" (CVI; "Like a salamander in burning flames"), for example, Cariteo's speaker appropriates one of Petrarch's more flamboyant figures, the salamander that lives in fire (from *Rime* CCVII, 40–41), but he extends the analogy in compromising ways.[22] At the end of the octave he uses it to plead for mercy: "Deh, mostra agli occhi miei benegno aspetto," ("Ah, show my eyes your benign aspect"). In the first tercet, on the other hand, he uses it to express his own endurance: "Non può frenar la voglia," ("I cannot restrain my will"). In the penultimate line, however, he reverts to his plea for mercy: "Non soffrir tu che 'n cener si converta!" ("Don't allow it to turn to ash"). The arbitrary discontinuity is sharper and more melodramatic than anything in Petrarch. Such discontinuity would not serve the hybrid, eclectic, smoothly integrated impulses of pastoral.

Sannazaro faced the challenge directly. To avoid imitative extravagance, and thus to make Petrarchist conventions amenable to pastoral, Sannazaro carefully modulated the emotional register of his sonnets and *canzoni*. In so doing he approached the Petrarchan model differently yet more respectfully than his bolder contemporaries. By the early sixteenth century, Sannazaro's good friend, Cardinal Pietro Bembo (1470–1547), had initiated a program for returning to Petrarch in a truer spirit than recent Petrarchists had shown. His *Prose della volgar lingua* enthroned Petrarch as the best exemplar of poetic style in Italian and urged other poets to eschew the flamboyant diction and syntax of his recent imitators. Bembo need not have articulated his program for Sannazaro. The latter had already declared his allegiance to the pure Petrarchan precept with his own youthful collection of Italian *Rime*.

Having composed several *rime* in his youth, Sannazaro spent the last years of his life revising them to eliminate vestiges of Neapolitan dialect or other idiosyncratic forms and to replace those varieties with the standard forms of Petrarch's own Tuscan. Most revisions exalt the Tuscan or Petrarchan model. Thus *arai* (XXV.37) became *avrai*, "have"; *aran* (XXXIV.10) became *avran*, "have"; *suspire* (XLV.4) becomes *sospiri*, "sighs."[23] Many revisions honor the Tuscan model by eliminating certain words altogether, even at the cost of recasting whole lines in order to accommodate new rhymes. Thus the revision of XI.14 eliminates *preggio*, formerly rhyming with *seggio*, because it lacks the purity of *prègio*, "worth"; the revision of LVI.9 eliminates *benegno*, formerly rhyming with *ingegno*, because it lacks the purity of *benigno*, "benign"; and the revision of LXXXVIII.8 eliminates *spalli*, formerly rhyming with *cristalli*, because it lacks the purity of *spalle*, "shoulders." Other revisions according to the Tuscan standard correct the plurals of feminine nouns whose singulars end in *e*: *lode* (IV.7, XXV.39) becomes *lodi*, "praises"; *virtute* (XI.31) becomes *virtuti*, "virtues"; *frode* (XXV.2) becomes *frodi*, "deceptions"; and *nube* (LII.10) becomes *nubi*, "clouds." Still other revisions effect a curtailment of contractions such as *parol* (XII.7) for *parole*, "words"; *car* (VII.3) for *caro*, "dear"; and *ristor* (XLIII.12) for *ristòro*, "refreshment." Occasionally the revisions reflect a stylistic rather than linguistic judgment. Some change acceptable Italian forms into Latinate ones. Thus *altiero* (XIII.2, XVII.2) becomes *altèro*, "proud"; *brieve* (LIII.75) becomes *breve*, "short"; *fuogo* (XL.10, LVII.5) becomes *fòco*, "fire"; and *luogo* (LVII.6) becomes *loco*, "place." More frequently, however, the emendations replace Latinate orthography with the current vernacular standard. Thus *mundo* (XI.86) becomes *mondo*, "world"; *vulgo* (LXIX.17) becomes *volgo*, "mob"; and *impii* (LXX.3, LXXXVII.8) becomes *empi*, "impious." In general, Sannazaro's revisions of the *Rime* follow a pattern that we will later observe in the revisions of *Arcadia*.[24]

The first printing of Sannazaro's *Rime* appeared a few months after the poet's death in 1530, in an edition that he had been personally overseeing. It consists of eighty sonnets, nine *canzoni*, five madrigals, four sestinas, and three laments in *terza rima*. Divided into two parts (*Rime I–XXXII* and *Rime XXXIII–CI*), the sequence unfolds according to no readily apparent order. Sannazaro dedicated the collection to Cassandra Castriota but noted (though, since the words echo a Petrarchan convention, perhaps we should not take them too literally) that he had composed most of the poems in his youth, "queste mie vane e giovenili fatiche" (Mauro ed., p. 135; "these empty youthful labors of mine"). The probable date of their composition is the

last decade of the fifteenth century, before the poet's close contact with Cardinal Bembo, though certainly Sannazaro emen-
ded his text afterwards.[25] Those revisions conforming to the
Tuscan linguistic model, however, represent only one aspect of
his labor. A more significant aspect was to attain a fully Petrarchan synthesis of moral drama and literary figuralism.

Sannazaro's appropriation of Petrarch's amatory and literary
motifs, his perception of their deep relationship, and his use of
the amatory motif to illustrate the nature of his literary endeavor distinguish his best lyrics. Often these enrich the amatory and literary motifs with other topics that are also adumbrated in Petrarch's poetry. In the *Rime*'s first part, for example,
the speaker addresses a number of sonnets to a lady who has
died young and a number of other sonnets to another lady who
scorns his poetry. In the second part the speaker augments
poems addressed to an unspecified beloved with sonnets and
canzoni on political and religious matters. Amatory and literary
motifs, however, dominate the collection, just as they do in the
Petrarchan model. In fusing them Sannazaro in fact attains a
superbly crafted imitation of Petrarch's most distinctive poetry.

Canzone XXV, "Ben credeva io che nel tuo regno, Amore"
("I well supposed, Love, that in your realm") in the *Rime*'s first
part is a good example. In that amatory lament the speaker as a
poet recognizes that his poetic complaints serve no purpose:
"Ma perché dopo 'l danno in van si piagne" (59; "But because
after the harm one laments in vain"). He therefore reduces his
production of sad poetry, but not so that he rejects his role as
poet altogether: "ma non sì che, pensando, / non torni a' suoi
dolori alcuna volta" (62–63; "but not so that in a rational manner I no more turn to its sorrows"). His dialectical surrender to
sorrow and his consequent resistance against it, powerfully recorded in the ebb and flow of his verse, lead the speaker to an
artistic crisis: "convien c'odii la vita e si distempre; / ché via
meglio è 'l morir che pianger sempre" (65–66; "it is wise to hate
life and be untuned, because it is far better to die than always to
be weeping"). The key word, *distempre*, echoes from Petrarch's

Rime sparse (LV.14, CCXXIV.13, CCLIX.38). It refers to the speaker's musical "distempering," his "unstringing" or "untuning" wrought by grief. To untune him means to deprive him of his poetic talent, and that deprivation amounts to death. Only by singing can the speaker hold on to life, even if his song is full of lugubrious notes.

The *Rime*'s first part sharply differentiates between the speaker's surrender to love and his pursuit of the muse. Towards its end the speaker advises several friends, associates, and younger poets to abandon amatory trifles for more serious endeavors. In "Al corso antico, a la tua sacra impresa" (XXIX; "To the ancient course, to your sacred endeavor") he urges his own soul to turn "al vero onore, a la famosa palma" (2; "to true honor, to the famous palm"). In the next sonnet he exhorts a friend to extricate himself from a hopeless love affair in order to secure a better place in recorded history: "e far chiaro il tuo nome in mille carte" (XXX.14; "make your name illustrious in a thousand pages"). In yet the following sonnet, "Fuggi, spirto gentil, fuggi lo strazio" (XXXI; "Flee, o gentle spirit, flee the torment") the speaker promises to reward in verse his friend's liberation from love: "ti inalzi insino al ciel con le mie rime!" (14; "I will lift you to heaven with my rhymes!") In this instance poetry serves as a vehicle that celebrates one's rejection of love; through it the poet sublimates his erotic desires.

The *Rime*'s second part explores other interrelationships between the poet's life and art. *Canzone* XLI, "Or son pur solo e non è chi mi ascolti" ("Now I am alone and there is no one who hears me"), outrivals Petrarch by referring also to Propertius's *Elegy* I.18, which Petrarch himself had echoed. In Propertius's elegy the speaker retreats to a silent desert in order to sing about his love for Cynthia. The beloved, however, seems less an object of the speaker's desire than its symptom. The speaker complains that she has misinterpreted the signs, *signa* (17) of his love given in the altered color, *mutato colore* (17) of his complexion.[26] His words resonate through the woods' delicate shades, "a quotiens teneres resonant mea verba sub umbras"

(21; "how oft do my passionate words echo beneath your delicate shades"), but they vanish into thin air. The speaker's problem is to lend those fleeting words substance and solidity. His
solution is to adopt the pastoral convention of engraving them
on the barks of trees. Thus he carves Cynthia's name throughout the forest, "scribitur et vestris Cynthia corticibus" (22; "how
oft is Cynthia's name carved upon your bark"). As Propertius's
elegy concludes, however, the pastoral convention only raises
another problem: how can the poet be sure that his audience
will interpret even those reified signs with suitable skill?

Sannazaro confronts that problem in his own *canzone*. There
in the woods the speaker addresses the stones and the trees as
"secretaries" with whom he has notarized expressions of his
woe: "O secretari di mie pene antiche / a cui son noti i miei
pensieri occolti" (4–5; "O secretaries of my old pains, to whom
are noted my secret thoughts"). Later he addresses the moon-
goddess. She knows well his silence, since love for Endimion
robbed her of speech: "Tu sai ben quanto tacque / la lingua mia,
e quanto in sé ritenne" (20–21; "You know well how silent was
my tongue and how much it held back in itself"). Yet in the
third stanza the speaker recognizes that silence only masks the
need to express oneself. He now mocks his taciturnity, "cre-
dendo che 'l tacer giovasse assai" (34; "believing that silence
was of much use"). Reticence has only vanquished him: "e dal
dolor mi vedea preso e vinto" (41; "and I saw myself crushed
and defeated by grief"). For relief he expresses his beloved's
name by carving it on trees: "scrivea di tronco in tronco sospi-
rando / de la mia donna il nome; e ben vorrei / che fusse or noto
a lei" (44–46; "while sighing I wrote from trunk to trunk the
name of my lady, and well I wished that it were noted by her").
As in Propertius's elegy, however, the pastoral convention of
engraving words on trees offers small consolation. It does not
guarantee that the audience will interpret those words correctly.

The final lines of stanza 4 suggest a solution. The audience's
reciprocal gesture of acknowledging the speaker's words prevents
him from withering away: "e mi togliesse a morte, / ché sola ella

il pò far con sue parole" (50–51; "and she would prevent me from dying, since she also can do so with her words"). Her words strengthen his. Nonetheless a troublesome distance separates them. In stanza 5 *desio* indicates the beloved's inaccessibility: "Tal guida fummi il mio cieco desio, / c'al labirinto, il qual seguendo fuggo, / mi chiuse, onde non esco omai per tempo" (53–55; "my blind desire was a guide that enclosed me in a labyrinth which I fled as it pursued, from which I henceforth will not exit early"). Self-expression relieves him to a certain degree, but not entirely so long as the beloved, the object of his expression, remains silent: "pur mi rileva lo sfogare alquanto" (70; "unbosoming myself still relieves me somewhat").

The agent of dissatisfaction becomes clear in the lines that follow. It is the beloved herself. She hides from the speaker by covering her eyes with her hands and hair: "Scusar non posso il velo, / e la man bianca, e i be' capei che spesso / mi fanno odiar me stesso" (72–74; "I cannot excuse the veil, both her white hand and her beautiful hair that often make me hate myself"). Forever inaccessible because of her scattered hair, *sparsi* (75), the beloved represents a deferred object of desire. Like the words of an ancient text whose deepest meaning is shrouded by uncertainties, the beloved remains finally an enigma. The pastoral convention of carving her name on trees has been an imperfect logocentric means of approaching her. It nonetheless affords the speaker some measure of relief. Without it he could not have completed this poem. With it he has managed at least to suggest the illimitable scope of his desire.

Another *canzone*, "Amor, tu vòi ch'io dica" (LIII; "Love, you wish that I should say"), relates the beloved's inexpressibility to both the speaker's amatory frustration and his poetic ambition. The speaker accuses Love of pressing him to say what he would rather leave unsaid, "quel ch'io tacer vorrei" (2; "what I would like to keep silent"). Wishing to make a powerful effect on his audience, he prefers to remain silent if he cannot do so. He sings in two styles, the first "con lacrimoso stile" (28; "with sad

style") when he complains of his amatory woes, the second
"con soavi tempre" (30; "with sweet temper") when he sings his
beloved's name. Now, however, he suppresses his "dolci rime"
and his "pietosi accenti":

> *Tacen le dolci rime*
> *e que' pietosi accenti*
> *che rilevar solean mie pene in parte;*
> *ché se non è chi stime*
> *queste voci dolenti*
> *né chi gradisca il suon di tante carte,*
> *a che l'ingegno e l'arte*
> *perder, sempre piangendo*
> *dietro a chi non m'ascolta?*
>
> (40–48)

My sweet rhymes and these sorrowful accents, which used
to relieve my grief in part, are both silent because if there is
no one who values these mournful voices nor appreciates
the sound of these pages, why waste talent and art by weeping after someone who does not listen to me?

The speaker's emphasis on the logocentric oral-aural aspect of
his poetry—its rhymes and accents, the sound of his voice and
(oxymoronically) the sounds issuing from the pages—is important. It implies his need for an audience, for, like thunder, his
poetry cannot exist without someone to hear it.

As yet, unlike thunder, poetry is an intentional act. The
poet controls its production. Departing from the two styles he
had earlier mentioned, the poet now exhorts his soul to a
higher purpose: "Alma, riprendi ardire, / e dal continuo pianto /
ti leva al ciel, che già t'affetta e chiama" (53–55; "Soul, regain
your courage, and away from continual weeping rise to heaven,
which already moves and calls you"). He will adopt a new style,
one that he associates with a nobler genre and a more ambitious
poetic mode: "rifrena il gran desire, / e con più altero canto /
ti sforzas d'acquistare eterna fama" (56–58; "Restrain your great
desires, and with a prouder sort of song strive to acquire eternal

fame"). The new genre, he intimates, is epic: "Drizza le voglie accese / a più lodate imprese" (64–65; "Raise your inflamed will to more celebrated endeavors").

The tension that this *canzone* depicts between competing styles approximates an autobiographical statement. One can of course read it as such, but only by situating it in the chronology of Sannazaro's life. Instead, within the context of the *Rime* it acquires significance as a meditation on stylistic options always available to a serious poet. The speaker's dilemma is to reconcile those options, high and low, amatory and divine, lyric and epic. One mode that accommodates them all is pastoral. There, under the guise of singing a humble song, the poet can treat of high matter. The pastoral mode can release all the speaker's pent-up energies without requiring him to sacrifice one option to another.

The speaker's recognition of pastoral's experimental, archaeological, and logocentric possibilities therefore pervades the *Rime*. Even when the speaker appears to reject them, he does so at evident risk. In Sonnet XXXV, "Or avess'io tutto al mio petto infusa" ("Now that I had infused all in my breast"), he claims to have advanced far beyond his apprenticeship in pastoral when he praises his beloved in the amatory mode. Thus he addresses his muse with the taunt that his pastorals would have acquired their own reputation earlier if they had such a beloved as this one to extol:

> Del tempo andato, o pastoral mia Musa,
> e del tuo rozzo stil so che ti dole;
> ché se 'l ciel ti scopriva un sì bel sole,
> non saresti or di fama in tutto esclusa.
>
> (5–8)

O my pastoral Muse, I know that you regret the past and your rough style; because if heaven had disclosed to you so beautiful a sun, you would not now be entirely excluded from fame.

In the sonnet's sestet, moreover, he asserts that the pastoral muse ought to thank his beloved for having earned his eclogues a place in literary history:

> Ma grazia a lui, c'a questa età più ferma
> ti riserbò, per farti in più felice
> e più bel foco empir gli ultimi giorni!
>
> (9–11)

But thanks to her whom I save for you in this more resolute age, to make you in more joyful, more beautiful flame fulfill your latest days.

The sonnet's final line, however, throws the speaker's assertion into jeopardy. The beloved has wounded him. On the one hand his love for her has enabled him to outdo his pastoral inspiration; on the other it has reduced him to tears:

> Dunque rinascerai nova fenice:
> così mel giura Amor, così m'afferma
> quella che vòl c'a sospirar ritorni.
>
> (12–14)

Hence you will be born a new phoenix: so Love swears to me, and so to me she affirms, who wishes that I revert to sighing.

Immune to this reduction, pastoral exerts a vitality that transcends the amatory lyric. It may yet harbor resources unknown to the speaker, resources that might later enable him to achieve a victory of poetic form.

Beyond referring to the speaker's apprenticeship in pastoral as well as in his subsequent triumph in that mode, the *Rime*'s sonnets pay homage to Petrarch. Sonnet LIV, "Cercate, o Muse, un più lodato ingegno," initiates a sequence of three poems in which the speaker shows his indebtedness to Petrarch. In the first he addresses his muses with the request that they help him to master a sweeter style for praising his beloved:

> Cercate, o Muse, un più lodato ingegno
> che con più dolce stil lode costei,
> che 'l suon de' bassi e fiochi accenti mei
> più non ascolta, e 'l mio dir prende a sdegno.
>
> (1–4)

Seek, o Muses, a more commendable talent that with sweeter style may praise her who no longer listens to my hoarse low accents and holds my speech in disdain.

Such a style would replicate Petrarch's as closely as possible. With that style Petrarch acquired for his beloved a form of eternal life, as the speaker asserts in sonnet LV, "Quella c'a l'umil suon di Sorga nacque" ("She who was born by the lowly sound of the Sorgue"):

> Quantunque in vile albergo occolta giacque
> e stiasi or chiusa in una oscura tomba,
> pur vive, per virtù di quella tromba
> che per tal grazia al suo morir non tacque.
>
> (5–8)

Although she lay hidden in an abject dwelling, and now is enclosed in a dark tomb, yet she lives by virtue of this trumpet that by such grace was not silent at her death.

With it the speaker can achieve a similar goal.

The keystone of Sannazaro's homage to his predecessor is Sonnet LVI, "Trentaduo lustri il ciel, girando intorno" ("Thirty-two lustra, heaven in its revolutions"). It measures the temporal distance between Petrarch's age and the speaker's own by celebrating the hundred-sixtieth anniversary (thirty-two lustra) of Petrarch's meeting Laura (6 April 1327). Establishing a precise date for its own composition (6 April 1487), it proclaims Petrarch's poetry to be as fresh now as the day it was conceived: "veduto ha sempre con bei rami d'oro / far più fresc'ombra assai che 'l primo giorno" (3–4; "it has always seen a green laurel with beautiful golden branches cast a shade as refreshing as on the first day"). Punning on Petrarch's name, the speaker asserts that if heaven had summoned (*impetrasse*) the older poet to return to life, he would be amazed to see how much his poetry has influenced other poets. Addressing Petrarch metonymically in the first tercet, the speaker applauds the happy product, his well-spent hours, the sacred ink and his fortunate pen, exclaiming their wide effect. It staggers the imagination to think how Petrarch initiated so much: "come il poteste voi sospinger tanto?" (11; "how could you have stimulated so much?"). Challenging the speaker's illusion in the final tercet, however, Love informs the speaker that his own work will bear as much influence:

> Ma—Rallégrati—dice il mio signore,
> —ché, se 'l tuo Febo il ver di te m'accenna,
> non ti spargerà in van tutto 'l tuo pianto.—
>
> (12–14)

But "Cheer up," says my master, "because if Apollo tells me the truth about you, your tears will not all be scattered in vain.")

He refers to the dissemination of pastoral under his influence. For the speaker, perhaps even despite his own awareness, the pastoral would mark his major contribution towards overgoing Petrarch's sovereignty.

The tension between merely copying Petrarch on the one hand and fully overgoing him on the other finds expression elsewhere in the *Rime*. In general the collection's first part evokes Petrarch's *Rime in morte di Laura*. Many of its twenty-eight sonnets, along with its two *canzoni*, one madrigal, and one sestina, summon a deceased beloved who has become an object of the speaker's mournful veneration. The same beloved also provides poetic inspiration. In "L'alma mia fiamma, oltra le belle bella" (XVIII; "My divine flame, beautiful beyond beauty"), a cento composed entirely of phrases and whole lines from Petrarch, the speaker addresses his beloved as a figure of the Blessed Virgin, God's handmaiden (*ancella*) summoned to heaven in her prime: "A Dio diletta obediente ancella, / 'nanzi tempo chiamata a l'altra vita" (5–6; "Obedient handmaiden, pleasing to God, called to the other life before your time"). The speaker now wishes some efficacious sign, some verbal demonstration that she protects him from above: "vèr me ti mostra in atto od in favella" (8; "show yourself to me in act or in word"). He petitions her to direct this gesture towards his inner life, his *ingegno*, which she has the power to transform: "Deh porgi mano a l'affannato ingegno" (9; "Offer your hand to my troubled genius"). She will be the active support not only of his art but of his life as well: "o usato di mia vita sostegno" (11; "o customary support of my life"); and she will prepare him for an artistic renewal whose consequences will touch upon his own moral development. As in Petrarch's *Rime sparse* where the moral life interacts with the artistic, this sonnet stresses their interrelationship: "di poner fine a l'infiniti guai" (14; "hasten to put an end to my infinite woe"). But though it forecasts a new development, it does not specify the innovative direction that it will take.

That direction emerges in the fifty-two sonnets, seven *canzoni*, four madrigals, three sestinas, and three *terza rima* laments of the *Rime*'s second part. For those poems in the amatory mode it marks the Petrarchan model with a contemplative, meditative, Platonic vein. Because of the work of the Florentine academy, the recovery of Plato in Sannazaro's own age provided for him what was inaccessible to Petrarch. The experimental grafting of Platonic motifs onto Petrarchan ones makes itself felt, for example, in "Ahi letizia fugace, ahi sonno leve" (LXIII; "Ah fleeting happiness, ah light sleep"). The anachronistic pressure of Platonic abstraction on Petrarchan concreteness, however, forces a conflict between the speaker's enjoyment of his new beloved and his inability to define it. Sleep, with its fleeting dream images and their dissolution upon his awakening, lays bare the conflict. Sleep generates good dreams and bad feelings at once because the moment of awakening dispels the dreams and returns the speaker to reality: "come le mie speranze hai sparte al vento, / e fatto ogni mia gloria al sol di neve" (3–4; "How you scattered my hopes to the wind and made all my glory melt like snow in the sun"). The speaker resolves this conflict with a mythic comparison. Addressing Endimion, he

evokes the former's happiness and grief in being loved by another without knowing it: "Felice Endimion, che la sua diva, /
sognando, sì gran tempo in braccio tenne" (9–10; "Happy Endimion whose goddess held him in her arms while he slept").
Yet another conflict is less easily resolved. It entails a recognition of still higher states of being than mere dreaming: "Ché se
s'un'ombra incerta e fuggitiva / tal dolcezza in un punto al cor
mi venne, / qual sarebbe ora averla vera e viva?" (12–14; "Because if an uncertain and fugitive shade brings such grace to my
heart all at once, what would it now be to have that grace true
and alive?" The phantom of Platonic beauty confounds the
speaker at the very moment that it inspires him. Despite the
temptation to cede to its allure, the speaker remains on his
guard against it.

Another innovative direction in the *Rime* lays stress on political themes. Petrarch had brooded on the tragedy of the Avignon papacy and Italian disunity throughout his own *Rime
sparse*, but usually in darkly veiled and obliquely allegorical
terms. Sannazaro's approach is straightforward. He measures his
praise for Naples and the Aragonese dynasty with enthusiastic
outpourings, and he locates Ferdinand at the center of his patriotic imagination. The gloomy vision that clouds much of *Arcadia* and the *Piscatoriae* and the satire that animates many of
the Latin epigrams are missing, but in their stead political encomium emerges with a full voice. Sonnet LXXXII, "Lasso me,
non son questi i colli e l'acque" ("Alas are not these the hills
and waters") exemplifies the political range. Celebrating the
Neapolitan landscape where the beloved herself was born, "ove
l'alma mia dèa dal ciel discese" ("where my divine goddess descended from heaven"), the poem also pays homage to Prince
Federigo: "non è questo il superbo alto paese, / onde il gran
Federigo al mondo nacque?" ("is not this the proud, noble
country where the princely Federigo was born into the world?")
The first tercet then establishes the speaker's own situation at
the moment of his exile, far from the beloved homeland where
he is not allowed to die: "dunque era pur nel fato acerbo e crudo

/ ch'io non gittasse in te l'ultimo strido?" (10–11; "then was it yet according to a harsh and cruel fate that I should not have cast my last breath within you?"). As a product of the speaker's exile the poem laments the "doppio sostegno" (13; "double support") of his beloved and the national sovereignty that he must forsake. The fusion of beloved and prince in his nostalgic imagination suggests the pastoral conflation of both in *Arcadia* and the *Piscatoriae*. Again Sannazaro's lyric composition refers ahead to his pastoral achievement.

Still another important direction emerges towards the end of the *Rime* in a group of poems on religious themes. There the speaker dedicates himself to Christ and meditates on His goodness and mercy. One sonnet, "È questo il legno che dal sacro sangue" (XCVI; "Is this the cross that with sacred blood") commemorates Good Friday in vivid imagery. The composition begins with the speaker's glimpsing the relic of Christ's cross. It provokes an analytical recollection of Christ's sacrifice and, in the first tercet, an exclamation addressing His divine compassion and the singular new law that He established: "Oh pietà somma, oh rara e nova legge" (9; "Oh supreme mercy, oh rare and new law"). In the last tercet the speaker addresses himself during a meditation on Christ's care for mankind: "Lassa, mente infelice, ogni altra cura" (12; "Abandon every other care, unhappy mind"). The sonnet's last remarkable gesture, however, restores to the crucified Christ His pastoral role as the shepherd of mankind: "vedi il pastor, che va per le sue gregge, / come agnel mansüeto a la tonsura" (13–14; "behold the shepherd who goes among his flock as a lamb meek for the shearing"). Even in this lyric meditation on the crucifixion, then, the pastoral impulse asserts itself with striking relevance. In such unexpected ways the resources of pastoral transform the *Rime*.

Pastoral accommodates the matter of loftier poetry to itself by rendering it in the guise of a humble style. The danger is both that pastoral's low style may debase high matter or, worse, that its low style may seduce the poet to other themes more congenial to it. *Canzone* LXXXIX near the collection's end, "Sperai gran tempo, e le mie Dive il sanno" ("I hoped for a long time, and my goddesses knew it") poses the problem obliquely. The speaker has hoped for a long time to elevate his frail low style: "quel mio dir frale e basso / alzar, cantando in più lodato stile" (3–4; "to raise my frail low style by singing in a more exalted one"). For more than a decade, however, he has limited the topic of his poetry to the torments of his love: "or m'è già presso il quartodecim'anno / de' miei mirtìr" (5–6; "now the fourteenth year of my torment is already upon me"). The speaker's gravest fear is that his fame as a poet will not outlast his death: "rimarrò io pur chiuso in poca fossa?" (21; "will I then remain enclosed in a small grave?"). Addressing the muses, he begs their aid to avoid that fate: "non mi lasciate, prego, in preda a morte" (28; "do not leave me, I pray, a prey to death"). With their help he might compose poetry that can grant him immortality.

The poetry will celebrate the deeds of his patrons and protectors, members of Naples's royal family. The speaker therefore renounces his enslavement to the amatory mode:

> Basti fin qui le pene e i duri affanni
> in tante carte e le mie gravi some
> aver mostrato, e come
> Amore i suoi seguaci alfin governa.
>
> (31–34)

It suffices until now to have shown the pains and hard anxieties in so many pages, and my difficult burdens, and how Love finally rules his followers.

He now vows to adopt a higher style:

> Or mi vorrei levar con altri vanni,
> per potermi di lauro ornar le chiome
> e con più saldo nome
> lassar di me qua giù memoria eterna.
>
> (35–38)

Now I would like to rise with other wings, to be able to decorate my hair with laurel and with a more solid name leave an eternal memory of myself here below.

The effort, however, begins in vain: "Ma il dolor, che ne l'an-ima si interna, / la confonde per forza e volge altrove" (39–40; "But the suffering that penetrates my soul confounds it against my will and directs it elsewhere"). The speaker confronts his own self-image in a moment of powerful recognition and he ad-mits the difficulty of achieving his newly announced goal.

The rest of the *canzone* subtly confirms the speaker's admis-sion of defeat, his resignation to a humbler poetic mode at the expense of achieving some greater poetic triumph. At first the speaker states his preference for higher matter as a taunt to the beloved:

> *Lasso, chi mi tien qui, che non mi sferra?*
> *Ché avendo di parlar sì largo campo,*
> *del desir tutto avampo,*
> *sol per mostrare a chi mi incende e strugge*
> *che, senza dir degli occhi o del bel velo*
> *o di lei che mi fugge,*
> *si pò con altra gloria andare in cielo.*
>
> (54–60)

Alas, who holds me here, that she does not let me loose? Why, having such a broad field for speaking, am I all aflame with desire only to show to her who burns and consumes me that, without speaking of the eyes or beautiful veil or of her who flees from me, one can go to heaven with other glory.

The taunt falls on deaf ears, however. The examples of Homer and Virgil, who tended to epic themes, not amatory ones, ought to encourage the speaker: "più chiari son di quei che 'l mondo vide / pianger dì e notte le amorose risse" (65–66; "they are more distinguished than those whom everyone sees lament-ing amorous quarrels day and night"). They encourage him to question his career in the pastoral woods: "Ché se viver qua giù tanto ne aggrada / errando in questo bosco, / che fia salir per la superna strada?" (73–75; "Because if living here below pleases us so much wandering in this wood, what would it be to ascend through the heavenly route?"). The speaker fails, however, to answer that question.

Questioning begets more questioning. Addressing Apollo, patron of the muses, the speaker asks of himself whether he is able to celebrate in some other kind of poetry a worthier undertaking than love:

> *potrò dir io con rime argute e pronte*
> *il bel principio altero, e la corona*
> *vittrice, onde Aragona*
> *sparce l'imperio suo per ogni gente?*
>
> (80–83)

can I explain with keen and ready rhymes the proud beginning and the conquering crown whence Aragon spread its command everywhere?

The *canzone's* conclusion outlines a possible epic on three generations of Neapolitan glory. It will depict the rule of Ferrante and his sons Alfonso and Federigo, "i bei rami che uscìr di tal radice" (96; "the fine branches that issue from such a root"). But the speaker's confidence in his abilities notably wanes. Twice at the poem's conclusion he qualifies his designs with a conditional *if*. Both clauses express uncertainty. First the speaker casts doubt on his power to complete such an epic design:

> *Indi, se aven che al viver frale e manco*
> *non lenti il corso il mio debile ingegno,*
> *ma con vittoria al segno*
> *pur giunga, si com'io bramando spero.*
>
> (106–9)

Thence, if it happens that in my frail and declining days my weak talent does not slacken its course but rather arrives victoriously at its goal, as I so longingly hope.

Then, at the poem's very end he casts doubt on his power even to initiate such a design:

> *Ma se pur fia che Amor non mi distempre,*
> *vedrai col suo poeta*
> *Napol bella levarsi e viver sempre.*
>
> (125–27)

But if only Love does not untune me, you will see beautiful
Naples rise with its poet and live eternally.

Love is the culprit as well as the motivating force. It inspires
him to compose poetry, but it prevents him from succeeding in
any mode other than the one associated with rustic compliment
and complaint.

As the *Rime's* final and longest *canzone*, this poem therefore implies the speaker's attenuation of plans to compose a political
epic. It simultaneously affirms his competence in the more
modest pastoral mode. In the hierarchy of genres, this mode
functions in a middle range that potentially accommodates
high and low without devoting itself exclusively to either. Here
the speaker feels more comfortable. If at this point he lacks
confidence in his power to engage the epic muse, he remains
content to exercise his humbler skill. Throughout the *Rime*, in
fact, he celebrates that skill, obliquely in *Canzone* LXXXIX and
overtly, as we have seen, in *Canzoni* XLI and LIII and Sonnets
XXXV and XCVI. In such ways the *Rime* dramatize the speaker's acceptance of pastoral.

Certainly the magnificent sestina that opens the *Rime's* second part dramatizes that acceptance.[27] It explicitly relates the
speaker's literary activity as a poet to his travail as a lover, and
it resolves both in the embrace of pastoral. Its first line, "Spente
eran nel mio cor le antiche fiamme" ("The old flames had been
extinguished in my breast"), indicates, with its allusion to Dido's "veteris vestigia flammae" from Virgil's *Aeneid* IV. 23, that
the speaker has emerged from one love affair only to find himself on the verge of another. Indeed, he now feels himself entrapped by Love and obliged to adjust both his amatory life and
his poetic style to a new register: "mi senti' ritener da un forte

laccio, / per cui cangiar conviemmi e vita e stile" (5–6; "I felt myself restrained by a strong snare which obliged me to change my life and style"). The conjunction of "vita e stile" at the end of the initial stanza suggests the interpenetration of life and art that the ensuing *Rime* will explore.

The sestina's most powerfully repeated rhyme word, *stile*, dominates the poem's development. In the first line of the second stanza the speaker complains that neither tongue nor pen (*stile* in its other Italian meaning) can adequately describe his torment: "Lingua non poria mai narrar né stile / quante spine pungenti e quante fiamme" (7–8; "Neither tongue nor pen can ever recount how many stinging prickles and flames"). The speaker responds to signs of new love by a retreat to his accustomed forest: "ond'io, scorgendo i segni d'altra guerra, / pensai di rimboscarmi a le mie selve" (10–11; "whence I, perceiving the signs of another war, thought to reafforest myself in my own woods"). Both *segni*, "signs," and *selve*, "woods," evoke the forest of words, linguistic signs that the poet uses to construct his art.

The association becomes explicit in the next stanza when the speaker addresses Fortune and begs her to modify her own harsh style: "e tu, Fortuna, muta il crudo stile" (14; "And you, Fortune, change your crude style"). He now beseeches his fates to send him back to the shepherds and the woods, to the strains of his earlier song: "rendetemi a' pastori et a la selve, / al cantar primo" (15–16; "send me back to the shepherds and the woods, to my first song"). He seeks the simpler, sweeter style of the pastoral mode that he had mastered in his youth. In the fourth stanza this wish begets a sharp exclamation: "Ch'io tornar possa al mio rustico stile" (22; "that I could return to my rustic style!"). The exclamation in turn begets a stanza of autobiographical narrative:

> *Tempo fu ch'io cantai per poggi e selve,*
> *e cantando portai nascoso il laccio;*
> *poi piacque al ciel suttrarme a quelle fiamme,*

> et a' caldi sospir prometter pace.
> Allor m'accinsi ad un più raro stile,
> non credendo giamai più sentir guerra.
>
> (25–30)

There was a time when I sang in the hills and the woods, and singing I wore my snare hidden from view; next, it pleased heaven to draw me from those flames and to prom- ise peace for those hot sighs; then I set about adopting a more exquisite style, believing myself no more subject to love's strife.

In his youth the speaker had used pastoral forms to conceal his amorous torment. Upon release from that torment, he began to develop "un più raro stile," referring perhaps to his preoccupa- tion with reviving the Latin style of classical antiquity. Now, however, he finds himself drawn back to the vernacular in a sig- nificant way.

The narrative parallels the evolution of Sannazaro's own ca- reer, from the vernacular *Arcadia*, which in part allegorizes the speaker's pursuit of a youthful love affair, to the Neo-Latin pro- duction of his maturity. At the same time it announces late in Sannazaro's life the poet's renewed interest in polishing these youthful *rime* for publication. In the sestina's concluding lines the speaker suggests the complexity of this integration of his life with art. On the one hand he is returning to a vernacular style that is *antico* for him because he had mastered it long ago: "e seguir mi fa pur l'antico stile" (33; "and [Love] makes me pursue even my old style"). On the other hand he is pursuing a ver- nacular style that is *novo* for him because he is continually re- vising it to meet current Petrarchan norms: "e novo laccio ordir con novo stile" (39; "to lay a new snare with a new style"). The juxtaposition of *antico* and *novo* describes Sannazaro's lifelong absorption in his pastoral endeavor. By returning to the old models of ancient pastoral he found new resources to develop his own vernacular art. Those models themselves conceal still more ancient traces of classical civilization. By applying them at a yet later period of his own life to a deepening interest in Latin composition, Sannazaro would restore the vitality of antiquity to the Latin style of his own age. This sestina records that project, just as the *Rime* as a whole represent it. They adumbrate for Sannazaro the importance of cultivating Neo-Latin verse.

NEO-LATIN EPIGRAMS AND ODES

The cultivation of Neo-Latin verse might seem to impose tight constraints upon the practicing poet. It subjects him to the rigors of an alien tongue, an abstract prosody, and a conventional set of themes, forms, and motifs that long since seem to have outlived their usefulness. In fact, however, they did not. For bilingual poets like Jacopo Sannazaro and some of his contemporaries, the cultivation of Neo-Latin verse proved to be a liberating experience. Intimacy and the expression of personal qualities came easier in the older language, where they had more of an expressive precedent in ancient than in modern literature. The precise demands of versification allowed the young poet to develop his craft in such a way that it could become flexible enough to meet all his needs. The conventions themselves in their very number opened to him a storehouse of materials apt for every use. An awareness of resources inherent in the Neo-Latin literary tradition, especially those inherent in the pastoral, therefore increased the poet's options rather than restricted them.

Sannazaro's freest verse in the vernacular occurs in a series of semidramatic *farse* on various topics and in a series of light-hearted verses on random topics called *gliuommero* (ball of thread.)[28] Cast in *frottola* verse, a form of eleven-syllable line whose fifth syllable rhymes with the last syllable of the preceding line, and a form that Sannazaro would employ extensively in *Arcadia*, the *farse* range from two masques written to celebrate the Moors' expulsion from Granada (they were performed on 4 and 6 March 1492) through two others drawing upon elements of exotic romance (*Farsa della ambasciaria del soldano*, The Farce of the Sultan's Ambassador) and classical myth (an untitled farce on Venus's search for Cupid), to two moralistic ones on the carpe diem theme (untitled) and on unrequited love (*Predica de' XII heremiti*, The Admonition of Twelve Monks). The *gliuommero* is also cast in *frottola* verse and rendered in a highly idiomatic Neapolitan dialect. It ranges from a catalogue of exotic foods (15–24) to gossip about contemporary individuals (66–74). Brief, seemingly spontaneous, this work clearly constitutes a youthful *jeu d'esprit*.

Paradoxically, however, the linguistic, prosodic, and thematic freedom of the *farse* and *gliuommero* does little service to Sannazaro's poetic powers. If it contributed at all towards the development of his pastoral, it did so in the give-and-take of its dialogue and colloquial language. The dialogue, however, is anything but pliant or spirited, while the colloquialisms are obscure and exasperating. Sannazaro attained much more substantial freedom within the confines of his own Latin verse. That verse includes epigrams, odes, elegies, and two short narratives, the *Salices,* and the *Lamentatio de Morte Christi*, in addition to his *Piscatoriae* and *De Partu Virginis*. There he attained his metier.

Of all his Neo-Latin poetry, the epigrams support the widest range of topics. By convention epigrams are short poems in several meters succinctly stating an attitude or point of view or summing up an action or event already known to the audience. Their length can vary from two lines to as many as thirty or forty (Sannazaro's longest is sixty-one lines), but rarely do they exceed ten or twelve lines. They owe their origins to inscriptional verse commending or reproaching the deeds of particular persons. In this respect they resemble the epitaph. The epigram's distinction is its witty turn or sententious comment that usually concludes the poem. This turn or comment almost always occurs as an antithesis, paradox, or pun that the speaker states or implies.[29] Its style aims at a concision and wit that Sannazaro would employ to great advantage in his pastorals.

As poetry of statement the epigram also resembles the maxim, though the latter is usually of an abstract, general nature while the epigram is nothing if not concrete, specific, and composed for a particular occasion. These last qualities figure prominently in the epigrams of *The Greek Anthology*. Their effort is to capture in as few words as possible the fleeting nature of a memorable deed or impression. Martial (ca. A.D. 40–104), on the other hand, developed a different kind of epigram by sharpening the wit and emphasizing the speaker's commentary. Martial's example prevailed throughout the Renaissance.

The structure of Martial's epigrams divides in half. The first part generates some expectation or anticipation, while the second affords a new disclosure or offers to explain the evidence. Sometimes the speaker tacitly assumes the audience's knowledge of the topic in question, and often he simply indicates the topic only in the poem's title. Both by its structure and by its elliptical nature the epigram demands a good deal of the audience's interpretative participation in its unfolding. Unlike elegies, epigrams are not subjective meditations or personal outpourings but rather rhetorical displays in the virtuoso epideictic vein. In sepulchral epigrams the speaker's moralistic stance enhances his commendation of the dead, just as in adulatory ones it enhances his commendation of the living. In reproachful epigrams it inclines towards satire, whether of a generalized type or of a type aimed at specific individuals, often with disguised names. This stance would serve Sannazaro well in the satiric portions of his own pastoral eclogues.

Sannazaro's epigrams also exhibit some of the broad range that his pastorals display. They develop conventional classical topics of praise, blame, friendship, love, funeral lament, and mythological fantasy. His laudatory epigrams honor his rulers and patrons, the royal Alfonso, Ferrandino, and Federigo; his aristocratic friends and acquaintances like Acquaviva, Assanio, Caudole, and D'Alvo; and members of the humanist circle like Pontano, Cariteo, Summonte, Compatre, and Cotta. Other epigrams make satiric fun of individuals in those circles: misers, cuckolds, pedants, and old fools, usually identified not by proper name but by role or class like "Quinzio," "Pretor," and "Vetustino." Sometimes the speaker quite clearly designates the object of his scorn, as when he names Poggio, Platina, and Poliziano, against the last of whom he directs four particularly cutting epigrams. Sannazaro reserves his harshest scorn for several contemporary popes and members of the Borgia family, whom he criticized on social, moral, and political grounds. These epigrams, together with other surprisingly obscene, lewdly pornographic ones, received ecclesiastical censure and were not printed until the Amsterdam edition of 1728.[30] Still, they bear the same stamp of Sannazaro's talent as the pastoral, amatory, and mythological ones that have long held esteem in the poet's canon.

A legend circulated by Crispo represents Sannazaro as composing the majority of his epigrams to amuse fellow soldiers and travellers during military campaigns with Alfonso in 1482–83.[31] Whatever the occasion, Sannazaro never judged them fit for publication in his lifetime. Late in his career he entrusted their manuscript to his friend, Antonio Garlon, who gave them to the famous Venetian printer, Paolo Manuzio, after Sannazaro's death. Manuzio's edition of the Latin poems in 1535 was itself incomplete.[32] Censorship prevented the publication of the antipapal epigrams, while the printer's own selection eliminated many poems on obscure or little-known people. To this date, the Amsterdam edition of 1728 remains the only complete one in print.

A mature epigram in honor of Pontano (I. 13/11) typifies Sannazaro's style. In it the speaker praises his humanist master for improving upon the text of Catullus's poetry in an emendation of 1489. If Catullus himself should return to life, he would be delighted to approve Pontano's corrections. Addressing Pontano, master of the pastoral flock directed towards the classical revival, the speaker says that Catullus would repeatedly embrace him and kiss him in gratitude, and would prefer the new version to his own original: "Ille tibi amplexus, atque oscula

grata referret; / Mallet et hos numeros, quam meminisse suos"
(5–6; "He would greet you with embraces and grateful kisses;
and he would prefer to have remembered these verses rather than
his own).[33] The epigram confirms the speaker's own youthful
enthusiasm about the humanist enterprise. It offers tribute to
Pontano as one who could revive the glory of the ancient past,
and even improve upon it; but still more it radiates the speaker's confidence that such an endeavor can succeed. The speaker
has not yet perceived the distance that separates him from the
past, nor has he yet imagined that each attempt to recreate the
past in conjectural terms betrays it. At the same time he has
not yet evolved for himself a sustaining concept of tradition
able to overcome the negativity of this perception. For the moment, his attitude on these matters is serene.

The speaker accords other humanist friends particularly touch-
ing tributes. An epigram at the beginning of Book II addresses
the soldier-scholar Andrea Matteo Acquaviva, the speaker's
friend and later an editor of De Partu Virginis. He had fallen
into disrepute when he supported the barons in their revolt of
1486, but Sannazaro took charge of rehabilitating his name. He
characterizes Acquaviva as such a superb soldier that it might
seem difficult to convince others of his literary talents as well:
"Quis mites illum Permessi hausisse liquores / Credat, et im-
belles excoluisse lyras?" (II.2/1 "Who would believe that he had
drunk from the calm waters of Permesso and had cultivated the
peaceful lyre?") At home in the pastoral fields of poetry as on
the battlefield, Acquaviva represents in II.38/27 an ideal for
the speaker to celebrate.

Within the circle of his humanist friends the speaker commemorates births, deaths, and other significant events in several epigrams. In I.7/5 he acknowledges the birthday of Gabriele Altilio, bishop of Policastro, poet, and tutor of young
Prince Ferdinand. In I.11/9 he pays an elegant tribute to Cariteo by celebrating his daughter's birth in 1495. The poem tells
what happened among the gods while the mother was in labor.
Led by Venus, Mars, and the Graces, half the deities wanted a

girl; led by Minerva, Apollo, and the Muses, the other half wanted a boy. Cupid teases the gods until Jupiter makes up his mind. When a girl is born, Venus rejoices because the Graces themselves have now increased in number.

In a different vein Sannazaro mourns the death of Ibla, the mistress of Marullus (I.43/38). As much as he honors the woman by evoking his own tender feelings about her (3), he honors Marullus as well by affirming the latter's fidelity to her. The longest epigram in the collection he devotes to the death in 1501 of Pietro Golino, il Compatre (II.16/14). Elsewhere he praises the thoughtfulness and *pietas* of Summonte, editor of Sannazaro's works as well as of Pontano's. By publishing their works, Summonte composed fit memorials for his deceased friends (II.10/8).

Even in dealing with the most lugubrious of topics, however, he can limn the weightiest sentiment with light touches similar to those in the pastorals. Thus, in his elegy on the death of Giovanni Cotta in 1510, he coyly chides Fate for having deprived Verona of its second Catullus. "Quae tamen ut vidit morientis frigida Cottae / Ora, suum fassa est crimen, et erubuit" (II.45/33; "Hardly had Fate encountered the cold figure of the dying Cotta than she confessed her crime and blushed"). In his own lifetime Sannazaro himself sought to repay the damage that Fate had done to Cotta's brief career. He insisted on the publication of Cotta's fourteen Latin poems along with his own in the 1529 edition of his works. Cotta's poetry soon earned the admiration it deserved, but only because Sannazaro had helped to bring it to light.

The form of the epigram has particular affinity for the kind of satire that pervades the pastoral mode. Short, hence pointed, and almost always elliptical in its assumptions and implications, the epigram derives its highest power from judicious irony. The epigrammatist can exult when he is sure that some members of his audience will miss the point entirely while others will share it fully. Specifically he hopes that the victim of his irony will see the point but prefer not to admit it. Shrewder members of his audience, on the other hand, will always perceive it. Whenever successful under such guises as those of pastoral, this irony enforces a bond between author and audience as they share attitudes towards textual signs that imply something different. It is the pulse of the communicative act.

The gallery of satiric caricatures includes many types. The most lengthy one (forty-seven lines) represents "a little old man," *Vetustinus*, intent on supervising the construction of his own tomb (I.41/36). The comic flavor results from his extreme stinginess. Although he has commissioned an enormous memorial for himself, he has spent his life in want and deprivation, living in the humblest quarters and surviving on leftovers. Now he wearies the architects of his tomb by making them search high and low for models and materials to build the monument, and in the afternoons he locks them inside their studies until they finish their work (33–36). The speaker concludes with a direct address to the old man, exhorting him to relax, rest, and give some respite to his workers.

The speaker addresses far more ironic epigrams to rival members of the humanist profession. Often he does so for personal rather than professional reasons. Surprisingly (I.67/56) he attacks his great Florentine contemporary, Poliziano, for courting the mistress of his friend, Marullus, though otherwise Sannazaro was close to Poliziano in artistic temperament and political conviction. The first epigram addressed to Poliziano is the most scurrilous. It concerns the topic of literary interpretation. The speaker begins with a pun on his opponent's name by relating it etymologically to Latin *pulex*, "flea." He says that one ought not call Poliziano a flea because as a grammarian he is inferior to fleas (I.66). Poliziano has glossed Catullus's poem about his pet sparrow to mean something that no reader can accept as modest. He interprets it as Catullus's homosexual proposition of a young boy. The speaker remarks that Poliziano ought to know by his own experience of such matters: "Solus qui bene calleas poetas" (I.66.17; "You who know such poets so well by experience"). He congratulates Poliziano for rising above the ignorant crowd with his superior understanding, and conjectures that perhaps Catullus's boy friend may have been none other than Virgil. When he hears the muses laughing, he chides them with mock indignation. Poliziano probably wishes that Catullus had propositioned him (I.66.26–28).

In a second epigram against Poliziano (I.67/56), the speaker compares his opponent's attempt to seduce Marullus's beloved with the Titan's attempt to unseat Jove. With such a comparison it was of course possible for the speaker to acknowledge Poliziano's real and prodigious merits as a poet. By the poem's end, however, he attenuates the comparison by reducing the Florentine poet and his compatriots to a pack of fleas, for not only Poliziano's name, but also that of Luigi Pulci (1432–84), is related etymologically to *pulex*.

On occasion the lambent wit of these epigrams can pass over into frank obscenity. The Aldine edition of 1535, and all subsequent editions printed in Italy, excluded three mythological epigram and four others on various topics because of their lewdness. The three mythic ones deal with the gods' homosexual affairs. In II.20 Deianira complains that Hercules has shifted his affection from her to Ganymede. In II.34 Jupiter comments with jealousy on Hercules' passion for Hylas. And in II.51 Juno coyly bids Ganymede entertain his lord and lover. Among the other obscene poems, the best is an erotic entreaty addressed to Nina requesting sexual favors (I.6). In an amusing vein is I.63 where an urbane gentleman asks Phyllis why her chubby buttocks appear to be biting her gown when she walks; she replies that her gown is merely wiping her "lips" so he can kiss them.

In addition to these epigrams there are others deleted from the canon for their controversial satiric nature. They criticize the popes whose political dealings Sannazaro experienced firsthand in his lifetime. Sannazaro regards these popes as perverse shepherds who have neglected their pastoral duties.

His attitude towards the first two popes of the sixteenth century is unambiguous. He resented Julius II (1503–13) for refusing to intervene in the exile of Federigo and himself. Addressing Julius in II.48/36 by his name and former title as Julianus Roverus (Giuliano Della Rovere), cardinal of St. Peter in Chains, he laments that he himself will perish unless that prelate change matters; "Nil meminit praeter vincula et exsilium: (4; "but Julius thinks only of chains and banishment"). Here the chains refer both to Federigo's exile and to the lucrative benefice of Julius's see, St. Peter in Chains. The pope is unwilling to look beyond his own self-interest. Julius's successor, the Medici Pope Leo X (1513–21), receives a different kind of criticism in II.57. Sannazaro never forgave Leo for taking the side of Cassandra Marchese's husband in granting him their divorce. Accordingly he characterizes Leo as shortsighted, *caeculus*, and, punning on the pope's chosen name as "lion," addresses him as more a mole than the king of beasts. Any other name, he concludes, would be more proper for him than "Leo." Later, in III.8 on Leo's death, the speaker asks whether his audience knows why the pope could not receive the last rites. The reason, he asserts, is that he had already sold them simoniacally.

Sannazaro resented the narrowness, self-absorption, and protectivism of these popes, but he positively loathed the political alliances, machinations, and duplicity of their immediate predecessors, Innocent VIII (1484–92) and Alexander VI (1492–1503). Both of them pursued explicitly anti-Neapolitan policies, the former aiding the barons in their revolt against the king of Naples in 1486, the latter aiding the French and the Spanish in their invasions of Italy. And both entertained dynastic ambitions for their own illegitimate issue. I.38 on Innocent VIII is a masterpiece of understatement. It is fair, the speaker says, that the ancient Quirites are indebted to this harmless man (the adjective puns on Innocent's name) for he replenished the depleted population with his own progeny. The joke alludes to the pope's children, whom he instated as heirs with full rights and privileges. Alexander VI would follow this precedent even more outrageously with his own offspring. Sannazaro's attitude towards Innocent was contemptuous, but his attitude towards the Borgia pope and his family would burn with hatred.

The Borgia Pope Alexander VI and his heirs, Lucretia and Cesare, received Sannazaro's scorn in the poet's eighteen most malicious epigrams. He ascribes to Alexander VI the direct cause of the wars that ravaged Italy in his time. Upon Alexander's death, Sannazaro addresses Alecto, chief of the furies, and asks whether she knows why peace had dawned and strife so suddenly fallen silent. The reason is this pope's death (I.22). In life he was indeed a fisher of men since he fished for his son's benefits with nets and snares laid for others (I.51). For his mistress he selected a woman named Julia, though one should rather say that he raped her. Sannazaro mordantly compares the rape of Europa by the fine young Tirian bull to the rape of Julia by this Spanish bull ("Borgia" derives etymologically from *bos, bovis,* "bull"). Among his predecessors he had affinities only with someone like Sixtus IV, whose name his own numeral parodies grotesquely. Sixtus (1471–84) was a munificent pope, one of the earliest restorers of Rome in the fifteenth century. When Rome thought it would see another Sixtus, it saw Alexander VI instead, and it groaned (I.57).

The diversity of modes and styles in Sannazaro's three books of epigrams is wholly admirable. Composed over a long period of time, those books reflect a wealth of tones, moods, and attitudes from amatory to funereal, mythological to historical, adulatory to satiric. They provided Sannazaro with a forum to raise his poetic voice on various occasions, and he in turn rewarded those occasions with all the polish, craft, and precision of which he was capable. He of course demonstrated that capability to much greater effect in *Arcadia,* the *Piscatoriae,* and *De Partu Virginis,* but his pastoral poetry there might not have been so rich if he hadn't honed it in the workshop of his shorter verse.

For all their variety, however, the epigrams tend to limit their prosodic range to hexameters and elegiac meters. Sannazaro would develop far more complicated rhythms in the various

stanzaic forms of *Arcadia* and in the flowing hexameters of the
Piscatoriae and *De Partu Virginis*. Part of his education in prosody came from his creative experiment with the Neo-Latin ode.
Sannazaro produced a thin output of eight odes. As individual
poems they are slender and slightly precious, not necessarily
bad poems, but not complex, dynamic ones, either. Their major contribution to Sannazaro's development was to expand his
prosodic ability. The diversity of his Italian meters and the suppleness of his later Latin ones surely owe something to his work
in the ode.

The ode is characteristically the most noble of lyric forms.[34]
With its strophic divisions it usually represents themes of high
seriousness and general importance. It addresses its audience as
a collectivity attending a public performance. It presumes that
audience's familiarity with the larger context of its topicality
and with the mythic and cultural allusions that it uses to illustrate its theme. In ancient Greece Pindar gave this form its
classical embodiment, but other poets managed successfully to
put it to varied uses. Anacreon, for example, conferred on it a
musical simplicity by making it the vehicle for drinking songs,
declarations of love, and short idylls. In Roman literature Horace identified it as the form most apt for expressing social and
ethical preoccupations of a serious sort, as well as his private,
personal, amatory preoccupations, all in a sustained lyric voice
that emphasizes the workings of the inner life.

Horace's concept of the ode prevailed in the Renaissance.
With the recovery of Greek influence, Francesco Filelfo (1398–
1481) reinstituted the more stately Pindaric form in his Latin
verse. The odes of Cristoforo Landino (1424–98) attest to their
popularity in Medici Florence. Among Sannazaro's friends,
Marullus and Pontano composed several odes in Latin. Afterwards Andrea Navagero (1483–1529), Ariosto (1474–1533),
Della Casa (1503–56), Bernardino Rota (1508–75), and Tor-
quato Tasso (1544–95) all wrote Latin odes. The Aldine edition
of Pindar in 1513 stimulated interest in the form, and within a
few years odes began to appear in the vernacular written by

Giangiorgio Trissino (1478–1550), Luigi Alamanni (1495–1556), Antonio Sebastian Minturno (1500–74), and Bernardo Tasso (1493–1569). In France the Pléiade accorded it a high formal status. In England such different poets as Drayton, Jonson, Herrick, Marvell, and Milton produced notable odes.

Sannazaro composed his Latin odes in the early years of the sixteenth century just before his exile with King Federigo. In the Aldine edition of his Latin works in 1535, they are interspersed throughout his collection of epigrams. Two of them (I, III) observe the Sapphic metrical form with three lines of ‾ ˘ | ‾ ˘ | ‾ || ˘ ˘ | ‾ ˘ | ‾ ˘ followed by a line of ‾ ˘ ˘ | ‾ ˘.[35] Two (5, 8) observe the Anacreontic form with octosyllabic lines followed by iambic dimeters. The others (II, IV, VI, VII) are variations on the Sapphic form. These eccentric meters reflect Sannazaro's confusion about the ode's form. He was writing when classical accomplishments in the ode were still imperfectly understood. The Anacreontics had been discovered in 1498, but Sappho and Pindar were not published until 1508 and 1513 respectively. Horace's long-standing example naturally afforded the best one for Sannazaro, but he overlooked a good many features of classical art: Horace's regular caesura, his avoidance of monosyllables, and the correspondence of his word accent with long syllables all find no consistent parallels in Sannazaro. The major similarities between the ancient poet and the modern one are tonal and thematic. Sannazaro had a good sense of the ode's capacities for personal, poetic, and religious topics, and he explored them deftly and often eloquently.

In Ode I the speaker addresses his beloved villa of Mergellina. He characterizes it as the dwelling place of pastoral nymphs and muses and emblem of time's passage and the endurance of art. Formerly the villa had been the jewel and delight of the Angevin kings ruling Naples. But time has passed and that family no longer holds power. The figure of the poet becomes now a connecting link that joins past and future in the present act of poetic composition. His patron, now the reigning king, has given him the villa as a reward for his earlier pastoral poetry and as a pledge that he will continue to honor the royal family in ensuing compositions. In thanks the speaker asks his servant to bring him his lyre (25–6). The praise that he sings will guarantee eternal fame for his patron and himself, all the more since the one has rejuvenated the other and the muses themselves have awakened to his gift of Mergellina:

> Principis nostri decus, atque laudes
> Fama, per latas spatiate terras,
> Evehat, qua Sol oriens, cadensque
> Frena retorquet.
>
> (29–32)[36]

Fame, having walked through far-off lands, bears the ornament and praise of my prince wherever the rising and falling sun pulls the rein on its horses.

Ode IV constitutes a better performance. In it the speaker on his own birthday offers Saint Nazarius a feast-day hymn from his present quarters in exile. He expresses surprise to his saint, whom he addresses as his own foster father, pater alme (9), that even in far-off lands during his exile he should find shrines dedicated to him. Apostrophizing the saint, he traces his own family's name, Sannazaro, to St. Nazarius, and he celebrates the coincidence that he himself was born on the saint's very feast day, 28 July (19–20). Now on the shores of the Saône the speaker feels himself not entirely isolated, however distant he may be from his homeland. A serving boy enters just as he is evoking memories of the river Sebeto. The speaker pauses to address the boy, instructing him to gather fronds to honor the saint (37–40). Then he recalls the Sebeto in an extended apostrophe: "O ubi dulces patriae recessus / Abluis, Sebethe, loca illa myrto / Consita" (41–43 "O where, Sebeto, are you washing the sweet recesses of my homeland, filled with woods and myrtle").

The rhetoric confirms the speaker's retreat to his inner selfhood. On the surface he is addressing Saint Nazarius, but in substance he is meditating on his own fate: why, he asks, is he not allowed to celebrate his own birthday and the saint's feast at home (53–6)? Why is it not enough that he has endured the hardships of travel without having to face the prospects of eternal exile? In the final lines his prayer shifts from laudatory to petitional as the speaker asks to see once more the smoke rising from his ancestral roof (59–60). The ode has advanced from a devotional exercise to a personal self-examination. In his *Piscatoriae* and even in passages of his epic *De Partu Virginis* Sannazaro would attempt a similar self-examination. It would be one of pastoral's virtues to encourage that kind of inner reflection amid dynamic and dramatic kinds of outer representation.

ELEGIES AND SALICES

In his Neo-Latin elegies, too, Sannazaro would cultivate an inner reflectiveness. His audiences must nonetheless approach the elegies from a properly classical perspective. The modern, post-Romantic concept of elegy implies a melancholy, meditative mode of poetry. The ancient concept, however, implied a meter, not a mode.[37] The Greek and Roman elegy was a sequence of couplets or distichs alternating a regular dactylic hexameter with a truncated one. As in epic meters, the regular hexameter line could combine heavy spondees with lighter dactyls, but the contrasting line would always omit unaccented parts (called the arsis) of the third and sixth feet; the two full feet in the second half of this line were normally dactylic; and a prolonged pause or quarter rest would follow each truncated foot:

$$\acute{}\,\bar{}\,\smile \mid \acute{}\,\bar{}\,\smile \mid \acute{}\,\bar{}\,\smile \parallel \acute{}\,\bar{}\,\smile \mid \acute{}\,\smile\,\smile \mid \bar{}\,\bar{} \parallel$$

$$\acute{}\,\bar{}\,\smile \mid \acute{}\,\bar{}\,\smile \mid \acute{} \parallel \acute{}\,\smile\,\smile \mid \acute{}\,\smile\,\smile \mid \bar{} \parallel .$$

The division of the pentameter into two similar, if not always identical, halves imparts a lyrical charm to the stately hexameter that precedes it. The line hesitates at the center and halts at the end with a quarter rest, only to lead into a rolling hexameter on the next line. Because of these pauses, each alternating verse falls into two natural halves. Because of its metrical symmetry, moreover, each alternating verse often lends itself to the use of internal rhyme in its spondaic feet. The overall effect is to modify the epic hexameter to express fugitive tones, subjective moods, and personal attitudes. Later Sannazaro would capture these same moods more subtly in his pastoral hexameters.

The earliest examples of the Greek elegy convey a wide range of feelings. In texts by Archilochus, Mimnermus, Philetas, and other older poets, elegiac topics include politics, war, friendship, love, pain, and death. With Callimachus and the Hellenistic poets it sometimes lent itself to mythological narrative with an accent on exploring the complex emotions underlying the events and juxtaposing them against the speaker's subjective predicament. In Augustan Rome the elegy became a vehicle for love poetry. Its greatest practitioners—Catullus, Tibullus, Propertius, Ovid—composed their poems within a span of less than fifty years, and the later ones gave evidence of considering themselves the earlier ones' comrades, *sodales*, all members of a group, *sodalicium*, a friendly circle, *convictus*.

To the humanists of the Renaissance, the notion of a sodality exerted a great appeal. Among them the elegy becomes almost a medium of exchanging common thoughts and feelings on a variety of topics. These include the ancient and especially Roman ones of politics, friendship, love, and death, but they also embrace the common pursuit of study, cultivation of the past, devotion to art, and the development of personal literary style.

One of the best Neo-Latin elegists of the Renaissance was Sannazaro's master, Giovanni Pontano. His two books of elegies entitled the *Parthenopeus*, whose title proclaims his adoptive Neapolitan citizenship, include several elegies on the development of his own poetic career. In II.18, for example, he tells how an Umbrian nymph summoned him to his career as a poet, and how Bacchus encouraged his composition of love poetry.[38] The *Parthenopeus* also reflects the Propertian and Ovidian modes in its subtitle, *Amorum Libri*. Into conventionally amorous themes and motifs Pontano incorporates others, too, such as the Ovidian one of metamorphosis. The collection's final elegy (II.14), for example, sings of how the sea god, Nereus, angry at his wife's adultery with Sebeto, transformed the handsome youth into the stream that Sannazaro later celebrated in his pastoral poetry. In yet another collection of elegies, *De Amore Conjugali*, Pontano sang of love for his wife, the fictionalized Ariadna. Finally, in *De Tumulis* Pontano used the elegiac distich for a series of laments on the deaths of loved ones, members of his family, and acquaintances high and low at the Neapolitan court.

Sannazaro's approach to the elegiac form in his Latin poetry was more austere than Pontano's. As with his epigrams and odes, Sannazaro did not rate his elegies high enough to publish them in his lifetime, and Antonio Garlon was ultimately responsible for their printing in Venice in 1535.[39] Sannazaro's elegies are much better poems than his odes and many of his epigrams. In them he treats of materials and motifs close to his personal interests. His elegies dramatize the life of a humanist in the Italian Renaissance.

The elegy on the ruins of Cumae (II.9) is a good example. Its brooding, impersonal, abstractly meditative tone is atypical of Sannazaro's elegies, for on the whole the latter evoke a record of the poet's life full of vibrant detail. The elegy on Cumae does, however, exemplify the metrical craft that distinguishes Sannazaro's competence in the genre. The poem's rhetorical argument divides into three equal parts. The first constitutes an eight-line comparison between the past city and its present ruins, followed by two lines that summarize the comparison. The second part (11–20) repeats the pattern of the first. The third part (21–32) constitutes a series of addresses to the audience, to the speaker's self, and to other major cities of the modern world, and it ends with a recapitulation. The structural symmetry, particularly of the first two parts, reinforces the sense of strength and solidity that time has undermined and destroyed in Cumae's ruins, while the rhetorical shifts and turns to various audiences near the poem's conclusion suggest the dissolution and change wrought by time's passage. At the end, time seems speeded up. The elegiac metrical scheme contributes brilliantly towards achieving that effect.

That metrical scheme is carefully controlled throughout the poem. The elegy's first eight lines compare Cumae's glamor in its prime with its decaying ruins in the present. Its seven opening lines introduced by *hic* explicate the glamor. The eighth line, introduced by *nunc*, initiates the decay.

> Hic, ubi Cumeae surgebant inclyta famae
>   Moenia, Tyrrheni gloria prima maris;
> Longinquis quo saepe hospea properabat ab oris
>   Visurus tripodas, Delie magne tuos;
> Et vagus antiquos intrabat navita portus,
>   Quaerens Daedaliae conscia signa fugae:
> (Credere quis quondam potuit, dum fata manebant?)
>   Nunc silva agrestes occulit alta feras.
>
> (1–8)[40]

Here, where the renowned walls of famed Cumae rose, the prime glory of the Mediterranean, where visitors often hurried from far-off shores to see your tripods, great Apollo, and the wandering sailor entered your ancient ports seeking recognizable signs of Daedalus's flight (for who could believe it, while fate held sway), now a deep forest hides wild beasts.

In metrical terms, the hexameter's odd lines represent the city's stateliness in the past, while the alternating lines with pauses in the third and sixth foot imply the vulnerability of that stateliness, the city's halting advance towards diminution and reduction. The poem's first dactylic hexameter, for example, extends grammatically into the second line with the subject, *moenia*, "walls," positioned at the beginning of that line. With the next word, *Tyrrheni*, however, the spondee and its concluding long syllable introduce a quarter rest into the line's midst that signals the start of Cumae's dissolution. In line 4 the address to Apollo, the Delian god, provides a distraction from the elegiac pause after *tripodas*, "tripods," while the tying of the arsis after *tuos*, "your," brings that line to its grammatical conclusion. In line 6 the pause after *Dedaliae* draws attention to the "conscia signa fugae" ("recognizable signs of flight") in the line's second half. Vanishing signs of the mythic flight are all that remain to testify its earlier occurence. At Cumae those signs are embedded in decaying rock and stones and may be visible to the perceptive eye as all that remains of the city. In this poem those signs are verbal ones in a pattern of metrical sound structure but attenuated in a pattern of fragile syntax and ambiguous semantics.

Lines 9 and 10 reinforce the preceding motif in miniature. The regular hexameter portrays the city in its past glory when the sibyls sheltered their prophetic enigmas, but the elegiac response of the next line depicts the present site as a grazing ground for sheep: "Atque ubi fatidicae latuere arcana Sibyllae, / Nunc claudit saturas vespere pastor oves" (9–10; "And where prophesying Sibyls keep their secrets, / now the shepherd keeps his well-fed sheep at evening"). The intrusion of the pastoral landscape is significant at this point. Emblematically it telescopes the career of ancient literary history from which the pastoral mode grew as a late development. Pastoral emerged as a hybrid of earlier forms that it appropriated for its own purposes, just as at Cumae the shepherds eventually took over the tract of that deserted city and tended it for their own purposes. The former is a record of poetic development, the latter of human history. Both represent a rehabilitation of abandoned materials, a conferring of presence upon elements marked by absence. In the pastoral literary mode the poet would begin with the classical evidence of that particular form and then work backwards to grasp its subterranean origins, its concealed first principles, the preconditions of literary history that generated the now absent grandeur of past cultures.

The elegy's next ten lines repeat the movement of its first ten. They too contrast Cumae's former glory with its present desolation:

> *Quaeque prius sanctos cogebat curia patres,*
> *Serpentum facta est, alituumque domus.*
> *Plenaque tot passim generosis atria ceris,*
> *Ipsa sua tandem subruta mole jacent.*
> *Calcanturque olim sacris onerata trophaeis*
> *Limina: distractos et tegit herba deos.*
> *Tot decora, artificumque manus, tot nota sepulcra,*
> *Totque pios cineres una ruina premit.*
> *Et jam intra solasque domos, disjectaque passim*
> *Culmina setigeros advena figit apros.*

> (11–20)

And the senate, which earlier invited revered elders, is made the home of serpents and birds. And courtyards everywhere full of noble wax effigies finally lie in ruins under their own weight. Thresholds once sturdy with holy trophies are trampled down, and grass covers the toppled statues of gods. So many works of art and artisians, so many famous tombs, so many holy ashes, one ruin covers all. And now among the lonely houses and fallen rooftops everywhere a stranger spears bristly boars.

In its metrical pattern each successive elegiac verse moves closer to a greater regularity, while in its syntactic pattern each moves towards paratactic simplicity. This movement evokes the shaping force of history, its patterning of diverse human action into discrete units that formally repeat themselves. The two halves of line 18, for example, present the final object of the verb's action, *cineres*, "ashes," and then the subject and verb themselves that summarize all the main clauses that preceded them: "una ruina premit" ("one ruin covers"). In line 20, finally, the metrical reduplication of the dactylic rhythm in each half evokes the repetition, predictability, climactic monotony of the city's long, slow fall to ruin.

The elegy's concluding section presents a series of stated or implied addresses. Lines 21 to 24 imply an attentive first-person plural audience. They contrast the incompleteness of the early Greek prophecies that did not predict Cumae's fall with the familiar topos of life's brevity. The emphasis on the first-person plural subject universalizes the complaint:

> Nec tamen hoc Grajis cecinit Deus ipse carinis,
> Praevia nec lato missa columba mari.
> Et querimur, cito si nostrae data tempora vitae
> Diffugiunt? urbes mors violenta rapit.
>
> (21–24)

Still, Jupiter never revealed this destiny to the Greek ships, nor the dove sent ahead across the wide sea. And do we complain if the time accorded to our lives quickly disappears? Violent death overwhelms cities.

Next the speaker accords an ironic voice to his own self-deprecation. Addressing himself he expresses the wish that his own account of universal doom may prove false:

> Atque utinam mea me fallant oracula vatem,
> Vanus et a longa posteritate ferar.
>
> (25–26)

And may my oracles deceive me, their prophet; and may I be thought foolish by distant posterity.

Finally the speaker addresses three cities concurrently famous for their power, wealth, and prestige. Rome, Venice, and even Naples, too, will one day decline:

> Nec tu semper eris, quae septem amplecteris arces,
> Nec tu, quae mediis aemula surgis aquis,
> Et te (quis putet hoc?) altrix mea, durus arator
> Vertet; et: Urbs, dicet, haec quoque clara fuit.
>
> (27–30)

Nor will you exist forever, you who embrace the seven hills, nor you who rise in emulation amidst the water, and you—

who would think it?—my nurse, the crusty plowman will
turn you up and say, "This city once was famous."

The elegy's final lines recapitulate the crushing force of destiny:

> *Fata trahunt homines; fatis urgentibus, urbes.*
> *Et quodcumque vides, auferet ipsa dies.*
>
> (31–32)

As Fate presses down, time carries off cities and whatever
else you see.

They also eulogize all of ancient culture. Amidst the decay, there
is survival; amidst survival, there is incentive to continue.

Despite its impersonal, abstract tone, the elegy on Cumae
exhibits certain concrete possibilities that Sannazaro would exploit in his other elegies. Its lines evoking the pastoral takeover
of Cumae presage the poet's own later enterprise in his pastoral
Piscatoriae. They articulate the central dilemma of the Renaissance humanist as Sannazaro himself came to experience it. For
the humanist who deals with the language and linguistic heritage of the past, the ruins of Cumae's clay and stone represent
only a bare surface. The decay that attacked them has also attacked the textual materials that the humanist seeks to restore.
Even if the texts that he analyzes are not visibly mutilated,
their language remains alien and impenetrable to modern philology. Sannazaro's other elegies also suggest that situation. On
the whole they present a full, rich, capacious moral vision able
to embrace a specific event in all its human complexity, but
they never lose sight of the speaker's central role as spokesman
for the humanist endeavor.

The typical Renaissance humanist lived in a world of concrete things that can evoke the past: texts, monuments, land-
scapes. The speaker of these elegies lives in a less substantial
world. As poet he tries to make poems out of the echoes of
older poems, with a gnawing sense that his artistic goals may
ever elude him. As lover he tries to ground his relationship
with his beloved in all too fleeting proofs of her affection for

him. Both as scholar and as poet-lover he lives in a world of absence that he strives to make present. The difference between these roles is that as scholar he can fulfill his desire with the unravelling of a text, the discovery of a monument, or the exploration of a landscape. As poet-lover, however, he can fulfill his desire only provisionally. He reaches out with words to supply the lack he perceives both in the poetry he writes and in his relationship with the woman he loves. He finds, moreover, that his functions as poet and lover are not unrelated. The lover, in seeking the other, tries to bridge the distance between them with words. Words can confer at least some kind of imagined being on what is absent and desired. If one cannot have what one wants, at least one can talk about it. Of course the lover runs the risk of articulating an idealized relationship that has no basis in reality, of turning the experienced situation into a fiction, of losing himself and his purpose in language. This risk is one that Sannazaro as elegist faces in every poem, just as he would in later pastoral eclogues.

The first elegy in Book I dramatizes this situation powerfully. The poem has three audiences—Luciano Crasso, the speaker's beloved, and Cupid. The first acts as a foil setting off the speaker's struggle with the other two. Its opening lines address Crasso, a humanist scholar, professor of poetry at the University of Naples, and the speaker's first mentor. The landscape's concreteness confers an immediacy and tangibility upon Crasso's world. The speaker's world, by contrast, has none of those qualities. It consists of pastoral songs handed down by the muses, mediated by Love, echoing through the woods and caverns: "At mihi paganae dictant silvestria Musae / Carmina, quae tenui gutture cantat Amor" (9–10; "But to me the pagan muses dictate silvan songs, which Love sings with a delicate throat"). In a second impassioned address to Crasso, the speaker emphasizes his own role as poet and contrasts it with Crasso's as scholar. The speaker has no wish to pull together these fragments and master their echoes as a scholar would, or even to compose poetry that would rival Homer's and Virgil's. He would

rather earn a lesser fame by articulating his love for Carmosina
Bonifacio: "Non mihi Moeonidem, Luci, non cura Maronen /
Vincere; si fiam notus amore, sat est" (27–28; "I don't care
to surpass Homer or Virgil; it is enough if I can become known
for love").

The irony is that such an attempt itself poses enormous difficulties. The poet and the lover share uncertain ground as both
seek to confer order and stability on their tenuous relationships.
The lover seeks to express his love and move his beloved to re-
ciprocate. The poet seeks to equilibrate words with things and
invest them with verbal artistry. In an address to his beloved,
the speaker betrays his desire to prolong the moment of their
union so that he might test its reality (33–34). Without this
assurance he faces the risk of acceding to an illusion, a pastoral
dream of what he desires rather than the reality itself: "Sed quid
ego, hei misero, ventosus inania fingo / Somnia; quae forsan
non feret ulla dies?" (39–40; "But why, poor wretch, do I like a
fool shape empty dreams that perhaps no day will ever give substance to?"). As poet, he craves a similar assurance. He wants
his pastoral verbal universe to square with the real one. The
lover's desire to possess his beloved emblematizes the poet's
desire to stabilize his verbal construction in yet another way.
Both the lover's world and the poet's face annihilation through
the power of magic: "Num rumpunt somnos carmen, et herba
meos?" (66; "Will song or herbs ever shatter my sleep?"). The
love-sick shepherd can seek relief through spells and incantations, *carmina*, but those very remedies can also absorb his powers to express his love. Song can defeat song, spell can wound
spell. The speaker's fears of losing both his beloved and his poetic grasp on reality are inseparably intertwined.

The resolution is not easy, and the speaker does not offer one
in this poem. Instead he disclaims the threat of outside inter-
ference and proclaims that the source of his trouble resides
within. Cupid, Amor, Love itself has brought misery upon him
(71–72). The poem's final address to Cupid conflates the speaker's roles as lover and poet in a unified gesture. The day he

ceases to love will be the day he ceases to live—the day, that is, he ceases to write poetry: "Quod si te nostrae ceperunt taedia vitae, / Ne cesset, quaeso, funeris atra dies" (77–78; "But if the boredom of our life becomes too much for you, I pray that the black day of death should be my lot"). Cupid animates him with life and inanimates him with poetry, so that to love is to live and to live is to write poetry.

Other elegies develop the same topos. In I.2 the speaker addresses two audiences. The first is his friend Giovanni Pardo, a Spanish humanist who attached himself to Pontano's circle in the 1490s. The speaker stylizes his own life in the pastoral manner as that of a shepherd who brings his flocks to pasture in the woods and fields, and he compares it with the life of a scholar who impassively contemplates the heavens and earth with their remote origins and present continuance. The speaker's existence in this pastoral landscape is an enforced one. His love commands him to reside there, limiting his very freedom of will: "At nos per silvas, et sordida rura, capellas / Versamus, quando Phyllis amare jubet" (13–14; "But we lead our goats through the woods and base countryside as long as Phyllis commands me to love"). Still, the speaker would not exchange this condition for that of the scholar. He gladly accepts it and prays to the gods, his other audience, to grant that he may continue in it (41–42). Love itself and the poetry he composes to honor his love will be a sufficient reward.

A pair of elegies brings the topos into Book II. The first of two audiences in II.7 is a scholarly humanist with a life-style different from the speaker's. This time, however, the speaker inhabits the city rather than the pastoral countryside. Playing on the name of his addressee, his former tutor, Giuniano Maio, he endows him with the qualities of a seer or magus (29–30). With his divinatory art Maio functions on a more secure ground than the speaker does. Cupid has not wounded him (57–58). The poet-lover, on the other hand, still suffers the pastoral torments of his earlier existence. Like Sisyphus, the Danaids, and Tantalus, he can know no repose or contentment. Thus in the poem's final lines he turns to his second audience, his friends (69), and bids them carve on his tomb the fatal words: "Actius. hic. situs. est. cineres. gaudete. sepulti. / jam. vaga. post. obitus. umbra. dolore. vacat" (71–72; "Here lies Actius. Rejoice, o ashes; his shade after death has now departed from sorrow"). Only death and the dissolution of his roles as poet and lover can provide release from the uncertainty he experiences.

The next elegy, II.8, honors the beloved on her birthday. Among this poem's multiple audiences, which include the beloved, Venus, Juno, and the deity of the present day, the speaker addresses his muses in an impassioned manner. In the poem's first line he bids his muse collect new crowns for Juno: "Junoni fer sacra, novas lege, Musa, coronas" (1). The act of collecting aptly describes what the pastoral poet does with his verses: he collects and weaves them into a texture (text) of meaning that inanimates his poem. The word *legere*, "collect, gather together," itself is significant because etymologically it undergoes a transformation of meaning through "survey" and "scan" to "read" and "peruse." The muse helps the poet gather meanings together, and in their written form the reader scans and collects them. In his second address the muses emerge in plural form as a group of nymphs, *Nymphae* (29), gamboling joyously in free rural space. Here the speaker promises to follow their songs and various steps on earth. He will bring pastoral poetry to the celebration of his beloved's birthday, and thus serve her in the role he is best equipped to perform.

The collection's final two elegies (III, 2 and 3) emphasize the speaker's private world and his role as pastoral poet in a deeply personal way. The penultimate one constitutes a short biography of his life as a poet. Early in the elegy he interlaces events in his life with his development as pastoral artist. His first direct inspiration came from the local shepherds at Merula, among whom he composed bucolic songs on various reeds (35–36). Their music, however, was *sibila*, "whistling," or even "hissing," and it belonged to the lowest of *silvestria* genres. "Calamis . . . disparibus" ("with reeds of unequal length; in various

styles") refers literally to the shepherds' pipes; it refers figuratively to the elegiac meter that alternates full hexameters with
truncated ones. It can also refer to the other meters, modes,
and styles that the young poet experimented with in his *Arcadia*. In either case, both the implied disparagement and the
implied variety function significantly in the context of the
poet's development.

The speaker's point is that he moved eventually from the pastoral eclogue, written in the vernacular, to the high genre, his
sacred epic, *De Partu Virginis*, written in Latin. Significantly,
not love or desire but rather numinous inspiration had led him
to this plateau: "Mox majora vocant me Numina" (45; "Soon
greater divinities call me"). Of course, the other attachments
remain. Devotion to his craft led him to compose the first
piscatorial eclogues (57). Desire for his beloved led him to compose amatory elegies and other short poems (63–64). Above
all, loyalty to his rulers led him to spend many years far from
bucolic tranquility, first in military life and then in exile, as he
claims in his plaintive address to Federigo (71–72).

Appeals to three audiences now underscore the pathos. Of
distant posterity the speaker begs pardon for allowing affliction
to diminish his powers (101–2). Next, to his close friends he
reasserts the "sincerity" implicit in his humanist name, Actius
Syncerus (107). Finally to Cassandra Castriota, his literary
executrix and the audience to whom he dedicates the entire
poem, he urges the preservation of his memory if he should
soon die (111–12).

Despite the poem's sudden termination, however, the poet's
career does not end. In a pessimistic moment he had simulated
an ending, much as he did when he evoked his own death in
order better to confirm his endurance. He now plays it out in
order to assert his control over it through poetry: "Parce tamen
scisso seu me, mea vita, capillo, / Sive: sed heu prohibet dicere
plura dolor" (115–16; "Yet do not mourn me, my life, with
shorn tresses, or, rather . . . but, alas, sorrow forbids me to say
more"). Thus the poem concludes, not with a halt after *sive* but

with the speaker's completion and rounding off of the line. In a yet deeper sense the speaker's control casts its spell over the entire poem. The retrospective nature of his account allows him to reconsider and revise his idea of the bucolic past. Thus he acquires a coherent narrative at the risk of misrepresenting what actually may have happened. The illusion of incompleteness still hangs over the poem, but only as a mere illusion. The poem and the poet's execution of it are both complete. The poet has expressed his inner life in a fully satisfying form.

The poet also devotes several elegies to depicting outer events in the contemporary history of Naples. An elegy in praise of his patron, Alfonso, opens Book II. In it, however, when the speaker comes to narrate Alfonso's campaign in northern Italy during 1479–82, he focuses his attention on certain antipastoral achievements to the unexpected exclusion of others. Perhaps out of respect for the Medici, who proved their friendship in later years, he does not mention Alfonso's crude offensive against Florence in the wake of the Pazzi conspiracy (1479) when the city was vulnerable to takeover; nor does he allude to its indecisive outcome when Alfonso suddenly headed south to confront the Turks. He does celebrate Alfonso's famous victory over the latter at Otranto, 10 September 1481, but he hardly lingers over the details of their expulsion, nor does he emphasize it as the most stunning achievement of Alfonso's career (65–66). Instead he proceeds directly to the less flattering events of 1482 with a curious twist of the narrative's structure.

In that year Venice revealed plans for annexing the Duchy of Ferrara, ruled by the genial Duke Ercole I d'Este, husband of Alfonso's sister Eleonora. Pope Sixtus IV's complicity with Venice gave Alfonso an excuse to march through Rome en route to the north, and to wreak as much havoc there as he reasonably could. The expedition was important for Sannazaro because it marked his first military engagement. The young poet had joined Alfonso's court in February 1481, and travelled with his army for the first time to Rome (75–76). Still, the expedition ended in an impasse. Alfonso's forces never fully penetrated Rome, and when Ercole managed to stave the enemy off from Ferrara, Alfonso withdrew. Sannazaro does not refer to the retreat in this poem. His silence about it may of course represent a pragmatic gesture of good will towards the man whose army he followed and the family whose patronage he enjoyed. It may also suggest something deeper about his mixed feelings upon invading Rome. Whatever depravity its popes may have been guilty of, Rome still held a special importance for the speaker.

The speaker continues his antipastoral elegy by strangely conflating events. He links Alfonso's first Roman invasion with a second one that occurred four years later and deliberately confuses the favorable outcome of the latter with the indecisive one of the former (77–78). In 1485–86 Naples was on the verge of collapse from the Barons' revolt, which was partly instigated and heavily supported by the new Pope Innocent VIII. Alfonso's father dispatched him and his troops to Rome to confront the papal forces. Sannazaro accompanied him. This time the Neapolitan army hit hard. By August 1486, Innocent VIII called for a truce, but only after Rome and its environs had suffered heavy damage. In another (long unpublished) antipastoral elegy on Alfonso's exploits, Sannazaro represented his victory with glowing praise; his Roman suppliant called upon him to enter the city in triumph as its veritable defender against the iniquities of his enemies.[41] In the elegy at hand, however, Sannazaro dims his commander's triumph by expressing his own misgivings (81–82). The poet had come to regret his part in defacing the ancient city. Personifying Rome and addressing it as a venerable mother, he asserts that he had acted badly only because he believed it right to obey his commander: "Parce tamen, veneranda Parens, si justa secutus / Signa sub Alfonso: Rex erat ille meus" (83–84; "still, pardon me, venerable mother, if I followed Alfonso's rightful signals: he was my king").

The elliptical linking of Alfonso's second invasion of Rome with his first one and the telescoping of events in between reveals perhaps more about Sannazaro's own persona than Alfonso's. It is as though the pastoral poet stood outside the gates of the city for four years awaiting entry, and then, upon succeeding, came to repent of the violent means that afforded him access. The Roman experience had a profound significance for Sannazaro. Here was the ancient city, home of the empire; the holy city, seat of Christendom. The site, landscape, geography, vestiges of ancient walls and streets and buildings spoke to him of the past. It would be wrong, however, to imagine Sannazaro as a Winckelmann *avant la lettre*, or a Goethe or even a du Bellay, all of whom felt themselves magically transported back into the past just by contact with the city's ruined artifacts. Ancient artifacts stood all around Sannazaro in his native Naples without comparable effect. Rome was special. Sannazaro entered it as part of an invading army, but what he sought to invade was less the city's battlements than its elusive classical heritage. He sought to penetrate, plunder, become one with, and revive for his own cultural milieu the ancient treasures of classical civilization. Alfonso's invasion of Rome did not permit him that wish. Indeed it threatened to prevent any fulfillment of it. In Alfonso's soldierly rage Sannazaro saw untold destruction. He could not abide the consequences.

If Sannazaro pays tepid tribute to Alfonso in the preceding elegy, he pays a much warmer one to Federigo in III.1. When Alfonso's son, Ferdinand II, died on 7 October 1496, after only one year and eight months of rule, the crown passed to his uncle, Alfonso's younger brother. A friend of political and intellectual leaders throughout Italy, a just and benevolent ruler and patron of the arts at home, Federigo earned Sannazaro's lifelong admiration and loyalty. His elegy glows with a sincerity missing from the one dedicated to Alfonso. The difference makes itself felt at the beginning. No frame belabors the speaker's concern with his own role as poet in III.1. Instead at the outset the speaker sets aside his amorous pastoral topoi in order to sing of Federigo's exploits: "Ergo ego fallaci tantum servire puellae / Natus, et adverso semper amore queri?" (1–2; "Was I therefore born only to serve a deceitful girl and always to lament an adverse love?"). Addressing his own verse, the speaker calls for a heightening of tone, a pursuit of more difficult tasks than he earlier set in his bucolic eclogues (11–12).

Every one of the elegy's 184 lines bears witness to the poet's respect for Federigo. Sannazaro wrote the poem after the exiled ruler's death in Tours in 1504. The fiction, however, is that he still lives. The speaker addresses Federigo throughout the poem, and at the end, in forecast of his death, he addresses the river Loire, beside which he will be buried (177–78). Envisioning himself as a pilgrim who comes from Italy to visit the grave, the same speaker offers a prayer in the poem's last lines (183–84.) The motif provides an appropriate conclusion since Federigo himself passes through most of the elegy as a traveller, whether as a young prince on diplomatic missions or as a military hero waging just wars, or as a dethroned king in exile.

At the ending of the poem, Federigo returns home to receive the kingship from his dying nephew. He is destined to sail north again, next time in exile. He therefore addresses his ships (167–68). The distant vision of Federigo's death in Tours, his tomb on the Loire's banks, and the pilgrims' visit end the account. The speaker has subtly distanced his tribute from ordinary reality and served to objectify it as an inspired pronouncement. At the same time he has rooted the tribute in the city of his own origin and testified to the greatness and endurance of its own institutions.

The Neo-Latin Elegies offer one other poetic mode that proved important for Sannazaro in his pastorals. It is the mythological mode. II. 10, for example, is a playful Ovidian performance in which a pomegranate addresses Sannazaro's learned humanist friend, Andrea Matteo Acquaviva. The fruit offers itself to him as a fit reward for his many endeavors. Its skin covers a richness of sweet red seeds (5–6). By comparison the wealth that multitudes hanker after seems paltry (11–12). The speaker's final advice is to ignore the ephemeral rewards that others esteem and rather to accept the simpler, homier joys (45–46). Structured on the commonplace pastoral topos of the vanity of human wishes, the poem echoes the forms and style of Pontano's pastoral garden poem, *De Hortis Hesperidum*. In this context the device of the speaking pomegranate is more than a novel rhetorical twist. It amounts to a double commendation of humanist endeavor, since it evokes Pontano's poetry while it praises Acquaviva.

Elegy II.4 is a more substantial Ovidian performance. It recounts the story of Morinna's transformation into a mulberry bush. In the first line the speaker requests the accompaniment of Erato, muse of love poetry, on a golden lyre while he narrates his tale (1–2). The setting is a pastoral society where the nymph Morinna dedicated herself to Diana. In a catalogue of evocative place names, all nature testifies to the way she rebuffed the amorous advances of gods and men alike (13–16). In particular, a satyr named Lucrinus had designs on her. One day, in order to take shelter from a hailstorm, she chanced upon him in a cave. His attempt at seduction was clumsy. The choice between what he offered and what she already enjoyed as Diana's nymph entailed no contest. Metrically the lines describing her flight from him are superb. Thumping spondees give way to quicker dactyls as she accelerates her pace (39–40). The rhythm stabilizes itself with dactyls as she approaches an area of brooding lakes and dead swamps (41–42). It asserts itself in spondees as she thinks she has found an exit (43–44). Upon the satyr's attack she calls out to Diana, whence the goddess tranforms her into the mulberry bush. A metrical ellipsis accompanies the transformation—"Fitque arbor subito: Morum dixere priores, / Et de Morinna nil nisi nomen habet" (55–56; "Suddenly she became a bush: the ancients called her Moro, and now she has nothing else besides her name, Morina")—and a series of spondees enforces its permanence:

> *Pes in radicem, in frondes ivere capilli;*
> *Et qual nunc cortex, caerula vestis erat.*
> *Brachia sunt rami; sed quae nitidissima poma,*
> *Quas male vitasti, Nympha, fuere nives.*
>
> (57–60)

> Her feet became roots, her hair turned into leaves, and
> what is now bark was once her blue tunic. Her arms are
> branches, and what is now its polished fruit, o nymph, was
> the hail that you scarcely avoided.

Faunus's song in praise of the mulberry finally restores balance
to the tone with its dominant anapests and its liquid m and n
sounds: "Tu numquam miserae maculabere sanguine Thysbes: /
Immemor heu fati ne videare tui" (71–72; "You will never be
stained by sad Thisbe's blood; so don't be forgetful of your
fate"). As poetic narrative the entire account foreshadows Sannazaro's longer experiment in the Ovidian mode with *Salices*
and the sacred narratives of *Lamentatio de Morte Christi* and *De
Partu Virginis*.

Salices (The Willows) is particularly important for Sannazaro's later pastorals because it demonstrates an approach to
Ovidian narrative purged of the moralizing, allegorizing commentary accorded to it in medieval renditions. Some modern
scholars have attached the term *epyllion* or *minor epic* to the
form that Sannazaro used, but others have pointed out that the
ancients did not recognize it as a type.[42] In his *Salices*, however,
Sannazaro's mingling of disparate elements from epic and other
narrative reflects the same kind of allusive, integrating, amal-
gamating imagination crucial to the development of his pastorals. Both *Salices* and the pastorals unfold within a frame that
dramatizes the speaker's personal involvement with their account. Both stress the importance of the setting and devote
many lines to rendering it with literary, mythic, and cosmological allusions. Both address an audience of sophisticated
readers conscious of the references and appreciative of the poetic effects. And both, finally, give full rein to rich, sensuous
imagery and rhythmically complicated meters.

The frame of the *Salices* defines the speaker's personal in-
vestment in the tale as an attempt to persuade his audience,
Traiano Cabanilla, Count of Troy and Montella, of the impossibility of taking flight from one's self and one's destiny in

the public arena. This frame hinges on two implied questions, both central for the Renaissance humanist: love and fame. The speaker's audience appears to have neglected the first while engaging in a single-minded pursuit of the second. He has upset a precarious balance between the two. The neglect of either leads to the loss of an essential part of one's humanity.

The frame depicts that loss in the implied contrast between Venus's activity and the absence of the audience. Venus comes born to life on the crest of a wave, carried by a flotilla of sky-blue sea-shells, and she maintains a constant, faithful watch over her tutelary islands, Paphos and Amathunta (2–3).[43] Traiano Cabanilla, however, is away on a military campaign, far from his community of friends and acquaintances and his protracted absences lead to a numbing sense of the void (9–10). In the final lines of the poem's prologue, Traiano endangers even the very fame that he sought to pursue. He does not wish the poet to call upon him, render him praise, or otherwise memorialize him (11–13). The speaker nonetheless entraps his audience, forces upon him a public recognition hitherto avoided, and guarantees—if his poem itself will achieve success—a living posterity even after death.

The narrative that he offers portrays entrapment, and it does so in a highly charged Venerean atmosphere. It tells of the assault upon a group of nymphs by a band of satyrs, the nymphs' efforts to flee, and their subsequent transformation into willow trees. The pastoral setting is the banks of the Saône river near Lyons—a city known to Sannazaro during his exile—where satyrs, fauns, and silvan deities gambol in the midday heat. Their lusty vitality exerts itself in stark contrast to the quiet pastoral landscape surrounding them:

> *Dumque leves aptant calamos, dum sibila pressis*
> *Explorant digitis, tenuique foramina cera*
> *Obducunt, vario modulantes carmina cantu,*
> *Auricomae viridi speculantur ab ilice Nymphae*
> *Dulcia clarisonis solventes ora cachinnis.*
>
> (22–26)

> And while they fasten together delicate reeds for a zam-
> pogna, while they practice whistling on it by pressing their
> fingers, and cover the openings with soft wax, playing songs
> with varying melody, the fair-haired nymphs spy out from
> behind a green oak, allowing their sweet faces to break into
> loud, clear laughter.

The contrast occupies several senses, not just visual but also aural, as when the satyrs' merry piping opposes nature's midday
silence. The hexameters become tactile and kinetic when the
nymphs' dancing upsets nature's calm repose. The nymphs gaze
on the satyrs from afar, partly in terror, partly in fascination,
and the latter feel their customary sensual urging when they discover their beholders.

In two different passages of hortatory rhetoric the satyrs invite the nymphs to join them. The phrasing recalls Dante's version of Ulysses's plea to his followers (*Inferno* XXVI) to join
him in his exploration of the Western hemisphere. In the first
exhortation the satyrs complain that their solitary pleasures are
fruitless; in the second they remind the nymphs of their own
divine pedigree and their perfectly legitimate inclinations:

> *Nos quoque non Lernae monstris, non igne Chimaerae,*
> *Scyllaeisve lupis geniti, aut latrante Charybdi,*
> *Qui vestra immani laceremus viscera morsu;*
> *Sed Divûm genus, et qui semper rupibus altis*
> *Vobiscum crebris venatibus insultemus.*
>
> (52–56)

> We were not begotten by the Hydra of Lerna, nor by the
> fire of Chimera, nor by the wolves of Scylla or barking
> Charybdis, who would tear apart your flesh with enormous
> teeth. But we are the offspring of gods, who with you are
> always leaping across high cliffs in frequent hunting.

Their rhetoric might will be aimed at Traiano, who himself has
forsaken the liberties and luxuries associated with their life-
style.

The satyrs' rhetoric succeeds with the nymphs. As they join

in dance the poem's rhythms open into full, rich, sonorous tones, alternating double spondees with double dactyls in sensuous harmonies. The nymphs lead the dance, inciting the satyrs to ever more lusty measures:

> *Tum manibus simul implicitis per gramina festas*
> *Exercent choreas; aliosque, aliosque reflexus*
> *Inter se laetae repetunt; nunc corpora librant*
> *In saltus, nunc molle latus, nunc candida jactant*
> *Brachia, et alterna quatiunt vestigia planta.*
>
> (60–64)

Then with hands entwined together they dance across the grass, and gleeful among themselves they repeat other turns; now they poise their bodies in leaping, now they thrust their tender flanks, now their fair arms, and with alternating steps they beat their feet.

At the moment of attack the speaker generates a long epic simile that transposes the lyric tone of the poem to a graver, more serious, even philosophical one (74 ff.). This shift carries rhetorical weight. At the moment of entrapment the nymphs appeal to the naiads and to the river god Sarno, but they are unable to give aid. Fate prevents them (91–93). For the poem's audience, entrapped into receiving an unwanted act of praise and entrapped, too, in a human condition that should make him sensible to the erotic impulses recorded in this poem, the analogy is powerful.

At that point the nymphs' magical transformation into willow trees becomes a measure of both salvation and despair: salvation because they succeed in escaping their pursuers' embraces, despair because the price of escape renders them immobile. The form of the willow tree is particularly apt, as the speaker reminds the audience: emblematically it figures forth sorrow; visually it traces the arching shape of the nymphs' arms and bodies as they prepare to dive into the river: thus their limbs become branches and their fingers and hair turn into willowy tendrils inclining downwards:

> Nec mora: pro digitis ramos exire videres,
> Aurotasque comas glauca canescere fronde,
> Et jam vitalis nusquam calor, ipsaque cedunt
> Viscera paullatim venienti frigida ligno.
>
> (105–108)

And immediately you would see branches extend instead of fingers, and golden hair turn hoary with grey leaves, and now nowhere any hint of body heat, but rather their cold bodies give way to bark that overtakes them.

And yet, though their fate might seem a living death, a flicker of vitality still animates the nymphs. For the rest of their days they will remain aware of their single-minded wish to elude the satyrs' grasp (111–13). They suffer an appropriately Dantesque *contrappasso* for trying to avoid the dance of life.

In 1546 the Lyonnais poet Maurice Scève translated this poem almost literally as a graceful exemplum within his longer pastoral eclogue, *Le Saulsaye*.[44] In that context the humanist Antire counsels the lovesick Philerme on the dangers of the solitary life that he has adopted after his amorous disappointment. He uses the story to exemplify the morbid, gloomy, melancholic atmosphere of Philerme's retirement. Scève clearly perceived Sannazaro's ambivalence about the nymphs' survival as willow trees after their transformation. On the one hand the narrative exemplifies the humanists' anxieties about survival in a transposed form, dramatizing the warning that to avoid nature's course is tantamount to pursuing death. On the other it exemplifies the inevitability of survival anyway: the nymphs have merely embarked upon a new form of existence.

Scève's adaptation of Sannazaro's narrative for his own pastoral purposes illustrates the extent to which pastoral style and technique are embedded in the texture of Sannazaro's verse. That style and technique, culminating among Sannazaro's minor poems in *Salices*, leads us to the threshold of Sannazaro's pastorals. His shorter poetry, both Italian and Latin, taught Sannazaro versatility in forms and modes, styles and expression, genre and length. When he applied that versatility to his longer pastorals, he was using resources culled from a lifetime of humanist experience. Sannazaro's *Rime*, epigrams, odes, elegies, and *Salices* all exhibit those qualities. *Arcadia, Piscatoriae,* and *De Partu Virginis* would elevate them to a higher plateau.

2 ARCADIA

It is no wonder that literary pirates coveted Sannazaro's *Arcadia* long before its author deemed his text worthy of publication. Its novelty consisted of three richly inventive schemes: it boldly transposed the form of the classical eclogue into the modern vernacular and versified it in the half dozen most popular measures of the day; it furthermore arranged the twelve eclogues into a narrative sequence that implies an affecting tale of unrequited love; and finally, it connected them with passages of luminously detailed prose that clarifies the main action. The time was ripe for this endeavor, and audiences greeted it with high enthusiasm.

The early pirated editions do not register the changes and revisions that Sannazaro soon wrought. They do, however, convey the originality of the enterprise. Even in their raw form—and perhaps because they show this rawness rather than attempt to conceal it—they demonstrate the experimental nature of Sannazaro's project. The text's archaisms and latinisms also attest to its archaeological intent. Above all, the evocation of classical tones, moods, and attitudes through literary allusion points to its philological importance. The mark of its success as pastoral is the nostalgia that it evokes—its sense of constituting a return to the past and the classical tradition. The mark of its success as a literary achievement is the polyphony of modes and styles that it sustains. To appreciate its nostalgic, polyphonic achievements, we might best approach the text through analyzing its composition, its implied audiences, and its distinctive styles.

TEXT AND COMPOSITION

Sannazaro's *Arcadia* consists of twelve chapters of prose discourse, each ending with a poetic eclogue. The alternation of prose and verse is consistent, but the quality of each varies considerably. Many portions of the prose are simply descriptive; some provide brief episodic narratives; others, particularly in the second half, are linked by a more or less continuous narrative. A prose prologue and a prose epilogue frame the entire work.

Like the prose, the poetry is highly varied. Some eclogues offer amatory compliments; others are amatory complaints; some are funeral dirges; a few deal with social and political issues in a satiric or didactic vein. Their poetic forms are also diverse. In Eclogue II popular measures like the *frottola* (eleven-syllable lines whose fifth syllable rhymes with the last syllable of the preceding line) alternate with esoteric ones like the *barzelletta* and madrigal (five and eight line stanzas respectively combining seven- and eleven-syllable verses). The form of Eclogues III and V is the thirteen-line *canzone* stanza combining seven- and eleven-syllable verses. Eclogues IV and VII are *sestinas* (IV is a double *sestina*) comprising stanzas of six lines whose terminal words repeat those of the initial stanza in different orders. By far the most common measures are tercets called *sdrucciole*, with lines of twelve syllables (VI, VIII, XII and parts of I, II, IX, and X) and tercets called *piane*, with lines of eleven syllables (XI and parts of II and IX).

Throughout the work the tones and modalities of individual units change greatly. The first six chapters and their eclogues present relatively straightforward, uncomplicated images of pastoral life. Starting with the seventh chapter, however, the focus is more sharply on the character of the first-person speaker and his account of amatory tribulation. The narrative of the last two chapters unfolds with unusual urgency as the speaker transforms it into an apparent parable for his times. *Arcadia*'s plenitude is at once its glory and its downfall. It is as though Sannazaro had discovered ever new principles of composition and organization as he went along, but was unable or unwilling to integrate them into a final synthesis.

One explanation for the text's untidy appearance may be the long history of its composition under trying circumstances for more than two decades. Another reflects both the frenzy and confusion of the publishing world in the first half-century of the printing press and the emergence of the vernacular as a newly constituted literary language. Literary perfectionist that he was, Sannazaro must have been reluctant to see the publication of *Arcadia*, but from his place of exile in 1504 he agreed to it upon the urging of his friends Cariteo and Pietro Summonte. A pirated edition had appeared in Venice two years earlier (June 1502) and it greatly embarrassed Sannazaro.[1] Not only did it retain an older Neapolitan style that he was already revising in favor of Tuscan usage, but it was also incomplete. It challenged Sannazaro to finish his work in its definitive form.

Sannazaro had probably composed Eclogues I, II, and VI of the present *Arcadia* in the early 1480s. By 1489, the date of its first extant manuscript, he had completed the first ten of the twelve chapters of its final version. Doubtless he began by imitating recently published vernacular eclogues, then conceived the idea of joining them in a sequence, and finally of adding the prose passages as links among them. The initial impetus was most likely the printing in Florence in February 1482, of a collection of various Florentine and Sienese eclogues by Francesco Arsocchi, Jacopo Fiorino de' Bonisegni, and Girolamo Benivieni, bound together with an Italian translation of Virgil's *Eclogues* by Bernardino Pulci.[2] These eclogues are alleged to constitute the first vernacular pastorals composed according to classical models. The volume immediately became popular throughout Italy and especially in Naples because one of Bonisegni's eclogues bearing the date 1468 had been dedicated to Alfonso the Magnanimous. Sannazaro evidently read them with enthusiasm. Their topics were amatory and political and consisted of compliments, complaints, and political satires.

Sannazaro echoed their motifs and verse forms (tercets and *frottole*) in the poems that he subsequently designated as Eclogues I, II, and VI of *Arcadia*.

There exists another unique testimony to the composition of *Arcadia* in the early 1480s. It is a group of six pastoral eclogues found in *Arcadia*'s manuscript codex of 1489.[3] Three are anonymous and three are attributed to a Neapolitan gentleman named Pietro Jacopo De Jennaro. They deal in allegorical figures with certain political events in the Aragonese kingdom during 1484–85, and in both style and treatment they show clear traces of interaction with the young Sannazaro's work. The evidence suggests mutual influence. It appears, therefore, that much of *Arcadia* had been written and circulated in manuscript form before 1484–85, and the inclusion of other eclogues in the codex of 1489 declares the impressive impact that *Arcadia* had made from its very inception.

The manuscript codex of 1489 is important in yet another regard. In orthography and many lexical details it differs significantly from the printed version of 1504. It reveals that Sannazaro's original style was unabashedly Neapolitan, with its dialect, vocabulary, and spelling all reflecting local usage of the day. Within a few years, however, Sannazaro came to accept most (though not all) of Cardinal Bembo's recommendations in the *Prose della volgar lingua* about using Tuscan. While no one knows how much his editor, Summonte, his friend Cariteo, and his brother Marcantonio may have contributed, the authorized edition of 4 March 1504 immediately proclaimed the text's Tuscan priorities.

True to the humanist traditions in the written vernacular, moreover, Sannazaro colored his lexicon with a great number of Latinisms. More than most other humanists, however, he derived the majority of them not directly from classical sources but from fourteenth- and fifteenth-century ones.[4] Not surprisingly Petrarch and Boccaccio are the authorities for many of these words: *ceruleo* for *azzurro*, "blue", *nubilo* and *nubiloso* for *nuvoloso*, "cloudy"; *inopia* for *scarsezza*, "scarcity"; *palestra* for *lotta*, "gymnastic exercise"; *pavido* for *pauroso*, "fearful"; and many others. The Petrarchan influence is especially notable in Sannazaro's choice of epithets and adjectives: *nocturne stelle*, "nightly stars"; *umida acqua*, "wet water"; *deserte piaggie*, "deserted slopes"; and *lacrimevole*, "pitiful"; *incurabile*, "incurable"; *misero*, "wretched." The reasons for this preference are often as much rhythmic as they are decorative or aesthetic since many of them fit the complicated verse patterns and stanzaic forms that Sannazaro used. In Boccaccio's prose, moreover, Sannazaro found traces of earlier Neapolitanisms that the author of the *Decameron* had imported to Tuscany: nouns ending in *-tore*: *evitatore*, "evader"; *guardatore*, "guardian"; and verbs ending in *-izzare* (the learned form) and *-eggiare* (the popular form), such as *beffizzare*, "ridicule."

In not every case, however, did Sannazaro substitute a classical or Tuscan form for a Neapolitan one in the revision of 1504. Often he deliberately retained Neapolitan forms like *lei for ella*, "she"; *gli* for *a lei*, "to her" and for *loro*, "to them"; *volno* for *vogliono*, "they wish"; and *potesse* for *potessi*, "I might" (imperfect subjunctive), which Dante and Poliziano themselves had used on occasion. Among lexical choices he preserved such Neapolitan forms as *ucel* for *uccello*, "bird"; *congiedo* for *congedo*, "leavetaking"; *ricoprar* for *ricuperare*, "recover"; and *e volta* for *talvolta*, "sometimes." Finally, for some of the shepherds' own locutions pertaining to their customs and their territories, their tools and their clothing, Sannazaro permitted more than a residual trace of Neapolitan diction to remain: *alvano* for *albaro*, "white poplar"; *fiscella* for *cesto*, "wicker basket"; *mantarro* for *mantello*, "cloak."

Beyond its stylistic revisions, the authorized edition of 1504 also afforded a definite conclusion for the narrative. The pirated edition had ended with an unresolved satiric eclogue. The augmented version added two final chapters and an epilogue. Through their emphasis the pastoral action becomes a thinly veiled record of the poet-humanist's literary vocation in its earliest growth and development. That direction is not always apparent in the initial chapters. It originates there as a subtext with only occasional significance, hardly emergent before the last chapters. Still, a reading of the entire text confirms its importance, and the following account will stress it throughout.

A barest outline of topics in each of the prose sections and eclogues suggests a mostly random and largely undifferentiated action. In Chapter I the speaker introduces two shepherds, Ergasto and Selvaggio. The latter prompts the former to unfold an amatory complaint in Eclogue I. Several days later, in Chapter II while he is grazing his own sheep, the speaker promises to reward another shepherd named Montano for singing a song. Montano offers first a sociopolitical satire in Eclogue II, and then he recounts a contest in amatory poetry between himself and Uranio. Next day the shepherds celebrate a holiday in honor of Pales, goddess of the shepherds (Chapter III). A shepherd named Galicio sings a song in praise of his beloved (Eclogue III). Two other shepherds, Logisto and Elpino, challenge each other to a singing contest (Chapter IV). They perform a complex double *sestina* (Eclogue IV).

The following day Opico, eldest of the shepherds, leads the company to a new spot (Chapter V). They come upon a group of ten cowherds sorrowing over the death of the shepherd Androgeo, and Ergasto joins them in a funeral lament (Eclogue V). At a distance from the others the speaker sorrows over his own amatory misfortunes (Chapter VI). A young shepherd named Carino arrives looking for a lost heifer. His plight causes Serrano and Opico to complain of the world's wretched state (Eclogue VI). When Carino asks him why he looks so sad, the speaker tells how overpowering love has driven him to separate himself from his lady (Chapter VII). He sings a song about his voluntary exile (Eclogue VII). Carino urges him not to despair and recounts how his own love affair had a happy outcome (Chapter VIII). Eugenio and another unrequited lover named Clonico challenge him to a song that will help him renounce his love (Eclogue VIII). Night falls and the shepherds seek shelter in the woods.

The next morning Opico proposes to take Clonico to a magician named Enareto who will cure him of his love (Chapter IX). Nearby they encounter a goatherd, Elenco, whose diffidence prompts a cowherd named Ofelia to challenge him to a poetic contest (Eclogue IX). Afterwards the shepherds enter Enareto's sacred grove, dominated by an altar to Pan, founder of pastoral poetry (Chapter X). Enareto describes the power of his incantations to Clonico, and the other shepherds take their leave. Near the tomb of Massilia, Ergasto's mother, Selvaggio relates a satiric antipastoral song about corruption in the city of Naples (Eclogue X).

The pirated editions of *Arcadia* ended with this eclogue. In Sannazaro's authorized edition two more chapters follow. In the first of these (Chapter XI), Ergasto, grieving over the anniversary of his mother's death, announces and judges a series of funeral games. He sings his own lament for Massilia (Eclogue XI). The speaker, grieving over his separation from the homeland and his beloved, resolves to return to Naples (Chapter XII). After a disturbing dream about abandonment and solitude, he meets a nymph who leads him to the subterranean source of the earth's rivers. From there he follows the Sebeto river to Naples. Upon emerging he listens to two shepherds, Barcinio and Summonzio, who recount Meliseus's lament for his dead wife, and he accompanies them on a visit to Meliseus (Eclogue XII). Biographically the characterizations of Barcinio and Summonzio and their action entail situations that evoke ones attending the publication of *Arcadia*. Barcinio's name refers to Cariteo of Barcellona, called "Barcinio" in Chapter II, while "Summonzio" of course refers to Pietro Summonte, the author's friend and editor who rescued the text from its pirated printings. As much as Sannazaro had been reluctant to publish *Arcadia*, it has now been done, and he can only look forward to publishing other, more ambitious texts. In the epilogue, therefore, the speaker warns his sampogna, or shepherd's pipe, that audiences may be unreceptive to it, and he closes with an indication that he will soon attempt to publish a nobler kind of poem.

THE AUDIENCES

Arcadia's epilogue raises explicitly a question that its last two chapters and their eclogues raise implicitly: what audience does *Arcadia* really address? To a greater degree than elsewhere in the text, these portions achieve a dynamic integration between poetry and prose, so that the poetry serves as a comment on the prose while the prose holds its own as something more than just a frame for the poetry. Prose, however, presumes a different kind of audience from the one that poetry does. Each form makes its own particular demands on the reader. Prose conveys information, commentary, and straightforward narrative. It addresses a casual reader eager to grasp its fictional elements. Poetry conveys the speaker's introspection, critical sophistication, and literary allusiveness. It addresses a more attentive reader than prose.

In *Arcadia* one function of prose is to reveal how the audiences of the poems have received the poetry. It analyzes, interprets, and evaluates their reactions. In the Prologue the author explicitly appeals to his readers. Among them he estimates that "woodland songs carved on the rugged barks of beeches no less delight the one who reads them than do learned verses written on the smooth pages of gilded books" (29/3).[5] In Chapter IV the speaker perspicuously outlines how the preceding eclogue "was marvelously pleasing to everyone, but in various ways" (48/25). Throughout *Arcadia*, his attention never wanders from the presence and immediacy of the reader's response.

Those responses grow more complicated as the work advances. After Chapter VII, when the speaker develops his own characterization more fully, he implicitly evokes the audience's recognition of and reading competence in a variety of literary forms. His narration of Carino's plight in Chapter VIII addresses an audience familiar with the conventions of romance fiction. His account of magic lore in chapter IX is designed for readers interested in that topic. His history of the pastoral mode in Chapter X implies an audience willing to learn more about the literary form that his present text is transposing. His description of funeral games in Chapter XI appeals to readers acquainted with epic poetry, where such descriptions are conventional. Finally, in Chapter XII his oracular vision and journey to the source of all waters demands an audience aware of motifs in Virgil's *Georgics* on the one hand and willing to go beyond them on the other.

The eclogues that spur these and other reactions in the prose address in turn their own kinds of fictive audience. The amatory ones, like I, II, and VII, address their speakers' beloveds both in compliment and complaint. The funeral lament in Eclogue V addresses the dead shepherd Androgeo. Poems concerned with problems of poetic expression, like III and XI, address the classical muses and Apollo, patron of poetry. Poems that contain poems within poems, like X and XII, address multiple audiences at various levels of their fictive performances. Throughout these poetic texts, different forms of rhyme scheme, metrical pattern, and stanzaic length correspond both to the diversity of topics encountered in the poetry and to the diversity of readers that the poetry might appeal to.

The demands made upon the audience to recognize the conventions embedded in the text as well as the profusion of fictive audiences dramatized there constitute some reasons for the phenomenal success of *Arcadia* in the Renaissance. Sixteenth- and seventeenth-century readers delighted in the multiplicity of roles that they were asked to play in reading the text. Its variety was the very source of its appeal. Later audiences grew impatient and hostile. Modern readers, committed to the romantic notion of organic unity and other critical shibboleths, judge the text confused and frustrating. In several important ways, however, Sannazaro anticipated their objections. He seems intent on making each chapter, each eclogue of *Arcadia* a satisfying reading experience for audiences familiar with a host of literary conventions from their earlier reading.

The epilogue's overt concern about the status of poetry in the author's own time underscores the important issue of his literary achievement in *Arcadia*. In its simplest terms the action of *Arcadia* records the singing of songs and, in its prose sections, the audience's responses to those songs. Most of the songs raise the issue of difficulties encountered in composing them, and all of them elicit from the speaker a specific comment about appreciating them. The last two eclogues in particular, rendered in the mode of funeral lament, deal with the relationship between life and art, poetry's power to memorialize the dead and at the same time to lend support to the living, the dignity of the poet's calling, and the speaker's resolution to pursue a serious poetic career. The final chapter records the speaker's leave-taking from the shepherd's domain, his return to Naples, and, along the way, a spiritual renewal that makes him especially aware of his homeland's literary, cultural, and artistic heritage.

When in the epilogue the speaker complains that audiences may misconstrue his endeavor, he is therefore bringing to a conclusion a more substantial complaint recurring throughout his narrative. He does not just indict the pirates of his manuscript, who published it in a premature form, nor does he stop short at complaining about the possibility of misinterpreting the pirated edition. Rather, he goes on to indict the failure of an entire generation of poets and audiences to achieve a new kind of poetry. The humanist revolution, the rise of the vernacular, and the invention of the printing press have changed the very nature of producing and receiving texts. Poetry generates poetry as individual poets inspire each other and ensuing ones to new heights, and as successive audiences respond to the poems intertextually, perceiving echoes, allusions, and connections among them. Now, however, the very flocks, here metonymically associated with the poets themselves, do not "deign any more, seeing themselves to lack milk, to nourish their own offspring" (130/108). The malaise affects even the bees, long a figure for humanist scholars who, as St. Augustine and Petrarch both explained, convert the flowers of classical civilization into honey for their own culture: "the piteous bees within their hives leave to perish unperfected the honey that they had begun. Everything is lost; all hope is vanished; every consolation is dead" (130/109). The speaker connects the poverty of his age's literary production with the decline of its humanist endeavor. The revival of the latter will insure a renewal of the former. The way forward is by a path backward, and the vehicle for the journey is the pastoral mode itself. The problem is to gather its seeds and signs, reassemble them to comprehend the past in all its richness, variety, and alien difference—to return in short to the literary origins of the present.

The pastoral mode epitomizes those literary origins. Fictively it represents a simple, unsophisticated, even primitive kind of poetry. Artistically, nothing can be further from simplicity. Its conventions, forms, and technical achievements represent a highly wrought, cultivated, complex kind of poetry. Historically the pastoral mode developed late in Hellenistic culture, incorporating a host of classical patterns and bequeathing them to an eager Renaissance. In *Arcadia* the speaker's desire to recover the ancient pastoral is emblematic of his desire to recover the whole civilization that preceded it and remains embedded in its roots. Such a late product of classical civilization as the pastoral might provide access to its earlier achievements as well. It signals a historical process in reverse: one enters at the end of its development and journeys back to the beginning.

That process was meaningful even to the ancients. For Virgil, the pastoral *Eclogues* served as an apprenticeship for the *Georgics* and the *Aeneid*. At the end of *Arcadia*'s twelfth chapter the speaker faces an important choice. It seems that he can continue with light amorous poetry or he can advance to another mode of serious, more difficult poetry. His own model, Virgil, took Theocritus as his model and moved beyond him. There are precedents in modern literature as well. Dante, after all, took Virgil as his model, while Petrarch suffered the anxiety of both Virgil's and Dante's influences. In Latin Petrarch composed his Virgilian *Bucolicum Carmen*, a series of twelve pastoral poems, while working on his epic *Africa*. In the vernacular he composed his *Rime sparse* to emulate Dante's Italian verse. For Sannazaro the task is to equal all of them by deconstructing the entire pastoral tradition and reconstituting it in his own Italian *Arcadia* before attempting things unattempted yet in Renaissance Latin.

THE RECEPTION AND STYLE

According to some critics, the sole merit of *Arcadia* is the number of imitations that it spawned.[6] As we have seen, those imitations began to appear even before *Arcadia* was published. The three anonymous eclogues and the three eclogues by Pietro Jacopo De Jennaro included in the codex of 1489 reveal Sannazaro's influence while *Arcadia* was still circulating in manuscript form. Contemporaries ranked Sannazaro with his friends Pontano and Cariteo among the greatest poets of their generation. His friendship with Cardinal Bembo and his willingness to adapt to the latter's Tuscan prescriptions assured him a wide audience throughout Italy. Ludovico Ariosto, surely the greatest poet of the era, represented Sannazaro in the first and subsequent editions of his *Orlando furioso* (1516–32) among celebrated Italian poets as "the man I have so longed to meet" (*Orlando fusioso*, 46.17). Eighty-three successive editions of *Arcadia* through the first half of the seventeenth-century attest to its popularity, as do elaborate commentaries appended to the Renaissance editions by Tommaso Porcacchi (Venice, 1558), Francesco Sansovino (Venice, 1559), and Giovambattista Massarengo (Pavia, 1596).

Much of *Arcadia*'s early fame in Italy was owing to its linguistic merits. Sannazaro's contemporaries felt not just that he had legitimized the vernacular—Dante, Petrarch, and Boccaccio had already done that—but that he had legitimized the use of various dialects of the vernacular. For while the revised *Arcadia* acknowledged the priority of Tuscan as the literary language of Italy with the elimination of many of its Neapolitanisms, it also challenged the hegemony of Tuscan. Its style was in some ways still too Neapolitan and in other ways far too Latinate to be mistaken for Florentine.

Sannazaro's younger contemporary Benedetto Varchi (1503–65) recognized the conflict. On the one hand he praised Sannazaro for writing like a Florentine even though "when he composed *Arcadia*, he had never, as far as I know, been to Florence."[7] On the other Varchi noted several deviations, both classical and vulgar, and commented: "Ought we not to marvel all the more and commend him because, though a foreigner, he wrote so well in another language both in prose and poetry, rather than be surprised and censure him for mistakes in a few matters of no great consequence?" *Arcadia*'s greatness was as much to have violated the Tuscan model as to have validated it. Its style created, in fact, a wholly artificial literary idiom never spoken by either Florentine or Neapolitan. Before Sannazaro, Virgil had created a similar language in his *Eclogues* with a Latin never spoken by any Roman. After him Spenser in his *Shepheardes Calendar* was to create an English never spoken by any Englishman. In each instance an artificial literary language belongs to the pastoral as its special provenance.

Because the linguistic surface of *Arcadia* resembles nothing ever spoken in Italian, its artificiality has both irritated and exasperated its readers since the sixteenth century. The reason for its strangeness was Sannazaro's desire to reconstitute an aura of Latin within the vernacular. Critics have misunderstood this purpose. Its central thrust appears in the complex, complicated syntax of both the prose and the poetry. Even more strikingly it appears in the diction, which evokes rare Latin forms of minor authors like Nemesianus, Claudian, Valerius Flaccus, and Pliny rather than the canonized "classical" forms of Virgil, Ovid, and Cicero. Sannazaro's stylistic procedure isolates a particularly Latinate sense of language and plays upon it for its exquisite rarity.[8]

Sannazaro drew upon his Latin models in two different ways. For the most part he borrowed from them directly, right from the source of their own texts, which he transformed for his own purposes. But he also borrowed from them indirectly, through already sanctioned modes of imitation that some of his forerunners in Italian poetry had established. Among these forerunners he could refer on the one hand to the great Tuscan triumvirate of Dante, Petrarch, and Boccaccio, and on the other hand to humanist writers of the fifteenth century who had elaborated upon the Tuscan example. Sannazaro's relationship to his Italian models is therefore always to be judged in the context of his models' proximity to classical origins.

The manuscript of 1489 shows that Sannazaro's orthography, if not his syntax and diction, was largely Neapolitan. For publication in 1504 he followed Bembo's advice in revising the orthography and adapting much of the diction to the Tuscan norm. In that final version, however, he still retained the flavor of classical syntax in his complex word order and extended periodicity. Thus, while the 1504 printing preserves the sentence structures of 1489, it revises lexical choices like *yo* to *io*, "I"; *nescuno* or *nissuno* to *nessuno*, "no one"; *vasi* to *baci*, "kisses"; *cuóyro* to *cuoio*, "skin"; *sperto* to *disperso*, "scattered."[9]

Sannazaro's revisions in the opening sentence of Chapter I exemplify the procedure. The 1489 manuscript reads:

> *Jace nella sommità de Parthenio non humile monte*
> *de la pastorale Archadia un delettevole piano, de*
> *ampiezza non molto spacioso, però che la statura del*
> *luogho non consente; ma de minuta et verdissima*
> *herbetta sì ripieno, che, se le lascive pecorelle*
> *con li avidi morsi non vi pasciesseno, vi si potrebbe*
> *de ogni tempo ritrovare verdura. (Scherillo, p. 4)*

The 1504 edition reads:

> *Giace nella somità di Partenio, non umile monte*
> *de la pastorale Arcadia, un dilettevole piano, di*
> *ampiezza non molto spazioso però che il sito del*
> *luogo nol consente, ma di minuta e verdissima erbetta*
> *sì ripieno, che se le lascive pecorelle con gli avidi*

morsi non vi pascesseno, vi si potrebbe di ogni tempo
ritrovare verdura.

There lies on the summit of Parthenius, a not inconsider-
able mountain of pastoral Arcadia, a pleasant plateau, not
very spacious in extent, since the situation of the place
does not permit it, but so filled with tiny and deep-green
herbage that, if the wanton herds with their greedy nib-
bling did not pasture there, one could always find green
grasses in that place. (31/5)

One sees that the orthography of *Jace* becomes *Giace*, *Parthenio*
and *Archadia* become *Partenio* and *Arcadia*, *humile* and *herbetta*
(which are Latinisms recurrent in Tuscan Petrarchism) become
umile and *erbetta*, *spacioso* becomes *spazioso*, *luogho* becomes
luogo, and *et* becomes *e*. Neapolitan grammatical forms become
Tuscan ones: *de* becomes *di*, and *li* becomes *gli*. *Pasciesseno* becomes *pascesseno*, equally derived from dialect but representing
merely a graphic variant. The only change in diction favors a
more Latinate form: *statura* becomes *sito*. The syntax of the
sentence remains exactly the same.

From a stylistic perspective that syntax is instructive. A single
intransitive verb, *giace*, "lies," governs an adverbial phrase,
"nella sommità" ("on the summit"), designating place-where,
and it precedes its subject, *piano*, "plain." The latter governs
two adjectival phrases, "di ampiezza non molto spazioso . . .
ma di erbetta sì ripieno" ("not very spacious in extent, . . .
but so filled with herbage"). The litotes of the first (whereby
"non molto spazioso" asserts a positive notion of "small") leads
through *ma*, "but," not to the contradictory assertion that *non*
would seem to imply, but rather to an amplifying one that offers
more information about the plain: it is "di erbetta sì ripieno"
("so filled with herbage"). Three subordinate clauses further
complicate the syntax. The first reinforces the idea of "non
molto spazioso" redundantly, if not tautologically, by explaining
that the geography does not permit a larger site: "pero che . . ."
("since . . ."). The second refines the idea of *ripieno*: "sì ri-

pieno, che . . ." ("so full that . . ."). The third subordinate clause, however, works to negate the preceding one: "se . . . non vi pascesseno" ("if the herds did not pasture there").

The marvel is that these complications do not render the periodic syntax wholly incomprehensible. Despite its length and the reversals inherent in the negative qualification, the sentence preserves its logical clarity. The problem is that it doesn't convey its thought economically or memorably or with vivid forcefulness. Dominating the prose are nouns, adjectives, and noun phrases that exclude verbs expressing strong action. The intransitive *giace* at the beginning of the sentence serves only to govern a long string of nominative modifiers. Even though the long train of subordinate clauses suggests a complex logical and grammatical hierarchy, its real function levels the thought to a fixed idea. On the positive side, the style heightens the expressive value of individual words. On the negative side it renders the action static, immobile, frozen in time and space, and wholly dispassionate.

These effects recur in later samples of the prose. The tendency towards a heavy use of adjectives, for example, turns noun phrases into epithets. Thus Arcadia's trees are described: "lo ombroso faggio, la incorruttibile tiglia e 'l fragile tamarisco" (31/5; "the shady beech, the incorruptible linden and the fragile tamarisk." These epithets, echoing Virgilian and Ovidian ones, contribute to the style's strongly classicistic flavor. There is also a tendency towards personifying inanimate nature, imbuing it with powers that vivify all things. Thus the *piante* are not *sì discortesi* that "le lor ombre vieteno i raggi" (31/6; "Nor are the trees so discourteous that with their shade they altogether forbid the rays of the sun to enter the pleasant little grove"). Finally, there is a tendency to incorporate persistent retentions of the author's own dialect or popular forms of the language that have since been modified, side by side with echoes of classical diction: *ricevano* for *ricevevano*, "receive"; *a pruova* for *a prova*, "in rivalry"; *sollacciare* for *sollazzare*, "to amuse."

If Chapter VII marks a great divide from the early chapters with its new emphasis on the speaker's character and his development of a continuous narrative, one might assume that it and subsequent chapters were composed at a later date than the former ones. In those later chapters adjectival epithets, frequent personification, complicated syntax, and dialect mixed with classical diction all become amplified. Thus in Chapter VIII Carino addresses a bird that he catches in his snare, attributing to it qualities of memory and foresight normally reserved for humans: "E tu, misera e cattivella perdice, a che schifavi gli tetti pensando al fiero avvenimento de la antica caduta, se ne la piana terra, quando più secura stare ti credevi, ne li nostri lacciuoli incappavi?" (80/57; "And you, poor wretched Perdix, to what purpose did you avoid the lofty roofs, thinking on the dolorous issue of that ancient fall, if on the level ground, when most you thought yourself secure, you became entangled in our snares?"). The Latinate *misera* and the Italianate *cattivella*, the Latinate personification of *perdice* (Perdix) rather than the Italian nominal *pernice*, and the profusion of Latinate adjectives (*alti, fiero, antica, piana*) are typical. Elsewhere Latinate diction and classical echoing coexist with standard Tuscan forms and Petrarchan echoes, as when Carino complains of his beloved: "O crudelissima e fiera più che le truculente orse, più dura che le annose querce, et a' miei preghi più sorda che gli insani mormorii de l'infiato mare" (82/60; "O most cruel and pitiless more than surly bears and harder than aged oaks and to my prayers more deaf than the wild murmurings of the swelling sea").

These tendencies recur strongly in the prose of the final chapters added after 1489 for publication in 1504. There one finds epithets that lend a poignancy to nature: "un nero e funebre cipresso" and "fosche campagne" (134/112; "a black and funereal cypress," "shadowy meadows"). They appear in classicistic epithets using Latinate diction, like "indeficiente liquore" (136/114; "unfailing current"); and in Petrarchan phrases like "da nubilosa caligine oppresso" (140/117; "oppressed by cloudy ignorance"). They appear there, finally, amidst traces of popular diction like the verb *attuffasse* (134/112), "overwhelm" and the noun *bassezza* (137/115), "lowliness."

Sannazaro's poetic style develops on similar principles. An early poem like Eclogue I displays the chief characteristics:

> Perisca il mondo, e non pensar ch'io trepidi;
> ma attendo sua ruina, e già considero
> che 'l cor s'adempia di pensier più lepidi.
>
> (I.40–42)

Let the world perish, and never think that I tremble, / but I await its downfall and already consider / that my heart is filled with thoughts that are pleasanter.

The Latinate *ruina*, the adjectival *lepidi* functioning as an epithet for *pensier*, and the verb *adempia*, which lends a personifying quality to *cor*, becoming a synecdoche as part for the whole of the speaker's emotions, epitomize the qualities of Sannazaro's poetic style.

A mature poem like Eclogue VIII shows great flexibility in adapting these qualities to the needs of particular verse forms. Thus the Dantesque *senio* (VIII.117) rather than the common *vecchiaia*, "old age," appears as part of the rhyme scheme *Eugenio-Genio-senio*; and the Neapolitan *neputa* (VIII.122) rather than *nepitèlla*, "calamint," appears as part of the rhyme scheme *neputa-deputa-reputa*. Personification turns into metaphor as the speaker declares that mortal life "reddens itself," *rinvermigliasi* (VIII.39), full of shame as it approaches its end, and that amorous hopes "find a haven," *albergano* (VIII.138), in the simple mind.

The metaphoric tenor of the late verse is strikingly dramatic. Occasionally it results in bizarre images. Thus in Eclogue XII the lover bids his deceased beloved "ma del mio lacrimar lo inerbi e increspilo" (XII.21; "put grass over [that hair] and curl it with my tears"). Another speaker prays for his comrade that "mai per vento o grandine / la capannuola tua non si disculmine" (XII.287–88; "never by wind or hail your cottage lose its roofing"), and that for hearing Meliseus's music "par che mi

spolpe, snerve e mi disiecore" (XII.309; "it seems that I am defleshed, unnerved, and dislivered"). The diction here attains its
unusual force through the addition of dynamic prefixes to verb
forms derived from nouns: *s-polpe, s-nerve*; and, in the cases of
dis-culmine and *dis-iecore*, through prefixes to verb forms derived
from nouns that are semantic Latinisms. The creative use of
such prefixes abounds elsewhere in Eclogue XII: "mi indrago e
invipero" (8; "I rage like a dragon, or viper"); "mi induro e in-
aspero" (XII.9; "I grow hard and bitter"); *infiorilo* (XII.20;
"beflower"); *"si ingordano* (XII.58, "hunger"); "si inolmi o im-
populi" (XII.105; "elmed or poplared"); *insolfasi* (XII.149, "becomes sulphorous"); *ingolfasi* (XII.151, "ingulfs itself"); *olfasi*
(XII.153, "becomes odorous"); "mi distenebre" (XII.213; "I am
out of the shadows").

Sannazaro's stylistic choices, however, do more than just direct attention to the surface of language. They bear full respon-
sibility to the substance of complex meaning. If critics have
been all too easily irritated and exasperated with *Arcadia*'s style,
they have been just as easily irritated and exasperated with its
content. Many have interpreted it simply as an exercise in evoking pastoral nostalgia. Others have interpreted it as an obscure
allegory of the author's life and times. Neither view does justice
to the text. Its pastoral nostalgia is richer than any mechanical
summoning of old conventions, and its allegorical possibilities
resonate on several levels. The drama of reading *Arcadia* should
uncover its genuine depth. The following pages may mark a
step in that direction.

THE PASTORAL NOSTALGIA

By deconstructing the pastoral tradition as he received it, and
reconstituting it in his own *Arcadia*, Sannazaro at once summa-
rized the tradition and carried it a step further. In the introductory prose passage of Chapter I, the speaker outlines the terrain
of "Partenio" (Parthenius), a mountain in Arcadia on whose
summit the shepherds often gather for sport and song. In his

Discorso sopra le Rime di Sannazaro (Venice, 1561) Francesco
Sansovino explained that Arcadia is a region in central Pel-
oponnesus, "highly pleasing, and full of mountains, meadows,
and flowing streams."[10] Sannazaro's Arcadia, however, is not
the geographical region cherished by the ancient historian
Polybius as the home of shepherds and singers, and of Pan, the
god of herdsmen and lover of Syrinx. It is instead an imaginary
realm, like the "other" world in central Italy that Virgil in his
Eclogues had populated with Sicilian shepherds.

Though Sannazaro suggests that his "other" world lies near
Naples, for the most part he exceeds Virgil in converting his
Arcadia to a wholly literary landscape. His description in Chapter I emphasizes pastoral's inner world with echoes from Theocritus, Virgil, Ovid, Claudian, and Dante. This echoing has
important consequences. For one, its inclusion of a modern author with the ancient ones asserts the importance of vernacular
texts side by side with Greek and Latin ones. For another, its
self-conscious allusiveness proclaims a particular aesthetics.
The trees admit such light and air that "rare is the tree that
does not take from them the greatest invigoration [*grandissima
recreazione*]" (31/6). The choice of the word *recreazione* is not
fortuitous. Nature renews and recreates itself, and so does poetry. It renews and recreates old forms in new modes and styles.

The evocation of earlier literature in the first paragraphs of
Arcadia demonstrates such a re-creation. It also establishes a
distinctive role for the speaker to play in the action's subtext
and for audiences to respond to. The passage's strongest resem-
blance is to Ovid's description of a landscape in *Metamorphoses*
X.86ff. Ovid's lines describe a hill in Rhodope and Haemus
where Orpheus retreated after losing Eurydice on their return
from the underworld. There the poet sang songs of Apollo's
abortive love for Hyacinth. The submerged references to both
myths establish at the outset the Orphic and Apollonian motifs
that the speaker develops in the later chapters. Orpheus and
Apollo were poets frustrated by lost loves; so is the speaker.

The alert audience will immediately sense the speaker's liter-

ary self-consciousness. His catalogues of trees, mythic references, and literary allusions establish an unequivocal subtext of
earlier poetry. In its sixteenth-century editions *Arcadia* was
printed with various commentaries and annotations. The major
ones were written by Tommaso Porcacchi (Venice, 1558),
Francesco Sansovino (Venice, 1559), and Giovambattista Massarengo (Pavia, 1596).[11] Besides indicating sources of literary
allusions, they provide good insight into how Renaissance audiences received the text. In analyzing the *Arcadia* it is helpful to
allude to them. Its most elaborate and detailed commentator,
Giovambattista Massarengo, was explicit about the narrative's
literary reflexivity:

It seems an Arcadia of infinite pleasure to whoever sees the heights of
poetic conceits: in its mountains, deep meanings; in its valleys, beautiful poetic descriptions; in its plains, delightful rhetorical periods; in
its trees, well-chosen diction; in its leaves, the most carefully wrought
narratives; in its fruits, attractive ornaments of style and poetic artifice; in its flowers, the occult secrets of philosophy. (Massarengo,
p. 205)

The proper audience of the *Arcadia*, then, must bring to the
text a double perspective allowing the pastoral tradition and
the pastoral landscape to merge into one.

The first chapter turns from description to narrative and then
to poetry by relating how the shepherds have come together to
celebrate early spring. One of them, Ergasto, sits apart from the
rest, pensive and forgetful of himself. His name, which in
Greek means "busy" or "active," contrasts with his withdrawn
behavior, but his friend Selvaggio soon encourages him to sing.
Selvaggio begins with *terza rima* stanzas consisting of a series of
three-line units with interlocking rhymes (*a b a, b c b, c d c,*
. . .). Each line is *sdrucciolo*, ending with an antepenultimate
accent that entails the addition of one more syllable than the
standard *piana* line does. In these tercets Selvaggio laments the
scarcity of shepherds who sit singing in the shade. Elsewhere in
the *Arcadia* "shepherd" will be synonymous with "poet." Here,

Selvaggio argues, it seems that the times require Ergasto to sing: "Deh canta omai, che par che i tempi il cheggiano" (I.30; "Come now, sing, for surely the times require it").

Later in the narrative Ergasto emerges as the foremost poet among the shepherds, and he comes to function as the speaker's own alter ego, the cultivated poet's rustic equivalent, whose poetry will serve as a stage in the speaker's journey towards artistic maturity. In the Renaissance, Massarengo readily identified him as Sannazaro "ora sotto nome d'Ergasto" (p. 213). Now, however, Ergasto needs to grow into that role. He rejects his friend's old-fashioned pastoral argument with a radically different set of modern rhetorical figures derived explicitly from Petrarch's *Rima* IX. He claims that neither the external signs of springtime nor dangers visible to the outer world have any inner meaning for him (I.34). Selvaggio asks him to explain what has happened (I.55).

At this point Ergasto shifts from *terza rima sdrucciola* (tercets with antepenultimate accents and an extra syllable on each line) to the freer structure of *frottola* verse. In the *frottola* form, the last syllable of each eleven-syllable line rhymes with the fifth syllable of the succeeding line, accelerating the pace of the narration. *Frottola* verse would not outlive Sannazaro's day as a sanctioned poetic form.[12] Francesco Arsocchi had used it in his eclogues, but it soon fell into such disrepute that Massarengo identified it in his commentary as fit only for rustic love songs and burlesques (Massarengo, p. 229). Retaining his elevated Petrarchan diction in this *frottola*, however, Ergasto tells how he saw a shepherdess whose beauty overpowered him:

> vide un bel lume   in mezzo di quell'onde
> che con due bionde   trecce allor mi strinse
> e mi dipinse   un volto in mezzo al core.
>
> (I.62–64)

I saw in the midst of those waves a lovely sight / that bound me then with two golden locks / and painted in the middle of my heart a face.

The lady, however, retreats from him, both pitiless and cruel—
"spietata e rigida" (I.91)—after expressing concern for his dis-
tress. Reverting to lugubrious *terza rima* verse in *sdrucciola* measures, Ergasto now echoes Petrarch's *Rima* CCLXXXVIII. He
laments that only an echo of the lady's speech remains with
him: "Eco rimbomba, e spesso indietro voltami / le voci che sì
dolci in aria sonano, / e nell'orecchie il bel nome risoltami."
(I.100–2; "Echo resounds, and often returns again to me / the
words that sound so sweetly in the air, / and in my ears her
lovely name reverberates"). Henceforth the quest for her radiance and her language will dominate his every action. Like a
poet who seeks to recover similar qualities in an earlier poetry,
Ergasto finds traces of his desire everywhere, but nowhere in a
fully present or complete form.

Selvaggio's astonishment epitomizes the shepherds' general
reaction. Pitying Ergasto, none of them has enough heart to return to the abandoned games. At sunset they begin their journey home, and gradually, as their mood lightens, they turn to
new songs. Here the speaker provides a partial inventory of the
poetic modes that they drew upon. The inventory, however,
omits naming the responsorial mode, where one singer answers
another in the same meter and verse form; it omits the erotic
carpe diem mode and the lugubrious funeral lament; it omits
the allegorical mode alluding to and satirizing the outer world;
and it omits poetry about the inner world of poetry that establishes aesthetic precepts. It seems as though subsequent
eclogues in *Arcadia* set out to remedy this lack.

Eclogue II marks a step in that direction. The speaker recounts that several days later he has allowed his flock to wander
from its usual haunts. Before he goes very far, he meets a shepherd named Montano, whom he encourages to sing by offering
a reward of a staff carved by the shepherd poet Cariteo, "who
came from fruitful Spain" (36/11). The reward of Cariteo's staff
should stimulate the lowly shepherd Montano to new heights of
song. And it does. Massarengo judged the ensuing eclogue the
most beautiful of all in the text "per la varietà della tessitura, e

per la diversità de' soggetti" (p. 238; "for the variety of its poetic texture and the diversity of its topics").

Diversity indeed characterizes the eclogue's form. It begins with *terza rima sdrucciola*, shifts at line 19 to *frottola* verse, and shifts again at line 39 to *terza rima piana* (tercets with regular eleven-syllable lines). The *frottola* alludes satirically but obscurely to a certain social and political climate in the outer world. In the larger narrative context, Montano challenges another shepherd, Uranio, to a singing contest. At line 57 the contestants undertake stanzaic units of two eleven-syllable and one seven-syllable lines with identical rhyme (A A a, B B b, C C c, . . .) as they answer each other in responsorial tercets. At line 81 they adopt a *barzelletta* measure of five-line stanzas combining eleven- and seven-syllable verses with the rhyme A b C c B, B c D d C. . . . Then at line 101 they employ a madrigal measure of eight-line stanzas combining eleven- and seven-syllable verses with the rhyme scheme A C c c A B D D. Finally at line 133 they return to *terza rima* alternating the *sdrucciolo* antepenultimate accent with the regular *piano* pattern.

The speaker himself constitutes the audience and ultimate judge of the singers' contest, and his response calls attention to the eclogue's form. He praises Montano's "marvelously fresh beginning," evidently appreciating his various innovations, but even more he praises the "prompt and secure responses" (41/17) whereby Uranio observes the stanzaic norms and poetic limits laid down by others. That observance defines the classical approach to composing poetry. Innovation is welcome, but it proceeds from the already extant. "Originality" means returning to origins.

Another of the speaker's responses entails his appreciation of the eclogue's disgressive quality. As he converses with the singers about their performance, he also listens to the faint sounds of pheasants singing in their nests. The interruption "seems sweeter than if we had continued our discussions in due order" (42/68). Counterpoint and digressiveness enhance the values of the performance.

Chapter III marks yet another departure. The speaker announces that it is the feast of Pales, the shepherds' revered goddess. His prose account of their festivities recreates Ovid's *Fasti* IV. 721–46, where a similar feast occurs. The speaker's curious description of figures painted on the frieze of the shepherds' holy temple becomes central. One of its by-products is to indicate how a painter's audience might view the work of art. The frieze depicts three stories. Two entail erotic frustration. The first shows the designs of four satyrs on a group of unsuspecting nymphs who soon recognize them and manage to flee. The third balances the first with a representation of Endymion viewed lovingly by the moon, and of Paris distracted from his love for Oenone by the three naked goddesses who ask him to judge their beauty. The dynamics of these paintings convey the fragility, mutability, and transformability of erotic desire, and these qualities can characterize an artist's mode of existence.

Yet another painting, the central one of the triptych, makes that connection clear. Referring to Ovid's *Metamorphoses* II.680, it shows the pastoral Apollo guarding the herds of Admetus while, unknown to him, Mercury steals his cows. Through his association with the muses, Apollo had been regarded as the patron—indeed the figure—of the artist. As a shepherd-singer Apollo plays his oaten flute while Mercury performs the theft. Mercury himself, trickster and deceiver, "astutissimo" according to Tommaso Porcacchi (p. 173), played another role in classical mythology as messenger of the gods; in this capacity he functioned as their interpreter. Here, then, Mercury, the figure of the interpreter, frustrates Apollo, the figure of the artist. The frustration is ironic. It is as though the artist lacks strength to determine the reception of his own work. The power of the interpreter is decisive. He can play tricks beyond the reach of the creator or originator. The latter is hobbled unless he controls his own artistic subtext.

Another allusion to Apollo appears again in Eclogue III. Its singer, Galicio, produces a flawless Petrarchan *canzone*, which contains five thirteen-line stanzas combining seven- and eleven-syllable lines with a rhyme (*a b C, a b C, c d e e, D, f f*), and an introductory stanza and a concluding tercet. In it Galicio retreats behind the identity of another shepherd singing his love for Amarantha.

The song welds the classical and Petrarchan modes into a perfect synthesis. In praising his beloved, the singer proclaims that the Golden Age may now recur (III.30–32). Three stanzas abound in references to the classical Golden Age poetry of Virgil (*Eclogue* IV), Ovid (*Metamorphoses* I.103–111), Horace (*Odes* V.16 and III.18), and Tibullus (*Elegies* II.1 and II.5). In the last two stanzas the speaker names his beloved and in oxymoronic Petrarchan fashion describes her contrary effects on him: "quella c'adolcir basta ogni mio tòsco" (III.63; "she who is enough to sweeten all my poison").

The audience of shepherds responds to this *canzone* in various ways. Some appreciate its harmony. Others commend its sweet and gentle Petrarchan rendering of amorous topics. Still others commend the technical feats of its versification, particularly in its beautiful rhymes; and some of the latter perceive a correspondence between the beauty of the poem's sound and the sagacity of its sense. Their diversity suggests the range of responses that the Petrarchan lyric may elicit from its audience. The speaker, however, probes deeper in Chapter IV. Wishing to discover the identity of the woman about whom the shepherd sings, he surveys the feminine audience for signs of recognition. Soon he finds one whose actions betray her.

Surprisingly he describes her in language that reflects the terminology of treatises on rhetoric. This terminology suggests that the woman's beauties bear analogy with the beauties of a good style. Her hair is covered by a veil ("un sottilissimo velo," 49/25), that could suggest the subtle veil of allegory covering the poem itself. Her features are of a beautiful form ("di bella forma") that could describe the form of the poetry. The beauty is strange and marvelous ("strana e maravigliosa leggiadria"), pleasing to contemplate ("piacevole a riguardare"), capable of making the audience think about her with more efficacy ("con

più efficacia"). "Efficacy" is indeed a quality of poetic persuasiveness that all classical and Renaissance handbooks of rhetoric announced as their aim. Significantly, one achieves efficacy
through the use of conventional figures and tropes known as
"colors." Here the beloved sows the earth with twenty varieties
of "colors" ("venti varietà di colori"), as Dante used the word
to mean "flowers" in *Purgatorio* XXVIII.68. The speaker understands the girl's identity as though by solid rhetorical proof
("quasi per fermo argomento"), and when she meets her companions, he enjoys the diversity of their charms (50/26). The
description seems to be less about a woman than about the diverse possibilities of poetic rhetoric.

Curiously Eclogue IV, which soon follows, does not attain
all those possibilities. It is a double *sestina* that demonstrates
nothing more than complex ingenuity in the deployment of its
rhyme scheme. In a traditional *sestina* as it was developed in
Provençal poetry and perfected in Italian by Dante and Petrarch, each of the poem's six six-line stanzas repeats the end
words from the lines of the first stanza, but in a different order.
In this double *sestina*, the singers use each order twice to create
twelve stanzas. Despite its ingenuity, however, this poem fails
with its other rhetorical resources. It depicts a poetic contest on
the topic of an unrequited lover's lament. The contestants, a
shepherd named Logisto and a goatherd named Elpino, are accompanied by Ofelia's pipes and subject to Selvaggio's judgment. Selvaggio declares both of them to be victors, and the
audience agrees.

Chapter V introduces the mode of funeral lamentation and it
demonstrates the radical differences between prose effects and
poetic ones.[13] The prose section of the chapter focuses on a long
lament by an anonymous cowherd for Androgeo, whose tomb
the speaker and his friends have discovered on a wooded mountain top. In its eclogue Ergasto sings a poetic lament for the
dead shepherd Androgeo. The difference between the two laments is incalculable. The prose version by an anonymous cowherd draws upon classical topics and motifs. Echoing Neme

sianus's *Eclogue* I and Virgil's *Eclogue* V, it nearly loses itself in
mere description. The poetic eclogue by Ergasto, on the other
hand, stands out sharply from the context and carries meanings
that reverberate beneath its surface. It reprises the classical topics and adds unmistakably modern motifs from Petrarch. Its
canzone form repeats the stanzaic meter (except for a final line
of eleven rather than seven syllables) and rhyme scheme
(*a b C, a b C, c d e e D f F*) of the earlier Eclogue III. Its verbal
echoes from Petrarch's "Chiare, fresche, e dolci acque" (*Rima*
CXXVI) are striking. They evoke Petrarchan reminiscences of
death freeing the soul from the body's bonds (V.2), of footprints
leaving traces among the stars, of the inescapability of death
(V.32), and of the immortality that will attach to Androgeo's
name (V.59). As Massarengo points out, however, the poem's
deeper sentiments are pagan rather than Christian. Instead of
grace, it is Ergasto's art that functions as a guarantor of Androgeo's immortality and of his own as well. The inner world
crosses the barrier erected by death.

Up to this moment, however, the shepherds' art has been
consigned to a particularly transient existence. They have composed their songs to answer certain felt needs, often without
premeditation and always without thought about preserving
them for future performances. If life is fleeting, so it seems, is
art. Now even before Ergasto finishes his song, he meets in
Chapter VI with a new kind of response. One of the shepherds,
Fronimo, the most crafty and ingenious of all, has been tran-
scribing the verse as it was sung. He has written it down on
green beech bark, which he later fastens near a tree (63/40). In
a direct and pointed way, writing bears to poetry the same relationship that the singer of the lamentation bears to the deceased. Writing confers permanence on the art, guarantees its
continuance in living memory, and endows it with a transcendence that it would otherwise not have.

Writing also serves to encode the law. In fact, in Italian the
word for "law," *legge*, is etymologically related to the verb for
"read," *leggere*. With the increasing pressures of civilization and

socialization, the shepherds should perceive a need to assert the dignity of law and distributive justice by singing about it. Eclogue VI therefore refers to this outer world. It delineates the corruption and dishonesty of the times and contrasts them with an image of the Golden Age. A young shepherd named Carino has been looking for a lost or possibly stolen heifer. When the shepherds mollify him with many courtesies, he asks Opico to sing. Not to be outdone in politeness, Opico replies that in his old age he has forgotten too many verses, but that a younger man like Serrano can perform them instead. Serrano then returns politeness to Opico by inviting him to join in song. Such courtesies freely dealt take the place of engraved law among the shepherds. Nonetheless, the problem of theft and other wrong-doing hovers in the background.

In Eclogue VI Serrano and Opico sing a lamentation about moral corruption in the outer world. Textual evidence from the 1489 manuscript, the 1502 pirated edition, and the 1504 authorized edition suggests that it was not only one of Sannazaro's earliest eclogues, but also a much revised one. Its difficult rhyme in *terza rima sdrucciola* and several verbal and topical echoes suggest Dantesque and Petrarchan analogues, but its conceptual models reach back further into classical antiquity. Horace's moral satires, Virgil's *Georgic* IV, and above all Calpurnius's *Eclogue* V supply the central motifs.

One of those motifs suggests a curious relationship between poetry and deceit, or fiction. Serrano points out that the thief used a magic language of his own that enabled him to accomplish his evil, "magichi versi assai possenti e validi" (VI.52; "magic verses very powerful and strong"). His transformability matches and supersedes that of the poet. Opico calls him a "Proteus" (VI.52), suggesting that his powers have produced wondrous effects. The problem is that Proteus has conventionally figured forth the role of the poet, too, as he will do explicitly in *Piscatoria* IV. Protean guises and the use of Protean language have therefore a double edge. On the one hand they enable the poet to create for his audience a number of forms and fictions that replicate reality. On the other they enable the thief to practice his deceits on unsuspecting victims, all for his own profit. Serrano's lament may constitute a warning against deceitful poetry as much as it does against theft. One harms its audience with false words while the other harms its victims with false deeds.

In response Opico evokes the topos of the Golden Age. The old man narrates how, when he was a young boy, his father described "olden times" (VI.68). The narrative situation of the aged father telling the young boy about the past mirrors and reverses the actual situation where the boy, who has now become an old man, tells Serrano about the days gone by. Opico provides the direct link with the past. He is able to draw a fine contrast between it and the present, and one of the contrasts that he mentions entails the practice of litigation (VI.80–81). Men make laws to regulate complex societies. Laws, however, can be construed as signs of decadence and corruption because they are written out of a need to control the misrule that has grown into fashion.

Eclogue VI therefore dramatizes a pessimism and despair about the outer world that brings *Arcadia* to a problematic juncture. Its remaining six eclogues will point through its inner world to a way out of the impasse. Poetry has already suggested a partial solution. The nostalgic references to Virgil and Ovid, Calpurnius and Nemesianus, Dante and Petrarch throughout the first six eclogues have dignified the poetic texture and elevated the style of Sannazaro's art. None of those eclogues, however, could be called truly distinguished. In the poetry that follows Sannazaro will attempt a more complicated task. By deconstructing the pastoral tradition as he has so far received it, he will reconstitute it anew in *Arcadia*'s last six eclogues.

THE PASTORAL POLYPHONY

Chapter VII marks a new turn by introducing conventions of romance fiction hitherto absent from the narrative. In it the speaker tells the story of his own amorous frustration. In the action that follows, Chapter VIII will extend the conventions of romance fiction with its focus on Carino's amorous plight. Chapter IX will introduce a discussion of magic lore. Chapter X will include a history of the pastoral mode that governs the entire text. Chapter XI will accommodate the conventions of epic poetry to pastoral with an account of funeral games. Chapter XII will unfold the speaker's visionary journey to the source of poetic inspiration. These various literary forms constitute a polyphony of modes and styles that distinguish the second half of *Arcadia*. They are the products of a long literary civilization.

Civilization breeds its discontents. In Chapter VII the audience's response to Serrano's and Opico's tercets is notably muted. When Carino turns to the speaker, he strikes a new note. He asks him to identify himself. Here a manifestly personal and autobiographical moment intrudes when the speaker calls modern Naples his home. He cites his aristocratic heritage in the service of his kingdom's rulers, and he allows the name of "Sannazaro" with the surname "Sincero" as his proper address. He also identifies himself as a victim of love in the literary mode made popular by Provençal and Sicilian poets, and by Dante, Petrarch, and Boccaccio. In an account echoing Dante's discovery of Beatrice in *Vita nuova*, he describes his enamorment of a young girl since the age of eight. The speaker's involvement with her is more sentimentally debilitating than Dante's, however. Echoing Francesa from *Inferno* V, he finds no greater grief than in remembering happy times amid misery: "not without bitterest sorrow can I call to mind the times that are past" (69/47), and as he recalls the simile of the doves in hell's circle of the lustful in *Inferno* V, he laments the joy of "amorous doves exchanging kisses with soft murmurings and then flying off" while he figures forth his own sorrow (73/50).

Driven to desperation by Petrarchan contrarieties in his love for her, he narrates how he sought release from his torment by going into voluntary exile among the shepherds. Like Florio, who separated himself from Biancofiore in Boccaccio's *Filocolo*, and like the heroine of Boccaccio's *Fiammetta*, the speaker hopes to recover his essential sensibility amidst the distraction of rustic life. As these intertextual reminiscences indicate, the recovery may be a primarily literary one.

The shepherds respond to his declaration through the comments of Carino. The latter's name, "dear little one," suggests a precious, polished, refined personality corresponding to Sannazaro's own "Sincero." Carino listens with "the utmost sympathy" (74/52). He begs Sincero to repeat the songs that he has heard him singing, and he offers as a reward a pipe of elderwood that he has gathered from the most distant reaches of the mountain. A privileged moment follows. Carino prophesies that the song Sincero will now sing will form only a prelude to future songs "in a loftier vein" (74/54).

The prediction heartens Sincero to pick up his lyre. The choice of that instrument confirms his sophisticated intentions and distinguishes him from the shepherds who play the less complicated sampogna. So does the form of Eclogue VII, his *sestina* in imitation of Petrarch's "A qualunque animale alberga in terra" (*Rima* XXII). Porcacchi hails the poet as a most adept master of its art ("diligentissimo maestro di quest' arte," Porcacchi, p. 179). Its first four stanzas dramatize the plight of the lover who finds no rest at night. Midway through them he addresses Mother Earth and petitions that someday he may find rest among the green hills (VII.13–14). In the fourth stanza he abandons his lady in order to seek repose among the shepherds, though to his grief he finds that even there the flowery hills have become fields of stubble (VII.22). In the fifth stanza he recalls a dream about his beloved's appearance.

Though the form of the *sestina* demands that its end-line words remain the same in each stanza, the tone changes remarkably. The lady bids him to leave his gloomy caverns and gather her flowers on the hills: "dicendo a me:—Vien, cogli a le mie piagge / qualche fioretto, e lascia gli antri foschi" (VII.29–30; "Saying to me: 'come, gather on my hills / a few flowers, and leave your black caverns'"). Her flowers may be the productive issue of his poetry, as Porcacchi suggests when he says that the *sestina* advances towards the inner world "con alle-gorie, con metafore, e con alcune convenienti comparazioni" (Porcacchi, p. 179). If so, she is then bidding the speaker to embark upon his poetic vocation without hesitation or regret. Her delivery of these lines within the formal constraints of the *sestina* furthermore implies the conventional discipline and al-legiance to tradition that his career will honor, while its tonal shift from dark to light indicates the freedom that he will enjoy in the use of such forms. Amatory desire becomes the well-spring of a deeper poetics.

The romance stories that follow in Chapter VIII entail vari-ous kinds of desire. The first of them, Carino's, narrates a youth-ful erotic passion. It radiates an enthusiastic optimism that its speaker directs against Sincero's pessimism. In his extended ac-count of the time spent with his beloved, Carino tells how they delighted in bird catching. His narrative could serve as a meta-phor for the speaker's own ensnarement in the nets of love. He does not tell the girl of his desire, but rather instructs her to find the image of his love by looking in the waters of a cool limpid spring. Shocked to find her own image there, she retreats from him (81/59).

Carino did not know how to articulate his desire, nor did the girl know how to receive it. Carino does know how to articulate his grief, however. He recounts the substance of a long lament that he uttered as he prepared to hurl himself from the neigh-borhood's highest cliff (82–84/60–61). His articulation in prose rather than poetry implicitly underscores Carino's youth. Unlike the older Clonico in the next eclogue, Carino needs to develop his control over the resources of language, and perhaps also to deepen his insight into human nature and the course of events. In the story's outcome it is only the lucky appearance of his beloved that deters him from suicide.

After Carino takes his leave, the speaker and his companions encounter another shepherd "so dishevelled and dolorous in his gestures that he made us wonder greatly at him" (85/62). In his physical dilapidation he seems the very opposite of Carino, who despite his grief still strikes a handsome pose. The shepherds recognize him as "enamored Clonico, a shepherd more learned than others and expert in music." He has fallen into a sorry state of frustrated desire. Carino's youth endowed him with a resilience that allowed him to survive love's torment. For Clonico, whose name in Greek means "disturbed, enraged," there is no hope. He has spent too many years in Cupid's snare, all the more to his discredit since his learning and artistic skill might have checked his erotic impulses. He is walking in the direction of the city, an ironic antipastoral movement counter to the speaker's own and one that establishes him as much as a foil to the speaker as an exaggerated extreme of Carino.

Eugenio, his best friend, prevails upon Clonico to answer him in song. Eclogue VIII duplicates the metrical pattern of Serrano's and Opico's eclogue in Chapter VI (*terza rima sdrucciola*) with something of a similar satiric effect. But whereas the latter aimed its scorn at moral and social corruption in the outer world, this one aims its at erotic and poetic distortions close to poetry's inner world. Eugenio taunts Clonico with conventional antiamatory—and antifeminist—barbs (VIII.10–12). Clonico responds by expressing a wish to be free from the influence of Cupid and Venus (VIII.25–27). Yet, while Eugenio assails love for its blindness (VIII.34–35), Clonico laments that all nature except for him is happy in love (VIII.60). Eugenio argues that lovers contradict the principle of life by nourishing within themselves a destructive death-wish (VIII.68). Clonico nonetheless finds death more attractive than life as it provides a release from his desire. It also provides release from the demands of art.

Here Clonico's pessimism leads him to negate his own poetic talent at the very moment he displays it so well. He asks the shepherds to bury his rhymes with him: "Allor le rime, c'a mal grado accumolo, / farete meco in cenere risolvere, / ornando di ghirlande il mesto cumolo" (VIII. 100–102; "Then the rhymes that I have somehow gathered / you will cause to be reduced with me to ashes, / adorning with floral garlands the gloomy pile"). It is the despair more of a poet than of a lover. Love, in fact, is merely incidental to the poetry. Desire for the wrong thing has driven him madly to renounce the talent that ennobled him among the other shepherds. Eugenio registers disbelief and then outrage, and the song ends with his promise to find a remedy for Clonico's mad desire.

The remedy will be homeopathic. It will entail an application of magic, which itself expresses one's desire to attain the unattainable, to control one's own world through an effort of intelligence and will with a concern for practical consequences. Opico therefore proposes to take the grieving lover to Enareto, a shepherd who is adept in white magic. Opico's long narration of Enareto's sacred incantations illustrates the power of words over things, intelligence and will over objects and blind forces, ingenuity and desire over intractable nature.

It turns out, however, that for Clonico's disorder Enareto has no magic cure. Before Enareto can respond, the shepherds hear the singing of a solitary goatherd. His name is Elenco, and his song is emblematic of one last form of desire. Desire in fact motivates song and all serious poetry. It begins with a discovery that one is lacking in something important, a discovery that impels one to reach out to fill the void. The soul reaches out by expressing itself. The poet learns to speak so that his words can confer at least an imagined being on what is absent and desired. Denial spurs articulation: if one cannot have what one wants, at least one can talk about it. Analogously, if one cannot understand what one lacks, at least one can seek words to aid in comprehension. Poetry is the artistic product of desire, and it can achieve results akin to those that magic begets. Porcacchi asserts in his commentary that he himself has more to say about the powers of poetry than he can articulate in a brief space, "ch'io potrei in questa Prosa dir molte cose più che non dirò, pertinenti all' imitazione" (Porcacchi, p. 182; "in this prose I could say much more than I will say about poetic imitation"), so rich are its powers.

As the shepherds approach Elenco, he falls silent. Ofelia, the oxherd whose pipes accompanied Logisto and Elpino in Eclogue IV, provokes him to resume his song. They then sing Eclogue IX in two parts, the first embodying the oxherd's taunts and the goatherd's responses in a series of *terza rima sdrucciola*, the second representing the poetic contest between them in *terza rima piana*. More than any of *Arcadia*'s earlier poetic contests (Eclogues II, IV, VI, and VII), this one captures the spirit and tone of the contest in ancient pastoral. Echoes of Theocritus's *Idylls* IV, V, and VIII, Virgil's *Eclogues* III, IV, and VII, Ovid's *Fasti* I.5, 51, and Petrarch's *Rime* dominate the poem. Towards the end of its first division, Montano, the contestants' judge, urges them to sing so that the mountains may know how much they renew the lost age (IX.49–42). In its faithful yet inventive treatment of ancient conventions, this poem accomplishes a minor renaissance of classical form.

The eclogue itself demonstrates poetry's power to survive the ravages of time and the incomprehension of distant audiences. Incomprehension is indeed a threat that every poet faces with his audience, and yet difficulty of comprehension contributes to poetry's durability and strength. All poetry speaks in riddles, some trivial, some majestic. Successive audiences may find different answers to these riddles, since each audience interprets them from the horizon of its own understanding. Inexplicit meanings invite renewals of meaning and guarantee the life of poetry. Like the phoenix of Ofelia's riddle in this eclogue (IX.136–138), true poetry rises from its own ashes. As the eclogue itself demonstrates in its revival of ancient pastoral conventions, not only individual poems, but whole poetic forms survive the pulse of time. Thus, says Massarengo in his commentary, poets are crowned with laurel because it decays

less quickly than other leaves and "thereby signals the eternity
of poetic verse" ("sì per dimostrar l 'eternità de' versi," Massarengo, p. 269).

Montano accords this particular eclogue a generous reception
in Chapter X. He judges neither singer the sole victor, but gives
the honor to Apollo, the sharpener of peregrine wits (101/79).
The group now leaves the stream and advances up the mountain slope towards the sacred forest where Enareto will work his
magic.

Pan reigns as the forest's deity, and an altar to him dominates
a cave inside the wood. The shepherds have carved his statue as
a work of art and have decorated it with scrolls recording the
work of farming and raising animals. Outside the cave stands a
huge pine tree from one of whose branches hangs a sampogna,
the instrument of seven reeds joined with wax that the shepherds fashion for their poetry. When they ask who is "the author" of this reed ("lo auttore," 103/81), Enareto tells them a
tale that in fact recounts the history of the pastoral mode. Pan
himself shaped the sampogna as the precursor of pastoral poets.
In love with Syrinx, he pursued her into the woods. Just when
he caught her, she scorned him by willing her transformation
into a reed. Left with the reed, Pan expressed such grief that his
sighs issued forth in sweet harmony. The process became complete when Pan divided the reed into seven successively shorter
pieces and joined them with wax to make a musical instrument.

Pan's poetry originally exemplified the complaint mode, but
it lends itself to other possibilities, too. The priest tells how the
reed came into the hands of a shepherd from Syracuse who sang
of Arethusa. The shepherd was Theocritus, originator of pastoral poetry, and his new and different mode in the *Idylls* was
mythic. Singing of Arethusa, he recounted her transformation
into a subterranean stream. Poetry undergoes such transforma-
tions, too. Theocritus brought the pastoral to his own homeland
and expressed it in his own dialect. From there he bequeathed
it to a Mantuan shepherd named Tityrus, who continued to develop it in new ways. This shepherd was Virgil, and the modes

he devised for it in his *Eclogues* were many, by turns amatory, didactic, political, aesthetic, funereal, mythic, and satiric. Virgil, moreover, fashioned a new reed to sing of greater things, as the prophetic poetry of *Eclogue* IV demonstrates. Indeed his eclogues served as a prelude for sounding the *Aeneid* with a more sonorous trumpet. Enareto concludes with an open-ended challenge when he states that few poets have been able to play it with accomplishment since then (105/82). The pastoral has lain neglected for ages, and no one has succeeded in reviving it, much less in elevating it to still higher forms.

Significantly the description of the setting carries no intertextual references to classical literature like those that abound everywhere else in *Arcadia*. Indeed, in Scherillo's footnote-laden edition of the text, the page on which it appears (p. 205) is the only one so far free from source annotation. The description of this place of origins is original with Sannazaro. The Neapolitan poet is, in effect, proclaiming his own originality.

Before Enareto actually performs his magic, the shepherds decide to return to their flocks. Along the way Opico commissions Selvaggio to praise their own noble century and its rich endowment of so many excellent shepherds. As it turns out, however, his song mounts an acerbic attack upon the sociopolitical corruption of the outer world. Selvaggio gives no indication of his intent when he urges that the shepherds gather around the tomb of Ergasto's mother, Massilia, to hear the song (109/87). Ergasto, who earlier functioned as an alter ego for the speaker, has recently embellished his mother's grave site. Her name itself suggests the name of Sannazaro's own mother Masella, who died in the poet's youth. The melancholy specter of death casts its shadow over the eclogue that Selvaggio begins.

Selvaggio's Eclogue X recounts a song-within-a-song, actually a paraphrase of an antipastoral about evils in Naples fictively composed by Gian Francesco Caracciolo, the historian of Ferdinand I's reign. Selvaggio presents this song (X.49–185) within the frame of *terza rima sdrucciola* (X. 1–48, 186–204) that he addresses to Fronimo, the scribe who earlier committed

Ergasto's Eclogue V to writing. The song-within-a-song casts
an enigmatic spell. In its first section Selvaggio repeats Caracciolo's complaint that the flocks and herds are hungry and that
the shepherds are abandoning Hesperia because of invading
foreigners (X.67–69). At line 79 he shifts from tercets to the
frottola form to describe the ills of the age. The description
composed by Caracciolo inverts all the pastoral values that
characterize the good society. Nature withers and wastes away
while the pastoral gods express outrage for the fault of one man.
Selvaggio repeats Caracciolo's admission that he sings in veiled
and obscure terms:

> Gran cose in picciol velo   oggi restringo.
> Io ne l'aria dipingo,   e tal si stende,
> che forse non intende   il mio dir fosco.
>
>   (X.157–59)

Great matter today I wrap in a thin veil; / I paint in the air,
and it is so much stretched out / that perhaps my darkened
speech does not convey meaning.

But he still refuses to identify the offender by name. In the concluding *terzetti* he suggests that a crow has already predicted disaster (X.169), while he alludes to the villain as a union of bear
and tiger (X.174). But whether he refers to a specific individual
or to a general situation is unclear. The style seems to glorify its
elusive vagueness; it relies on puns and wordplay more than on
concrete reference. For example, the singer advises a shepherd
to solve the problem by cutting down a nut tree, *noce*, that in-
jures, *nòce*, the grain with its cold shade (177–78). The fuller
meaning remains impenetrable.

The eclogue nonetheless delights each member of the fictive
audience, commanding the closest attention with obscurity that
invites varied interpretation (118/95). For the speaker in particular the reminiscences of Naples have a powerful effect. At
once pleasing and disturbing, they move him to tears and in-
duce him to think that he is standing once more beside the
placid Sebeto stream. The abrupt transposition of mood from

obscure invective to nostalgic sentimentality stands as evidence of Sannazaro's discontinuity in composing *Arcadia*. The text's pirated edition of 1502 ended with his eclogue; Summonte's edition of 1504 adds two more chapters and eclogues that were surely composed later.

THE PASTORAL DECONSTRUCTION

The praise of Naples that opens Chapter XI might seem a conspicuous rhetorical irrelevance, both with its rarefied style and its sharp break from the preceding action. Indeed in it the speaker reasserts the dignity of the city that Selvaggio and Caracciolo have just degraded and lamented in the previous eclogue. He does more. Superseding the earlier pastoral vision, he reclaims the sophisticated, self-conscious urban values that he had timidly advanced in Chapter VII. There he declared his impatience with Arcadian solitude and his belief that even woodland beasts would find little pleasure in it (72/50). Now he lauds the city as a center of art and culture, learning and skill (118/96). The city nourishes his literary development and that reason alone is sufficient to guarantee its worth. By choosing to return to the city, however, the speaker in fact reverses pastoral values. The last two chapters of *Arcadia* amount to a deconstruction of those values.

The first of these chapters implies the speaker's own logocentric literary development. It records a series of funeral games honoring the first anniversary of Massilia's death. Modelled "diligentissimamente," as Porcacchi says (Porcacchi, p. 188), on the games in *Iliad* XXIII, *Aeneid* V, and *Thebiad* VI, it demonstrates the speaker's aspirations towards higher literature than the pastoral, his propensity towards the epic, and his skill in adapting the latter's conventions to the demands of his own genre. It functions also as a promise that he will one day compose his own epic.

The observance begins, appropriately enough, with music. The shepherds pass the night in a vigil singing soft lamentations (119/97). They move the birds to compete with them and they charm even the wild animals. The games themselves allow for a reprise of the characters who had earlier performed throughout the *Arcadia*: Carino, Logisto, Elpino, Ofelia, Galico, Serrano, Montano, Eugenio, Ursacchio, Uranio, Selvaggio, and Fronimo. The eldest shepherd, Opico, too infirm to compete with the others, tells how he had himself shown great prowess in his youth at the games for the great shepherd Panormita. The last name echoes the pseudonym of Antonio Beccadelli, the humanist predecessor of Pontano and founder of the academy that came to bear the latter's signature, and by association it returns the action to a learned humanistic context. Through elegant variations on their customary role-playing, the shepherds contending in the games seem to be so many members of the academy. Thus in its last pages *Arcadia* revives the life and spirit of the intellectual group to which Sannazaro belonged. The deeper concerns of his fictional shepherds have all along matched the cultural, social, political, and aesthetic concerns of Pontano's humanist fellowship.

Eclogue XI, in *terza rima piana*, which Ergasto next sings in memory of his mother, raises that brigade's literary ideals to a new level. In the mode of a funeral lament, it uses its material to promulgate an emphatic statement of the poet's higher ambitions. An occasion for honoring the dead becomes an occasion for renewing the inner artistic life. The first tercet evokes this inner life when Ergasto claims that his mother's death has deprived him of hope for extending his gentle style and sweet song: "Poi che 'l soave stile e 'l dolce canto / sperar non lice più per questo bosco, / ricominciate, o Muse, il vostro pianto" (XI.1-3; "since hope is not permitted any more / for gentle style and sweet song in this wood, / begin again, o Muses, your complaint"). The poem subsequently records his quest for a more substantial style and a different kind of song.[14]

Its initial lines recall Moschus's classical lament for Bion, though the speaker soon develops his own concerns in a different manner. Moschus's verse may not have succeeded in restoring Bion's actual presence, but it did succeed in reestablishing his fame. More importantly, it established Moschus's own fame. It preserves his memory as well as Bion's, and it testifies to the Orphic power of poetry to raise the dead to life. The myth of Orpheus is the central one that holds out the possibility of human return. Ergasto summons that myth (XI.64–66), but ironically he neglects its unhappy issue. Orpheus failed to recover his beloved in bodily form. Ergasto's silence on this matter suggests that other sorts of recovery might still be possible. In particular, it might still be possible to recapture the spiritual form of the lost being and invest it with some kind of remembered permanence.

In the poem's middle section (XI.70–114), however, Ergasto comes to denigrate his own literary talent. Elaborating upon his implied comparison with Orpheus, Ergasto doubts whether he can achieve as much as his predecessor. Still, if his attempts at recovery should fail, he would prefer to remain in the underworld with what he tried to recover rather than emerge without it: "Ma se schernendo nostra umanitade / lei schifasse il venir, sarei ben lieto / di trovar all'uscir chiuse le strade" (XI.76–78; "But if, scorning our humanity / she should refuse to come, I would be happy / at finding the paths closed to my exit"). This idea of recovery suggests something different from reuniting with a single human person. The word *umanitade* evokes the larger program of recovering classical civilization that the humanists of Pontano's academy proposed. Similarly Ergasto's emphasis on his role as poet suggests his mission to recover the spirit of ancient poetry in his own art. Short of achieving that goal, he would prefer the life of a scholar bound to the past without the effort of a new production.[15]

Ergasto now arrives at a new accommodation with his art. If his style cannot match his intention, he ought to find a new style; or, alternatively, he ought to bequeath it to some other poet to fulfill. Still, he does not wholly despair. He now requests aid for his own rough style:

> *Fa che costei ritrove un'altra tromba*
> *che di lei cante, acciò che s'oda sempre*
> *il nome che da se stesso rimbomba.*
>   *E se per pioggia mai non si distempre*
> *il tuo bel corso, aita in qualche parte*
> *il rozzo stil, sì che pietade il tempre.*

(XI.94–99)

See to it that she find another trumpet / to sing of her, so
that the name be heard / forever, that of itself reverberates.
/ And—so may your lovely course never be disturbed / by
the rains—give aid in some degree / to my rough style, that
pity temper it.

It may never merit the permanence that writing can confer, but
it does have the right to some form of existence:

> *Non che sia degno da notarsi in carte,*
> *ma che sol reste qui tra questi faggi,*
> *così colmo d'amor, privo d'ogn'arte.*

(XI.100–102)

Not that it may deserve to be written on pages; / but only
that it remain here among these beeches, / as full of love as
lacking in all art.

This idea unlocks the stranglehold of negativity that has ham-
pered him, and it frees him to develop a wholly new attitude:

> *E perché al fine alzar conviemmi alquanto,*
> *lassando il pastoral ruvido stile,*
> *ricominciate, Muse, il vostro pianto.*

(XI.112–114)

And because at the close it behooves me somewhat to rise, /
abandoning my rude pastoral style, / begin again, O Muses,
your complaint.

If his poetry ought to exist, then it ought also to exist in as fine
a form as possible. This premise enables him to advance towards a new level of poetic production.

The poem's final section (XI. 115–60) then recounts Ergasto's triumph over self-doubt, his reconciliation with his own aims, and his prescience about future success:

> Non fa per me più suono oscuro e vile,
> ma chiaro e bello, che dal ciel l'intenda
> quella altera ben nata alma gentile.
>   Ella coi raggi suoi fin qui si stenda,
> ella aita mi porga, e mentre io parlo,
> spesso a vedermi per pietà discenda.
>   E se 'l suo stato è tal, che a dimostrarlo
> la lingua manche, a se stessa mi scuse,
> e m'insegne la via d'in carte ornarlo.
>
> (XI.115–23)

For me no more a sound obscure and low / but clear and lovely, that she from heaven may hear, / that proud blessed courteous soul. / May her soul with its radiance reach down to here: / may it offer me aid and often when I am speaking / for pity may it descend to have sight of me. / And if its state be such that my language fails / in shewing it forth, may she find excuses for me / and teach me the way of adorning it in my verse.

In particularly striking language he praises the achievement of shepherd-poets whose desire motivated serious poetry, and he encourages the attempts of those who have not yet done so:

> Fortunati i pastor che, desïando
> di venir in tal grado, han poste l'ale!
> benché nostro non sia sapere il quando.
>
> (XI.142–44)

Fortunate are the shepherds who in desire / of coming to such state, have aimed their wings; / although it be not ours to know the when.

With emphasis on poetry as the product of desire, its metonymic reference to the "wings of the poet," and its use of the conjunctive quando as a noun, the style achieves a palpable

density. Envisioning his own work, Ergasto prays that laurels
may cover him so as to make him at one with what he seeks to
regain:

> *impetra a questi lauri ombrosi e folti*
> *grazia, che con lor sempre verdi fronde*
> *possan qui ricoprirne ambo sepolti.*
>
> (XI. 148–50)

gain the grace for these thick and shady laurels / that they
have power with their evergreen boughs / to cover us over,
both of us buried here.

The result will be a true logocentric renaissance of the old in
what he produces anew. His ambitions are high, but Ergasto
ends with every hope of being able to accomplish them. And
he will, if every poem he produces has a comparable effect on
its audience.

Ergasto's performance has a decisive impact on Sincero, who
listens in admiration and suspense. The impact is profounder
than he realizes. That night he has a disturbing dream that sub-
liminally evokes his own central concerns as a literary artist
(134/112). The speaker's dream of abandonment amidst deserted tombs had transposed him to an antipastoral "other"
world evoking the dead past. His effort to relate to his environment represents an attempt to clear away the detritus of centuries. An uprooted orange tree and its disseminated fruits may
refer to the political collapse of Naples's royal house of Aragon
and the exile of its last king in 1501, but in broader humanistic
and literary terms it may also emblematize the state of classical
civilization and the need for its renewal.[16] Nymphs tell the
speaker that the fates have unjustly severed the tree, and they
direct him to a grove of funereal cypresses to sing his verses.
Distressed by the thought of singing dead poetry to a dead audience, the speaker awakens in turmoil.

In tears he begins walking towards the mountain slope bor-
dered by a great, rushing river (134/117). A nymph leads him
into a cave from whence the river issues. As he penetrates

deeper to the source, he sees other nymphs sifting the river's water for pieces of gold, spinning them into a pliant thread, and weaving it with silk into a series of tapestries. One of their tapestries distresses the speaker. It recounts once more the myth of Orpheus and Eurydice, but now with particular emphasis on Orpheus's loss of his beloved. The speaker interprets the meaning of the tapestry in its most abstract sense as a failed attempt to recapture what has been lost (136/113). In the context of the longing and frustration of his earlier dream, the speaker wishes to recover the past, and yet he fears lest he may not be able to do so.

Deeper inside the cave the nymph shows him the source of all the earth's rivers. The classical reference is to Virgil's fourth *Georgic*, but for Sannazaro's own texts it foreshadows the conclusion of *De Partu Virginis*, where the speaker would resolve his anxieties about creating new poetry out of old. Here the speaker expresses great amazement at discovering this subterranean world, the secret origin of life-giving waters, the womb of civilization, the hidden subtext that begets and nourishes visible manifestations that all might see. It is hollow and abundant, without an apparent center, but teeming on all sides with inexhaustible fluidity (136/114). There the tutelary deities of all the world's rivers honor Rome's triumphal Tiber, crowned not like the others with willows or reeds, but with the most verdant laurel, in token perhaps of its ancient poets' labors and as a reward for that city's literary offspring (137/114). Seeking a further flash of insight, one more buried diamond of revelation, the key to his own cultural heritage, the speaker asks to be shown the source of the Sebeto stream that runs through his native land, and the nymph consents to lead him to it.

En route they pass the caves of giants, Vulcan's forge, and the fiery depths of Mount Vesuvius. The speaker marvels to see the ancient city of Pompeii buried and preserved intact beneath the volcanic ash (138/116). Here the discovery that beneath the earth's crust lie the remains of an ancient civilization, signs of its daily life, and confirmations of its active existence parallels the conviction that literary texts themselves offer evidence of their own vital subtexts. Intertextually they carry traces of their own origin, the seeds of their own development, the possibilities of repetition from the past and in the future.

When the speaker arrives at the source of the Sebeto, he finds the nymphs there mourning Sebeto's failure to produce a distinguished compatriot. Two of them rise to greet him and accompany him away from the source as though to offer him a choice of something else. To return to the countryside would entail his resuming the pastoral mode that he is now on the verge of abandoning. To proceed to the city would entail his starting on some new form that awaits him. As a literary figure, the choice could pertain to the selection of a genre, mode, and style for further artistic development. The decision lies with him (149/117).

Two other nymphs appear and augment and clarify the possibilities. The one who speaks identifies herself and her companion as two minor streams. One, barely recognizable, "washes the beloved nest of the singular Phoenix" (140/118). Petrarch's epithet for Laura, the "singular phoenix" whose kindness reasserts itself every time she seems most cruel, refers to the speaker's own beloved. The speaker has shed many tears in love for her, and now he has the option either to devote himself wholly to her or to attend to what the other nymph represents. The latter "can be found under the slopes of the mountain where she lies" (140/118). The verb in its present tense, *posa*, suggests that the beloved is now dead, and that the speaker must decide whether to continue mourning her indefinitely or to move on to other experiences. The epilogue will confirm her death.

The unexpected revelation of that outer fact again indicates the broken continuity between the last two chapters of *Arcadia* and its first ten composed much earlier. But its significance also relates to the inner question of poetic development that the speaker raises throughout this section. The present option to mourn the beloved or to move on may mean either to remain in the amatory mode or to engage in some more complex mode as a poet of greater substance. The pastoral and amatory modes should comprise only an apprenticeship and an interlude. The greater task lies ahead. Again the decision lies with the speaker.

At this point the speaker breaks the veil of illusion and he directly addresses the reader in the manner of Dante: "Lettore, io ti giuro, se quella deità che in fin qui di scriver questo mi ha prestato grazia, conceda, qualunque elli si siano, immortalità agli scritti miei, che io mi trovai in tal punto sì desideroso di morire, che di qualsivoglia maniera di morte mi sarei contentato" (140/118; "Reader, I swear to you [even as that goddess who had thus far lent me grace for writing this, may grant me an immortality to my writings, such as they may be] that I found myself at that moment content with any manner of death whatever"). He gives the impression of being unsure about whether he has just reported a dream or reality, but he leaves no doubt about the intensity of his feelings. As he emerges from the depths he enters the world of concrete contemporary actuality, where he encounters two Neapolitan shepherds. Their names, Barcinio and Summonzio, directly evoke those of Sannazaro's close friends, the poet Cariteo of Barcelona (called "Barcinio" in Chapter II) and the editor Pietro Summonte, both of whom helped Sannazaro to publish his definitive Arcadia. Even though his ears ring with the music of Arcadia, he pauses to listen to their songs in order to compare them with others. He hesitates to rank them in merit, but he indicates that Arcadian songs, with their ancient overtones and classical conventions, have the edge; still, the Neapolitan poems deserve attention (141/119). Admittedly lacking the depth of their classical precursors, they nonetheless have a sweetness and charm of their own. After all, the speaker says that his native clime has drawn unto itself shepherds from many other regions, among whom were Boccaccio (from Tuscany), Beccadelli (from Palermo), Pontano (from Umbria), and Cariteo (from Spain). Nonetheless, one senses that the speaker's pause to listen constitutes a detour, and that his real task lies ahead in the composition of some greater work.

Eclogue XII, which follows, constitutes at once a hommage to Pontano, the most ardent devotee in Naples of the classical revival, and a concluding statement about the difficulty of re-covering the original voice of the genuine poet. Massarengo judged it the finest eclogue in the entire work, and a fit conclu-sion for it: "bellissima Eglog si può dir veramente, che il nostro Poeta abbia osservato quel detto: *Omnis laus in fine canitur*" (Massarengo, p. 287; "A most beautiful eclogue where our poet has observed this dictum: All praise should be sung at the end"). In it two shepherds, one a figure of the speaker, the other a figure of the audience, discuss the poetic achievement of yet a third shepherd, who sings about the grief of having lost his beloved Phyllis. The shepherd's name, Meliseus, is one that Pontano adopted for himself in his own poetry, and indeed the verse attributed to him in this eclogue represents a free trans-lation in *terza rima sdrucciola* of Pontano's own funeral lament upon the death of his wife, the *Meliseus*, an eclogue in 248 Latin hexameters.

The date of Pontano's eclogue, 1492, indicates the earliest possible date of Sannazaro's late addition to the *Arcadia*. As such an addition, it admirably catches and expresses literary ideals elsewhere animating Sannazaro's work. It fully unites the speaker's concern for the outer world where he lives with the inner world of his own poetic development. As an Italian trans-lation of Pontano's Latin poem, moreover, Sannazaro's eclogue would seem to refer to his own intentions henceforth to com-pose in Latin, both to match Pontano's ability in it and to con-front the classical language head-on. Biographically, of course, Sannazaro was already working on his *Eclogae Piscatoriae* when he composed this portion of *Arcadia*.

This translation, then, becomes an intermediary between the author's Italian production and his Latin one. In it Barcinio is a poet who reads for Summonzio some epigrams that Meliseus has composed in honor of his dead mistress, Phyllis. Then Barcinio encourages his audience to read some verse himself. Here and now Summonzio, the audience, performs the poetry in its author's absence; the poetry so moves him that he sets out to hear the author directly.

He undertakes this attempt because, as Barcinio confesses, Meliseus did not commit all his verses to writing. Some of them remain in his memory alone, and Barcinio must exert himself to recall them: "Taci, mentre fra me ripenso, e provomi / se quell'altre sue rime or mi ricordano, / de le quali il principio sol ritrovomi" (XII.55–57; "Hush, while I take thought within myself, and make proof / whether I can now remember his other rhymes / of which I have only recovered the beginning"). The situation suggests a clear analogy with the recovery of classical literature. Not all of it exists in writing, and even the part of it that does requires skill and patience to recover and unfold. At the end Barcinio readily acknowledges that writing can extend words, increase their availability, disseminate them in time and space, but it does not necessarily guarantee their adequate reception and understanding: "Summonzio, io per li tronchi scrivo e vergole / e perché la lor fama più dilatesi, / per longinqui paesi ancor dispergole" (XII.271–73; "Summonzio, I write them and trace them on the trunks, / and in order that their fame be extended further, / I scatter them even through far-distant countries"). Writing demands decipherment. The burden is on the audience.

Writing thus constitutes only a very indecisive guarantee of permanence. Barcinio now reveals that Meliseus stands apart from the rest, remaining by an altar on the summit of a hill (XII.283–85). The very admission is enough to inflame Summonzio's desire to see him. That desire defleshes, unnerves, and dislivers him: "Non consentire, o ciel, ch'io mora indecore; / ché sol pensando udir quel suo dolce organo, / par che mi spolpe, snerve e mi disiecore" (XII.307–309; "Do not consent, Heaven, that I should die unworthily; for only thinking of hearing his sweet instrument / it seems that I am defleshed, unnerved, and dislivered"). Barcinio agrees to lead him to Meliseus.

In the eclogue's concluding lines Summonzio encounters Meliseus directly and hears his lament. Like the song of Arnault Daniel in Dante's *Purgatorio* XXVII, when the pilgrim finally reaches the terrace of poets, Meliseus's fourteen-line poem betrays a certain modesty and impenetrability. Meliseus himself calls his verse lowly, slender, and poor, yet he admits to its effectiveness as long as he may be permitted to sing. Using the Dantesque verb *rinverdesi*, from *rinverdare* (*Purgatorio* XVIII.105), he proclaims this poem's power to make the world green again. Its secret resides in the active memory: to preserve the song means to rescue it from oblivion, to hold on to it despite one's passage though Lethe:

> Basse son queste rime, esili e povere;
> ma se 'l pianger in cielo ha qualche merito,
> dovrebbe tanta fé Morte commovere.
> Io piango, o Filli, il tuo spietato interito,
> e 'l mondo del mio mal tutto rinverdesi.
> Deh pensa, prego, al bel viver preterito,
> se nel passar di Lete amor non perdesi.
>
> (XII.319–25)

Lowly are these my rhymes, narrow and poor; / but yet if weeping has some merit in Heaven / so much fidelity ought to move Death. / I weep, O Phyllis, for your cruel passing: / and with my grief the world grows green again. / Ah think, I pray thee, on the good life gone by / if in the passing of Lethe love be not lost.

Paradoxically the song can thus achieve a monumentality through the fleeting articulation of a living voice. Even though that particular voice may be doomed to extinction, the logocentric power of the word will survive, passed on from poet to poet in a never-ending transmission.

In *Arcadia*'s final pages the speaker's address and injunction to his sampogna constitute an epilogue. It is not a negligible part of the text, as Massarengo warned by remarking that he could comment as much on it as the rest of the *Arcadia*: "Ed io per me se avessi a notare sopra questa ultima Prosa, tesserei più volumi, che sopra tutto il precedente dell' Arcadia non ho fatto" (Massarengo, p. 289; "For my part, if I commented upon this last prose passage, I would produce more pages than I had done for all the rest"). The circumstances of the text's publication color its meaning. The speaker complains that he is bequeathing it prematurely, "per malvagio accidente" (151/129), like a gardener who plucks unripe fruit to prevent theft. Doubtless he is alluding to the unauthorized publication of the earlier text in 1502, and his subsequent decision to publish this one in 1504. He recognizes, however, that even this careful edition is fraught with problems. *Arcadia* is "more apt to please shepherds than cities" (151/129), and the speaker beseeches the text to content itself with its rusticity and remain in solitude. Its proper audience is not the high-spirited one of nobler poetry like epic (151/129). It must be of a more particular sort, one appreciative of its model and stylistic conventions and inclined to respect them.

The speaker's last injunction to his sampogna then concerns his advice to ignore the ill-founded judgment of unsympathetic audiences. Some audiences, "accustomed to hear more exquisite sounds," perhaps of such refined forms as contemporary Petrarchan and courtly lyric modes, may have criticized "a fastidious taste" that scorns the experiment while it denies the vitality of other equally valid modes. Different audiences, more knowledgeable about the conventions of the pastoral mode, may object that "in some places you have not kept the laws of the shepherds" (153/131). To their pedantry the sampogna should assert " 'No plowman was ever found so expert in making his furrows that he could always promise to make them all straight, without one deviation.'" The word *verse*, of course, derives from *versare*, "turn," and metaphorically implies that as the poet exhausts the meter of one line he turns from it to another as a plowman turns from one furrow to the next. Whatever fault these audiences may find, *Arcadia* will stand up on merits of its own. It was, after all, innovative in being "the first in this age to reawaken the slumbering woods, and to show the shepherds how to sing the songs they had forgotten." Moreover, with its stylistic variety and poetic richness, it contains within itself the seeds of many other poetic forms. It is the prelude to a yet more ambitious artistic enterprise, and Virgil showed the way when he advanced from his pastoral *Eclogues* to the epic *Aeneid.*

Arcadia closes, then, with this promise of greater poetry to come. The speaker's final remark is in fact even more modest. If its audiences continue to complain about its low style, *Arcadia* should simply remain hidden, "to live secretly and without pomp amid the woods" (154/132). Unsought, unasked for, not urged, its publication has been gratuitous. Should audiences not respond properly, its best defence may be concealment, a return to the oblivion of the pastoral "other " world from which it came.

In an important sense Sannazaro would never leave the pastoral far behind even when he turned to other endeavors in his major Latin poetry. In the middle of his career he wrote his *Piscatoriae,* where he used pastoral conventions to depict the lives of fishermen off the coast of Naples. In that way he domesticated to his own maritime habitat the landlocked environments of Theocritus, Virgil, Dante, and Petrarch. Late in his career Sannazaro lavished all his energy upon *De Partu Virginis.* Even this brief epic on Christ's birth assimilates a large amount of the pastoral into its narrative framework. There the Infant is an archetypal pastoral hero, literally a descendant of the shepherd King David, born in a herdsman's stable-cave in Bethlehem, and visited by guardians of the local flocks. More than his other poems, however, *Arcadia* is at once a summation of the multifaceted hybrid pastoral conventions that Sannazaro received and a harbinger of the later, even more capacious pastoral conventions that the Renaissance would receive from Sannazaro. To understand these conventions aids one's reading of *Arcadia* in its historical breadth and poetic depth. *Arcadia* is in a single text the epitome of its own past and future tradition.

3 MAJOR LATIN POETRY

Sannazaro's formal return to the pastoral in the *Eclogae Piscatoriae* (Piscatorial Eclogues) represents more an extension of his interest in the mode than a mere resumption of it. He embarked upon their composition sometime after 1490 and, though he did not publish them until 1526, he was well on the way to completing them before he published *Arcadia* in 1504.[1] Thus he appears to have been working on both pastoral texts simultaneously. The result was a deepening of his pastoral sensibility. The *Piscatoriae*, along with the epic *De Partu Virginis* with which it was first printed, reveal Sannazaro's full mastery of pastoral's experimental, archaeological, and philological uses. *Arcadia* had represented a creative reworking of ancient pastoral into modern vernacular, but the *Piscatoriae* revived the Latin language at the root of ancient pastoral, while *De Partu Virginis* used that language to transpose pastoral into epic.

PISCATORIAE: THE PASTORAL TRADITION RENEWED

During the composition of his major Latin poems, Sannazaro enjoyed an exposure to several classical texts of which he seems to have been unaware when he conceived *Arcadia*. One text was Theocritus's *Idylls*, printed by Aldus Manutius in 1495, though circulated in Latin translations during the 1480s. While it is difficult to find direct traces of Theocritus in either *Arcadia* or the *Piscatoriae*, *Idyll* XXI may have had at least an indirect bearing on the latter. Its authenticity as one of Theocritus's own poems is questionable, but it is nonetheless piscatorial in its setting. In it two fishermen awake before dawn and recount their dreams. One reports nightmares and anxieties relating to sea voyages; the other narrates his dream of catching a splendid golden fish. At the end they conclude that dreams are mere fictions. Sannazaro would have enjoyed the poem's inventiveness as well as its treatment of the motif of dream and fiction.

Sannazaro would have approached quite differently another important pastoral text published in 1498. It consisted of ten Latin eclogues by Battista Spagnuolo (1447–1516), familiarly named "Mantuan" after his birthplace. Mantuan wrote eight of them as a student in Padua before he entered a Carmelite monastery in 1463. Thirty-five years later he added two more satiric eclogues about the state of affairs in his religious order. Published widely as *Adulescentia seu Bucolica*, they soon outdid all other Latin pastorals in popularity.[2] Accompanied by the detailed commentary of Badius Ascensius, they eventually found their way into school curricula despite Julius Caesar Scaliger's judgment that they were "non sine ingenio, sed sine arte" (vi.4)

Mantuan's pervasive moralistic tone, religious in flavor and filled with acute sociological observations on the life of the poet and the temper of the times, resembles nothing in Sannazaro. Whereas Sannazaro embraced his classical models wholeheartedly, infusing them with a modern Petrarchan outlook, Mantuan overtly Christianized those models. His outlook is austerely clerical and antifeminist. Two eclogues entitled "De amoris insania" (II; The Madness of Love) and "De insani amoris exitu infoelici" (III; The Senseless Issue of Unhappy Love) record the debilitating effects of love-madness on the young shepherd Amintas, who dies insane after being rejected by Diana. Two others, "De honesto amore" (I; Sincere Love) and "De natura mulierum" (IV; Women's Nature), denigrate women as the cause of men's ruin. And two, "De conversione iuventum ad religionem" (VII; The Conversion of Young Men to Religion) and "De rusticorum religione" (VIII; The Religion of Country Folk), record the speaker's conversion and retreat to Mount Carmel. It is undeniable, however, that Mantuan's eclogues shaped the attitudes of Sannazaro's own audience towards the pastoral, and that for better or worse they enjoyed a popularity that Sannazaro's never sustained.

Closer to the *Piscatoriae* in style and tone were the pastorals of Pontano. His *Meliseus* was, of course, a model for *Arcadia's* twelfth eclogue, and Sannazaro's rendering of it in Italian signalled his own transition from the vernacular to Latin. Pontano composed that poem as a lament for the death of his wife in 1491. The shepherds Ciceriscus and Faburnus discuss the sadness of their friend Meliseus, who inscribes on trees poems about his grief for the dead Ariadna. They tell how the nymph Patulcis mourns her, too, in her own poem-within-the-poem (20–144), and how Meliseus echoes her with his own dirge (151–80).³ Ciceriscus and Faburnus note that all nature sympathizes with the widowed husband. This sympathy provokes a gentle, hopeful conclusion. Remembering the myth of Orpheus, who consoled himself with song, they prophesy that Meliseus, too, will regain his composure (242–43). The poem's profusion of voices, its sense of distance from Patulcis and Meliseus as the original speakers, and its evocation of classical sources as traces from the past that yet impinge on the present all would suggest to Sannazaro the central direction for his own Latin pastorals.

Pontano composed other eclogues, notably one entitled *Lepidina* in seven parts celebrating connubial happiness.⁴ The representations of family life attain a degree of realism often absent from the conventional, idealized pastoral. Still, a sense of poetic self-consciousness and the motif of the poet's artistic development pervades the composition. In the last part a nymph speaks of Virgil, who brought honor to Naples, and she prophesies the birth of other poets—Pontano and Sannazaro—who will increase its honor. Already the sheer variety of modes in the *Lepidina*—lullabies, epithalamia, dirges, didactic discourses —extends Naples's poetic traditions, while its virtuosity of style proclaims an assured sense of craft.

Other Latin pastorals, mostly on the model of Petrarch's *Bu-*

colicum Carmen (printed in 1473, but composed between 1346 and 1352), proliferated in the late fifteenth century and early sixteenth century. Among them were Boiardo's ten eclogues (1476), Tito Vespasiano Strozzi's occasional eclogues (before 1505), Castiglione's *Alcon* (1506), Vida's *Quercus* (1521), and Navagero's short pastorals in the *Lusus* (1530), and their themes included amatory, panegyric, eulogistic, satiric, moralizing, and devotional topics. More than any of his contemporaries, however, Sannazaro modelled his eclogues on Virgil's. From the *Eclogues* he took dramatic situations, emotional effects, hexameter rhythms, even diction, since specific words and turns of phrases in Sannazaro's poems echo their great predecessor. On every level the quality and consistency of the influence is wholly palpable.

In *Piscatoria* I, for example, the fisherman Lycidas laments the death of his beloved Phyllis. The Virgilian model is Mopsus's lament for Daphnis in *Eclogue* V. The difference between the poems, however, is appreciable. Whereas Mopsus reaches a positive conclusion in the apotheosis of Daphnis, Lycidas finishes his dirge with little release from his sorrow. The opposite relationship prevails between Sannazaro's *Piscatoria* II and its analogue, Virgil's *Eclogue* II. In Sannazaro, Lycon complains of Galatea's unresponsiveness towards him, and he soon comes to acquire a greater understanding of his own emotional life. In Virgil, on the other hand, Corydon attempts in song to gain relief from love's pain, but in the long run he fails to resolve his problems.

Affinities among the remaining poems are straightforward. *Piscatoria* III and *Eclogue* VII represent singing matches on the theme of distance and separation. *Piscatoria* IV and *Eclogue* VI represent poetic performances by mythic personages; Sannazaro uses Proteus while Virgil uses Silenus, and both constitute figures for the poet and his craft. Finally *Piscatoria* V and *Eclogue* VIII represent contests between singers who complain of their beloveds' infidelities.

Above all in the *Piscatoriae* Sannazaro strikes a balance be-

tween the inner and outer worlds similar to the balance that
Virgil achieved in the other world of his pastorals. Earlier Renaissance eclogues tend to emphasize one at the other's expense, as Petrarch had done in his satiric eclogues. In them the
pastoral "other" world served only as a thinly disguised allegorical vehicle for commenting on action in the real world. With
Sannazaro this "other" world nearly collapses into a realistic
rendering of the Neapolitan landscape. It nonetheless gains resonance as an inner world from its allusions and its references to
Virgil and other classical poets. These echoes establish it as a
wholly literary landscape.

In one important respect, however, Sannazaro's references to
Virgil differ from those in earlier Renaissance eclogues modelled
on Virgil. The most important lesson that Virgil's *Eclogues* had
taught posterity was how to integrate personal, political, and
poetic meanings into a single metaphorical, allegorical, and
often ironic discourse. The text of Virgil's *Eclogues* may appear
to say one thing, but its author and audience both share an
understanding of something else. Medieval audiences largely
understood Virgil's poetry as an allegory figuring the Christian
life. His most celebrated pastoral, *Eclogue* IV, proclaims the
birth of a child who would transform the world; his *Eclogue* V
laments the death of a shepherd who would be apotheosized in
the heavens. Medieval readers felt that both poems referred to
Christ: the former to His nativity, the latter to His death, resur-
rection, and ascension. A vast body of commentary supported
these interpretations. The commentators of Sannazaro's age are
different. They reveal on the one hand a growing secularization
of interpretation and on the other a growing distrust about the
possibility of absolute confidence in any one interpretation.[5]
Sannazaro's own use of the Virgilian pastoral in his *Piscatoriae*,
and especially his later use of Virgil's *Eclogue* IV in *De Partu
Virginis*, would exemplify the secularizing process.

In 1488 Cristoforo Landino published his edition of Virgil's
works with full commentary. There he explicitly sought to
extract Virgil's philosophical significance and to underline its

relevance for his own age: "Hoc auctore ac duce maiestatis pub-
licae dignitas, quae pene iam extincta esset, non solum in pris-
tinum gradum revocata est, sed amplior multoque illustrior
reddita" ("In this author and guide, the dignity of public greatness which is now almost extinguished, is not only called back to
its early rank, but is also restored more fully and more clearly").[6]
Mindful of how speculative his endeavor might become, Landino also referred readers to the meticulous philological work of
his former student, Angelo Poliziano, "virum multa ac varia
doctrina eruditum, poetam vero egregium egregiumque ora-
torem, ac denique totius antiquitatis diligentem perscruta-
torem" (p. 254; "a man learned through a good deal of varied
instruction, an excellent poet and an excellent orator, and furthermore a diligent researcher of all antiquity"). By 1529 printed
editions of Virgil juxtaposed different interpretive commentaries by Servius (fourth century), Antonius Mancinellus (1490),
Badius Ascensius (1500), and Pierius Valerianus (1523). The
juxtaposition itself would proclaim the manifold variousness of
all interpretation. These commentaries imply the role of the
reader in the later Renaissance not just by what they say about
the texts in question, but more powerfully by how they show
the reader to read the text. In their divergences and outright
discrepancies they teach the reader to suspend several different
interpretive judgments on several different levels of understanding. They exemplify a way of accommodating alternative meanings to the text, and that way departs radically from the medieval fourfold strategy of interpretation. It eschews systematic
moral, allegorical, anagogical, and tropological levels of meaning for freer, more flexible, and often ironic ones.

    The commentaries on Virgil's *Eclogue* IV show how the in-
creasingly secularized understanding of Virgil's poetry could
modify the appropriation of it by a modern poet like Sannazaro.
Juan Luis Vives offered what was probably the last unquestiona-
bly divinatory reading of Virgil's *Eclogue*. His commentary,
written in 1537, was published posthumously in 1544. In it the
child whose birth Virgil depicts as ushering in a new age is Jesus

Christ, and divine inspiration has led Virgil to make this prophecy: "Taceant impii; nam vel simplici verborum sensu, absque
ullis omnino allegoriis, de nullo prorsus alio potest intelligi
quod hic dicitur, quam de Christo" ("Let skeptics be silent, for
even in the simple sense of the words, without any allegories at
all, what is said here can be understood to concern absolutely
nothing else than Christ").[7]

Long before Vives, however, other commentators voiced
skepticism. In the fourth century Servius had suggested in his
abstractly allegorical interpretation that the *virgo* announcing
the child is Justice, "Virgo Iustitia," and that the child is Good
Fortune, *felicitas*, and, by extension, a figure for the emperor
Augustus: "Nam felicitas temporum ad imperatoris pertinet
laudem" (p. LVII: "for the good fortune of the times relates to
the praise of the emperor). Servius showed the way to a new
interpretation in the fifteenth century. In 1488 Cristoforo Landino commented that the poem refers explicitly to Augustus,
but that it also implicitly prophesies the coming of Christ: "Sed
ut ostendit Augustum multa etiam de Christo est vaticinata"
("But while it represents Augustus, much is also prophesied
about Christ").[8]

In 1490 Antonius Mancinellus broke decisively with the medieval identification of the *virgo* as Mary and the child as Christ
by elaborating upon Servius's explanation. For Mancinellus,
the *virgo* is the mythological Astrea, and her child personifies
all justice and world order: "quoniam virgo (teste Hesiodo)
Iovis, & Themidis filia (teste Arato) Astrei, & Aurorae, quae
in aureo saeculo fuerat, eorumque princeps propter diligentiam,
& aequitatem, iustitia appellata" ("since *virgo*, according to
Hesiod, means daughter of Jove and Themis, according to Ara-
tus, of Astreus and Auora, who lived in the Golden Age, and
their chief one on account of attentiveness and equity, called
Justice").[9] Mancinellus adds that Christian allegory is patently
impossible because Virgil died before Christ's birth.

In 1500 Badius Ascensius tempered skepticism with ingenuity. If divine inspiration had revealed Christ's coming to Vir-

gil, the pagan poet nonetheless misinterpreted the revelation. It came to him through the prophecy of the Sibyl, but Virgil's Roman ears heard only a secular reference. Here Badius Ascensius suggests a range of possibilities that throws all interpretive sureness into doubt: Virgil could have understood the Sibyl to refer to Pollio's son, or even Pollio himself, or possibly Augustus, or even Augustus's nephew Marcellus. We have, Ascensius maintains, simply no way of knowing: "Magna est inter doctos, sanctosque viros controversia de carminis huic argumento" ("There is great controversy among learned holy men concerning the argument of this poem").[10] By 1523, in the commentary of Pierius Valerianus, the issue of a Christian interpretation seems to have become completely irrelevant. Valerianus is silent about the possibility of a Christian allegory.[11] By not even mentioning it, he assumes its unliklihood. He focuses instead on the text's purely grammatical, philological, syntactic cruxes, following the secular lead of the recently rediscovered Berne scholiasts of antiquity, whose philological explorations aimed at razor-sharp exactitude.

Before the late fifteenth century, then, the standard interpretation of Virgil's *Eclogue* IV accepted its Christian allegory without much question. The procedure was to ignore the difference in time between Virgil's age and the present, and to project one's own contemporary attitudes on to the poetry. But with Landino, Mancinellus, and Ascensius there is doubt and skepticism, and finally a rejection of this procedure. With Valerianus there is no mention of Christian allegory, as though the very possibility were absurd. Through philological study and the imaginative re-creation of antiquity, then, these commentators sought to uncover the original meanings of texts. Their model for encouragement was one of the earliest humanists, Petrarch himself.

Petrarch too had composed pastoral poetry on a qualified Virgilian model. He had conceived his *Bucolicum Carmen* as one long pastoral poem divided into twelve eclogues, but he resolutely refused to turn it into a vehicle for continuous religious allegory. If it reflects Christian concerns, it does so not as an allegory of the life of Christ in man (as tropological or anagogical readings might fashion it); rather it does so because it perceives its Christian concern as a fundamentally timeless one shared by the Roman poet in the guise of Roman virtues. Petrarch could therefore appropriate Virgil's content as well as his form. From Petrarch's personal copy of Virgil's *Opera* with marginal notations in Petrarch's own handwriting, one can gauge in fact Petrarch's interpretations of Virgil. In that edition Virgil's text appears with the commentary of Servius. Sometimes Petrarch's notations refer to the text; sometimes they refer to the commentary. In both cases they emphasize the secular at the expense of the Christological interpretation. For Servius's commentary on Virgil's *Eclogue* IV, Petrarch underlines the interpretation of the *Virgo* as *Iustitia*, not as Christ's mother, and he recapitulates "pro illos, justitia" ("for these things, justice"). [12] For the dead Daphnis in Virgil's *Eclogue* V, often interpreted as a figure for the crucified Jesus Christ, Petrarch's handwritten notation "J Cesar" (sic, p.9ʳ) reinforces Servius's secular interpretation of the figure as Caesar.

These notations and others show how Petrarch sought to bracket the medieval interpretation of these eclogues which saw Jesus Christ as an allegorical reference for each figure. Petrarch's approach to Virgil's form is no less radical. From Virgil and early Virgilian imitators like Calpurnius and Nemesianus, Petrarch adopted the hexameter line with an occasional bucolic diaeresis, or break between units of meaning, after a trisyllabic fourth foot. Like Virgil he cast his eclogues variously in the forms of dialogue and monologue. And like Virgil he developed topics of personal, political, and poetic concern. Of Petrarch's twelve pastoral poems, five focus on personal issues such as the rejection of monastic life and the threat of the Black Death (I, III, VIII, IX, XI); five others on political issues concerning the papacy, Italy, and Avignon (II, V, VI, VII, XII); and the remaining two on the author's own poetic vocation (IV, X).

Sannazaro's *Piscatoriae* complete the Petrarchan project. They fully resist allegorical, anagogical, tropological readings and at every turn they urge a secular rather than Christocentric form of interpretation. They adopt the hexameter line of Virgil's *Eclogues*, and much more consistently than Petrarch's pastorals they incorporate the bucolic diaeresis. They carefully alternate dialogue and monologue, and they closely interweave the Virgilian motifs of personal, political, and poetic concern. The landscape, or rather seascape, however, is Sannazaro's own. This striking innovation in the pastoral mode demonstrates how fully Sannazaro had appropriated its uses for his own purposes.

PISCATORIAE: THE PASTORAL SEASCAPE

The collection's early eclogues dramatically integrate the pastoral seascape into the poetic action. *Piscatoria* I is a funeral lament by the fisherman Lycidas on the death of his beloved Phyllis. Framing it at the beginning (1–43) and end (106–30) is a dialogue between Lycidas and his friend Mycon. There Lycidas takes his first tentative steps towards confronting Phyllis's death more honestly than he had done before. He advances from a general perception of sorrow experienced metonymically in nature (3–5) to a specific articulation of her death as its cause (8–9). More dramatically, he advances from an abstract recollection of her funeral (16–17) to a particular recollection of the solemn ritual associated with it (18–20), and, from attributing sorrow to the community at large (10–11), to attributing it to himself as the most ardent mourner (21–23). The dialogue moves gracefully from the speaker's recognition of the outer world to his confirmation of the power of his inner world.

Lycidas answers Mycon's challenge to sing with enthusiasm: "Immo haec quae cineri nuper properata parabam" (33; "Yes indeed I shall begin these hurried verses"), and further asks his friend to cover her grave with cypress boughs and myrtle while he sings his song: "Sparge manu et viridi tumulum super intege myrto" (37; "Scatter with your hand and cover the grave mound over with green myrtle").[13] The forms of the verbs are important. Lycidas addresses Mycon in the imperative singular, but Mycon replies in the first person plural: "Afferimus" (41; "We are bringing"). In the next line this plural comes to include more than Lycidas and Mycon when the latter points to yet another fisherman, the silent Milcon; "Incipe, dum ad solem Bajanus retia Milcon / Explicat et madidos componit in orbe rudentes" (42–43; "Begin while the Baian Milcon lays out his nets to the sun and coils in a circle his dripping lines"). Up to now the reader has assumed the presence of only two characters within the poem's landscape. The sudden multiplication of personae, though thoroughly conventional in classical Latin eclogues, often indicating the presence of silent auditors, registers a curious effect. In this poem about death and absence, the new character's unanticipated appearance evokes a wider community of living beings within earshot of the grieving speaker, and it implies a still larger community outside of it. Likewise it expands the range of the speaker's audience inside the poem. The silent presence of Milcon acts as a foil to the lamented absence of Phyllis, as a buffer to the apparent solitude of Lycidas and Mycon, and as a complement to the role of Mycon as eager audience.

This expanded audience performs an important function as the theme of the poetic inner world begins to unfold. In the final lines, after Lycidas has completed his lament, Mycon urges his friends to repeat the song. Lycidas refuses, partly on the grounds that he cannot bear the grief of repetition (115). More substantial grounds entail Lycidas's commitment to his own poetic career. He vows one day to inscribe his poetry at the seashore as palpable and tangible traces in the sand or on cliffs, so that passing sailors may see the poems: "Quin et veliferis olim haec spectanda carinis" (121; "But these too I shall someday inscribe to be seen by the passing ships"). In this form the poems will become entities existing in their own right apart from their creator and in the public domain, perceived by various audiences on various horizons, unfolding at different times in human history. His articulation of this vision seals his commitment. Its reward comes in his signature. His name and proof of authorship, carved in rust on stone, will outlast the ravages of time and earn him true poetic glory: "Inscribam grandesque notas ferrugine ducam / Praeteriens quas nauta mari percurrat ab alto / Et dicat: 'Lycidas, Lycidas haec carmina fecit" (123–25; "I shall trace in rust great letters which the passing sailor may scan from the open sea and say: 'Lycidas, Lycidas made these songs'").

The precedent for this striking topos is in Virgil's *Eclogue* V. There the elder poet Menalcas asks the younger Mopsus to sing a song. The topic is unimportant, but Mopsus embarks upon a funeral lament for Daphnis. It so impresses Menalcas that he acknowledges Mopsus's attainment of maturity, mastery, and skill. Sannazaro's poem, like Virgil's, dramatizes a young poet's coming of age. The lament for the dead beloved provides a vehicle for the young poet's performance, but emphasis falls on the poet rather than on the deceased. Milton would attempt a similar feat in his own pastoral elegy entitled "Lycidas," perhaps not without reference to Sannazaro's poem.

The clearest imitation of Virgil's *Eclogue* V in *Piscatoria* I occurs in the poem's second half. There Sannazaro's speaker vows to honor his deceased beloved with carefully prepared rites:

> *Nos tibi, nos liquidis septem pro fluctibus aras*
> *Ponemus septemque tibi de more quotannis*
> *Monstra maris magni vitulos mactabimus hirtos,*
> *Et tibi septenis pendebunt ostrea sertis,*
> *Ostrea muricibus variata albisque lapillis.*
>
> (79–83)

Seven altars for you will we raise beside the wet sea-waves, and seven rough sea calves, deep-water monsters, will we sacrifice to you in yearly ritual, and oysters will hang for you in sevenfold wreaths, oysters varied with murex and shining pearls.

In Virgil's eclogue Menalcas proposes a land-bound memorial to honor Daphnis:

> *Sis bonus o felixque tuis! en quattuor aras:*
> *ecce duas tibi, Daphni, duas altaria Phoebo.*
> *pocula bina novo spumantia lacte quotannis*
> *craterasque duo statuam tibi pinguis olivi.*
>
> (65–68)

> Be kind and gracious to thine own! Lo here are four altars—two, see, for thee, Daphnis; two for Phoebus! Two cups foaming with fresh milk, will I year by year set up for thee, and two bowls of rich olive oil.

Sannazaro's appropriation notably secularizes Virgil's altars. The Virgilian interpreters had long emphasized Daphnis's deification. In 1490, for example, Mancinellus, basing his commentary on Servius's gloss, suggested the likeness between Daphnis and Apollo. Mancinellus pointed out that just as Apollo merits two altars because of his dual role as supernal sun god and as infernal nighttime deity, so Daphnis merits two altars: "Quanquam coelum ascenderit, eius tum simulacrum apud inferos esse dicit. Propterea ergo duas Daphnidi aras posuit, duas etiam Phoebo, propter superum et inferum hemisperium" (Mancinellus, p. LXIX; "Although Daphnis has risen to heaven, Virgil says his image remains also in the lower world. Therefore he appoints two altars to Daphnis and also to Apollo on account of his supernal and infernal residences"). Sannazaro does not deify the object of Lycidas's lament. Instead he renders her more concrete as an emblem of the best in humankind. To her Lycidas will erect seven altars, signifying her position as the sum and substance of God's six-day creation and seventh-day rest.

Likewise Sannazaro secularizes the role of the poet. At the end of *Piscatoria* I Lycidas engraves a final song on Phyllis's tomb for fishermen to read as they prepare their lines: "Interea tumulo supremum hoc accipe carmen, / Carmen quod, tenui dum nectit arundine linum, / Piscator legat et scopulo suspiret ab alto" (101–103; "Meanwhile receive for your tomb this final

song, that, while he ties the line to the slender rod, the fisherman may read, and utter a sigh from the lofty cliff"). In Virgil
the corresponding verses inspire Menalcas's address to Mopsus
as a "divine poet": "Tale tum carmen nobis, divine poeta, /
quale sopor fessis in gramine" (45–46; "Your lay, heavenly
bard, is to me even as sleep on the grass is to the weary"). For
Badius Ascensius, Virgil's sixteenth-century commentator, the
address signifies the poet's likeness to divinity as a creator in his
own right: "aut quia divini officij imitatricem, nam sicut deus
solus ex nihilo creat, ita poetae saepe quasi de nihilo fingunt"
(Badius, p. LXVIII; "And the poet is said to be an imitator of
divine work, for just as God alone creates from nothing, so
poets often fabricate as though from nothing"). Sannazaro's
hexameters, however, base the composition in the concrete reality of everyday human action. The poet engraves his words on
Phyllis's seaside tomb while the fisherman ties his lines to a fishing pole. The response that the poet demands is nonetheless
analogous to the fisherman's act of tying his lines. It is the act of
reading, a binding (*legere*) of lines of verse into varied metrical
units, an act that epitomizes the human capacity to construe,
understand, and interpret.

The topic of *Piscatoria* II is the most artificial and conventional of all pastoral topics, the amorous lament. In the Renaissance, however, Julius Caesar Scaliger judged this eclogue as
Sannazaro's best: "Ecloga vero Galitea optima est."[14] In it
Lycon complains of Galatea's unresponsiveness towards him.
He alludes to a misunderstanding between them occasioned by
a false rumor of his infidelity to her. To defend himself he balances the rumor, which is one kind of fiction, against another
kind of fiction, which is myth, and he fashions his lament as yet
a third kind of fiction, the pastoral poem. Fiction therefore
plays against fiction on a number of levels, and all of them emphasize the inner world of the poem as an overarching fiction.
Its center shifts with the imposition of each new level, and the
shifting imparts an elusive beauty to it.

The beauty is hard won. As one result of shifting the ground so often, the poem risks losing its center altogether. The speaker seems conscious of this danger as he iterates the emptiness of the landscape dominating Lycon's lament. Lycon sits wearied in a vacant cave composing his poem throughout the dark night (1). He complains that his own words are as useless as hollow waves hurled against the cliffs (9–10). His audience, Galatea, has denied her hand to him (47–48). The cause of her displeasure is the rumor about his relationship with Lyda (59–60). To answer the accusation, Lycon can only resort to vain pleading (69). At the poem's end the speaker underscores the emptiness of his lament. Lycon's discourse is insubstantial; he can only fling his words hopelessly at the deaf wind. And yet the lament carries a strange beauty, a warm glow. The poem ends not with a sense of uselessness but with an image of soft morning light suffusing the sea and sky with rosy brightness (83–86). Dawn brings new hope, a promise of continuance, an impulse to take up the burden and try again. For all its negative feeling, the poem has achieved something positive.

Midway through the poem Lycon offers Galatea a fleece that had been a present to him from the shepherd Meliseus (44–45). The reference has biographical significance for Sannazaro because "Meliseus," as we have seen in *Arcadia*, was the name that Pontano had adopted for the fictive persona of his own poetry. This detail reinforces the significance of the speaker's own role as poet. To underscore the wit of his own invention, the controlling poet even weaves the letters of his own name into the verse as a clever anagram: "Quandoquidem nostra cecinisti primus in acta" (45; "since you have been the first in singing on our shores") "Actius Syncerus, Jacopo Sannazaro."

The fictional recounting of the past leads to a more complex recounting of fictional materials in the poem's second half. Fearing that Galatea despises him as the sailor of a mere skiff, he evokes the myth of Glaucus (53–55). Countering that innocent fiction is a vicious one, the ill-founded rumor that a

certain Lyda won his love with bribes (56–58). He exhorts
Galatea to disbelieve the *fabula*. Her disdain, itself a kind of
fiction dictated by amorous convention and imposed perhaps
artificially upon her true feelings, prompts him to seek out
solutions.

Exile is one. By journeying far and wide he may test travellers' reports of the North's eternal winter and the South's
nearness to the sun. But the recognition that he carries his fate
within himself causes him to renounce this solution (69–70).
His recognition itself is based on a pastoral fiction insofar as the
lines closely echo Gallus's hopeless complaint in Virgil's *Eclogue*
X.64–69. They also echo the self-address from Virgil's *Eclogue*
II.58, "Ah demens, quem fugis?" ("Ah, madman, whom do you
flee?"). The only fiction that Lycon cannot construe as such is
the immediacy of his own torment. It leads him to seek a de-
spairing release: "Jam saxo meme ex illo demittere in undas /
Praecipitem jubet ipse furor" (73–74; "Now does this very madness command me to hurl myself headlong from that rock into
the waves"). In the rhetorical artificiality of his address to the
nymphs that follows, however, one senses Lycon's growing real-
ization of its inadequacy (74–76). The dilemma is a purely literary one. The speaker exults in the conventions of his role. He
delights in constructing the fiction of a future when sea captains
will turn their ships away from the cliff of his doom: "'Vitemus
scopulos infames morte Lyconis'" (82; "'Let us avoid the cliffs
made infamous by the death of Lycon'"). Ironically this self-
indulgence in fiction-making redeems the speaker. It allows
him to vent his grief and regain equilibrium. His words are mere
artifice, but the artifice helps him to acquire a perspective on
his personal grief.

By comparison Sannazaro's central model for this poem, Virgil's *Eclogue* II, offers a less optimistic conclusion. There Corydon laments that he has rejected all women for the love of a
single boy, Alexis, who now ignores him. Corydon invites
Alexis to accompany him on the pastoral pipes that Pan has
bequeathed them and that the shepherd Damaetas has taught

them to use. He hopes that art will cement their relationship, but by the poem's end, when sunset drives the flocks home, he has come to perceive the futility of his imagination. He must now turn to other pursuits: "Invenies alium, si te hic fastidit, Alexim" (73; "You will find another Alexis, if this one scorns you"). In Sannazaro's poem, on the other hand, the final lines depicting the passage of night and the return of morning met-onymically reflect the speaker's recovery. Even though his vows are empty, *irrita* (84), and he hurls them in vain, *nequiquam* (83), against the deaf winds, *surdas* (83), he still treasures them, *fovebat* (84). Of course, he recovers only to renew his grief with the return of night. But the important point is that a resolution does occur, and that the play of fictions within the poetic discourse has brought it about. For all the speaker's amo-rous irresolution, he has not lost faith in his art.

The poem's Virgilian focus occurs at its climax, when the speaker despairs of escaping Love's power over him. Addressing himself, the speaker questions whether foreign travels and in-tense labors can help him forget his love:

> Quid loquor infelix? an non per saxa, per ignes,
> Quo me cumque pedes ducent, mens aegra sequetur?
> Vitantur venti, pluviae vitantur et aestus,
> Non vitatur amor; mecum tumuletur oportet.
>
> (69–72)

Unhappy man, what am I saying? Will not my sick mind follow me through rocks, through fires, wherever my feet shall lead me? Winds are avoidable, rains and heats are avoidable, love is not be be avoided; it needs must be bur-ied with me.

The lines evoke a similar climax in Virgil's *Eclogue* X with its famous conclusion that love conquers all:

> non illum nostri possunt mutare labores,
> nec si frigoribus mediis Hebrumque bibamus
> Sithoniasque nives hiemis subeamus aquosae,
> nec si, cum moriens alta liber aret in ulmo,

Aethiopum versemus ovis sub sidere Cancri.
omnia vincit Amor: et nos cedamus Amori.

(64–69)

> No toils of ours can change that god, not though in the
> heart of winter we drink the Hebrus and brave the Thra-
> cian snows and wintry sleet, not though, when the bark
> dies and withers on the lofty elm, we drive to and fro the
> Aethiopians' sheep beneath the star of Cancer! Love con-
> quers all; let us, too, yield to Love!

It may not be fanciful to see in Virgil's hexameters a literary
self-referentiality that Sannazaro adapts in his own manner.
Virgil's Gallus laments his inability to alter Love's will even
after the change of seasons when bark, *liber* (67) dies on the
trees and shepherds turn, *versemus* (68) their sheep in new directions. Both *liber* and *versare* suggest literary production by
evoking the paronomastic book (*liber*) and act of turning metrical verses (*versare*). Likewise Sannazaro's hexameters refer par-
onomastically to their own literary production, first in the
speaker's explicit questioning of his own verbal performance
("quid loquor"), next in his use of literary topoi that link classical Latin conventions to Petrarchan vernacular ones ("per
saxas, per ignes"), and finally in his curious evocation of feet
(*pedes*, 70) that lead him onwards, suggesting the propulsion of
metrical feet that draw the poem towards its conclusion. If in
this context Virgil's final line, "omnia vincit Amor: et nos
cedamus Amori," implies the complicity of poetic activity in
the experience of love, Sannazaro's reworking of it, "Non vi-
tatur amor; mecum tumuletur oportet," seals that complicity.

Piscatoria III extends the topic of literary self-referentiality by
dramatizing the effects of absence and separation on three different levels. It moves from the outer world of the speaker's political exile to the inner world of his composing poetry. An initial comparison with its Virgilian model, *Eclogue* VII, shows
how much Sannazaro emphasizes this movement. Virgil's Meliboeus, searching for a lost goat, encounters Corydon and Thyr-

sis, whose singing contest he judges. Sannazaro's frame is more elaborate. In it Celadon asks Mopsus to recount what happened when storms forced him and his fishing party to a standstill. Mopsus responds with an account of how they lamented their king's exile, and of how he judged a singing contest between Chromis and Iolas. Celadon's request, Chromis's lament, and the singing contest with Iolas all reflect various forms of discontent. Celadon's is personal, yet friendly; his companions have been detained at a remote harbor for twelve days. Chromis's is initially social and political: his countrymen have sadly followed their king into exile. The singing contest is private and amatory: the singers complain of their beloved's coldness.

Still other forms of discontent mark the poem's witty development. Mopsus is addressing an audience (Celadon) already unsatisfied by an earlier account (Aegon's) of a speech (Chromis's) that has itself retreated into past history. Mopsus moreover implies that Chromis's account itself is flawed. The king's physical separation has left him with only a secondhand report of the journey. Relying upon his memory of this report, "Nam bene si memini, Rhodanum referebat Amilcon" (19; "For if I remember rightly, Amilcon spoke of the Rhone"), Chromis has reconstructed the king's itinerary in his own words. Celadon is thus receiving Mopsus's account of Amilcon's account at several removes.

Emotionally, however, these words have the power to bridge the distance between the separated parties. The lover's ensuing rhetorical performance, then, becomes a test of language's power to compensate for absence. The lover can remove the barrier between himself and the beloved if his imprecations move her. For that very reason, however, the lover's imprecations impose on him as a speaker a more arduous task than other forms of discourse might impose on their speakers. Because this task promises at least some chance for success, whereas the others do not, there is more to hope for, more to aim for, and ultimately more to lose. The stakes are higher.

The singing contest proceeds in alternating quatrains, with Iolas duplicating each theme that Chromis announces. In it Chromis's attachment to his own beloved loses its linguistic moorings. Her name shifts from Chloris to Hyale, and he will repeat the shift on line 72. Nor is the confusion merely verbal. Chromis has in mind not the presence of a real beloved, but rather the idea of a conventional beloved, an idea attached more to words than to things, embodied in fictive language and the inner world of poetry. The reappearance of Chloris's name in the fifth quatrain brings Chromis's discourse full circle, as though the speaker had moved from a real woman to artful convention by citing Hyale and Phoebe, and finally back again (80–81). For Iolas, meanwhile, Nisa's continued proximity affords reason enough to stay on the island (92). Her presence assures a secure haven against the storms of adversity.

Nor are these storms idle imaginings. In this sea-enclosed landscape storms constitute a very real force in the fishermen's lives. The singing contest has led the speaker to assert that landscape's importance. There the beloved's presence or absence makes all the difference between the joy and pain that the speaker feels. In the eclogue's final lines Mopsus reestablishes Celadon's presence by addressing him as his immediate audience (94). Summarizing his story of the singing contest, Mopsus inserts a participial phrase that confers a final perspective on the action: "Inter se vario memini contendere cantu / Horrida ventosi ridentes murmura ponti" (94–96; "I have called to mind how these lads contended between themselves in various song, laughing at the savage rumblings of the windy sea"). *Ridentes* is the key word because it establishes a human and civilized reaction to the pressures of nature. The presence of the sea and its savage rumblings is inevitable. One seeks the presence of another—a lover, a friend, a king—to laugh and face the storm with confidence.

PISCATORIAE: THE PASTORAL ACHIEVEMENT

During the 1490s and early 1500s when Sannazaro was writing his *Piscatoriae*, political and personal storms raged everywhere around him. In 1502 he finally accompanied his king into exile. The poetic achievement of the *Piscatoriae* is to represent that storm in the texture of its pastoral verse. The collection of eclogues focuses insistently on the topics of absence, love, and memory. *Piscatoria* IV relates the topic of absence to the themes of love and memory in a new way. With its perfect balance of pastoral's inner and outer worlds, it is Sannazaro's most sophisticated piscatorial eclogue. It records both the speaker's desire to return from exile and his recognition of the impossibility of doing so. He articulates his desire in an assemblage of myths about the homeland that underscore his frustration. It is as impossible to return to his beloved Naples as it is to return to times past. The speaker feels distant not just from the political kingdom in the outer world but also from its mythic context in the inner poetic world. He desires their presence, moreover, not because they afford a peaceable haven, but because they challenge his productivity. They stimulate the speaker's forward striving, his impulses toward transcendence in the arena of public, political, and poetic activity.

The poem acquires extra resonance from comparison with its Virgilian model, *Eclogue* VI. There the shepherd boys, Chromis and Mnasylus, bind Silenus with flowery garlands while the nymph Aegle urges him to sing songs. Silenus responds with verses on creation and early mythology. His quest for origins and wish to return to the beginning of things animate the poem. For Virgil, Silenus functions as a figure of the poet. He is drunken but inspired; sensual, yet endowed with omniscience and incomparable memory; free-wheeling and variable, yet conscious of his craft. He must be bound with garlands before he can sing, just as his poetry must be constrained by formal technique before it can impress his audience with its worth. Virgil's eclogue moreover addresses the poet's friend and fellow student of poetry, Quintilius Varus, with apologies for singing a humble song rather than a heroic one: "deductum dicere carmen" (5; "to sing a humble song"). The poem records the state of Virgil's poetic activity and his desire to enhance it and improve upon it.

Sannazaro goes farther than Virgil in construing the action as an emblem of poetic activity. He dedicates the poem to Ferdinand of Aragon, son of the late King Federigo, now absent as a political prisoner in Spain. Sannazaro's dedication echoes lines that Virgil addressed to the dedicatee of his own *Eclogue* VIII. Virgil's lines are:

> *Tu mihi, seu magni superas iam saxa Timavi,*
> *sive oram Illyrici legis aequoris, —en erit umquam*
> *ille dies, mihi cum liceat tua dicere facta?*
> *en erit, ut liceat totum mihi ferre per orbem*
>
> (6–9)

> But thou, my friend, whether even now thou art passing the crags of great Timavus, or skirting the coast of the Illyrian main—O will that day ever come when I shall be free to tell thy deeds? O shall I ever be free to spread through all the world these songs of thine?

Though modern scholarship identifies Virgil's addressee as Pollio, Servius postulated that it was Augustus. Thus he glossed the passage as meaning "ubi es, O Auguste" (Servius, p. LXXXV; "wherever you are, O Augustus"). In the fifteenth century Mancinellus likewise considered Augustus to be the poem's audience: "faveo Auguste eum siquidem per apostrophem alloquit" (Mancinellus, p. LXXXV; "I favor him to be Augustus if indeed he speaks through apostrophe"). More significantly, Servius compared the emperor's deeds with those of the poet. Both wear, and both deserve, crowns of laurel and ivy: "Nam victores Imperatores, lauro: hedera coronantur poetae" (Servius, p. LXXXV; "for as conquerors, emperors are crowned with laurel; poets are crowned with ivy"). The emperor earns his crown through heroic exploits; the poet earns his by writing about those exploits. Political and military events provide the poet with material for his song, but the poet eventually surpasses the emperor in glory because his art lives forever, while the emperor's achievements only pass with time. The celebration of the prince therefore becomes a celebration of poetry.

Sannazaro's speaker underscores this connection between the celebration of the one and the other. In his address to Ferdinand he hopes that old memories will stir the prince to sue for release, return to Naples, and expel his father's enemies:

> *Tu vero, patriae juvenis decus, edite caelo,*
> *Spes generis tanti, seu te nimbosa Pyrene*
> *Pro dulci Latio, pro nostris detinet arvis,*
> *Seu vagua objecto munimine claudit Iberus,*
> *Rumpe moras.*
>
> (7–11)

Do you now, the youthful ornament of your country, spring from very heaven, the hope of so great a race, whether the stormy Pyrenees withhold you (alas) from sweet Latium, from our native fields (alas), or whether wandering Ebro close you within his spreading barrier, do you now break through delays.

The injunction not to delay also takes into striking account the speaker's own ambitions:

> *Nam mihi, nam tempus veniet cum reddita sceptra*
> *Parthenopae fractosque tua sub cuspide reges*
> *Ipse canam; nunc litoream ne despice Musam*
> *Quam tibi post silvas, post horrida lustra Lycaei*
> *(Si quid id est) salsas deduxi primus ad undas*
> *Ausus inexperta tentare pericula cymba.*
>
> (15–20)

For to me will come, for the time will come when I myself shall sing the scepters restored to Parthenope and kings broken under your lance. Meanwhile do not scorn the seaside Muse which after the forests, after the shadowy glades of Mount Lycaeus (if that be anything) I first have brought

for you to the salty waves, daring to make trial of their dangers in my inexperienced skiff.

Ferdinand's challenge to his captors and usurpers in the outer
world will provide high matter for the speaker to convert into
the inner world of epic poetry (15–17), but the prince's absence will delay the epic. The speaker must therefore coax Ferdinand away from Spain's luxury to resume the Herculean task
awaiting him in Naples. This poem becomes an attempt at such
persuasion. The speaker urges Ferdinand not to despise his rhetoric, however lowly it might appear from his "seaside muse"
(17). Pastoral poetry has noble precedent as a prelude to epic.
Virgil's career affords one instance. The speaker's will afford another. His craft may be *inexperta* (20), "inexperienced," but it
promises to transport him and his audience on an imaginative
journey back to the homeland.

The vehicle for this journey is the account of another speaker,
who acts as a surrogate for the poet. Virgil assigned this role to
Silenus in his *Eclogue* VI. Sannazaro, however, assigns it to Proteus. In his capacity as seer, Proteus becomes an apt figure for
the poet's own role because his variform changeability matches
the poet's ability to adapt to many poetic forms.[15] As shepherd
of the sea he is an especially apt figure for this piscatorial poet.
The latter, moreover, has received these words through the
agency of still other speakers, the fishermen Melanthius and
Phrasidamus, who heard Proteus's song from the helm of their
ship (24). The linguistic distance of this recorded event corre-
sponds to the mythic distance of what Proteus sings about. His
very language is nonhuman, irreducible to familiar speech:
"Ipse autem haudquaquam mortali digna referri / Verba sono
vacuas laetus cantabat ad auras" (28–29; "The god himself
moreover in happy mood was singing to the idle air words not
properly reduced to mortal sound"). He tells how Typhoeus
called up the Giants to war against the gods, and how the rocks
they hurled became the islands of Ischia and Procida off Naples's coast (30–40); how Hercules labored near Naples and

settled there (41–42); how Apollo and Diana frequented nearby Cumae (43–45); how Nesis sought to escape from Posillipo (46–58); how the siren Parthenope became patron of Naples (59–62); and how Proteus himself guided the waters underground through the city to irrigate and fructify it (63–68). These half-dozen vignettes imply a heroic standard against which to gauge the careers of both audience and speaker. Ferdinand must measure up to the work of the city's mythic founders, while the speaker must measure up to Proteus's poetic craft.

Certainly Sannazaro measures up to the example of Virgil's *Eclogue* VI. The Virgilian focus of *Piscatoria* IV defines how Proteus begins his account of the history of Naples:

> *Ipse autem haudquaquam mortali digna referri*
> *Verba sono vacuas laetus cantabat ad auras;*
> *Terrigena ut quondam matris de ventre Typhoeus*
> *Exsiliens infanda deos ad bella vocasset;*
> *Ut fratrum primus furiis et hiantibus hydris*
> *Instructus densas ductaverit ipse catervas;*
> *Ut nisu ingenti partes de monte revulsas*
> *Aenariam Prochytenque altis immiserit astris*
> *Ac totum subito caelum tremefecerit ictu.*
>
> (28–36)

The god himself moreover in happy mood was singing to the idle air words not properly reduced to mortal sound; how once earth-born Typhoeus springing from his mother's womb called up the gods to impious war; how as first of the brothers armed with furies and with gaping hydras he led the swarming bands; how with huge effort he hurled against the lofty stars the fragments torn from the mountain, Ischia and Procida, and made the whole sky tremble with the sudden blow.

These lines emulate those in Virgil's *Eclogue* VI where Silenus begins his account of the world's origin:

> *Namque canebat, uti magnum per inane coacta*
> *semina terrarumque animaeque marisque fuissent*

et liquidi simul ignis; ut his exordia primis,
omnia et ipse tener mundi concreverit orbis;
tum durare solum et discludere Nerea ponto
coeperit et rerum paulatim sumere formas.

(31–36)

For he sang how, through the gread void, were brought together the seeds of earth, and air, and sea, and streaming
fire withal; how from these elements came all beginnings
and even the young globe of the world grew into a mass;
how then it began to harden the ground, to shut Nereus
apart in the deep, and, little by little, to assume the forms
of things.

In his lengthy note to these lines, Servius offers a short history
of abstract philosophical opinions on such matters: "variae
sunt Philosophorum opiniones de rerum origine" (Servius,
p. LXXIII; "the opinions of philosophers about the origin of
things are various"). He surveys theories of Anaxagoras,
Thales, Empedocles, and finally Epicurus and Lucretius, from
whom Virgil derived his account. In 1488 Cristoforo Landino,
Sannazaro's Florentine contemporary, approves this synopsis of
ancient philosophy and to it he adds the Christian perspective
about God's act of creation *ex nihilo*. In a wholly temporal vein,
however, he speculates that every culture has proposed its own
myth of origin, "de temporibus et historiis Hebraeorum, et Gre-
corii, et Persarum, et Macedonum, et Alexandrinorum, item
Romanorum" (Landino, P. LXXV; "the same myth about time
and history of the Hebrews, the Greeks, the Persians, the Mac-
edonians, the Alexandrians, and the Romans"). The fact that
all contributed to the lore suggests the relativity of their accounts in the light of Christian revelation. To balance his perception of cultural relativity, however, Cristoforo Landino attempts a rhetorical synthesis of all these views. They gain in
validity when one considers them as metaphors for explaining
the human condition, the union of matter and spirit that constitutes a world unto itself: "Et microcosmus, idest parvus mundus, idest homo. Ergo mundus, idest omnia, quae in mundo vis-

ibili sunt, et est intellectio" (Landino p. LXXV; "A microcosm, i.e., a small world is what man is; therefore the world consists of everything that is visible in the world, and intellect as well"). For Landino, Virgil's eclogue encompasses the life of man within the life of the cosmos.

Despite this vague gesture towards Platonic abstraction, however, Landino does not naively moralize Virgil's poem as a Platonic allegory about the life of the soul. He instead grounds Virgil's cosmological myth in the life of the private individual. Landino's exegesis grasps the narrative on its high cosmological plane without sacrificing its concrete, personal, immediate relevance. That relevance is important for Sannazaro. He avoids both Servius's broad philosophizing and Landino's rhetorical platonizing. He refuses to imitate Virgil's poem as either world history or spiritual allegory. Instead he emulates the Virgilian model as a dramatic experience. If Landino had suggested Virgil's concrete, personal, immediate relevance, Sannazaro now exploits it. He focuses not on the origins of the world or of the soul, but of Naples; and he roots the landscape of his pastoral in the political soil of his homeland. Sannazaro's eclogue records the mythic history of Naples. Its motive is public and patriotic.

It is also to some degree self-referentially poetic. With the seventh vignette Proteus approaches the speaker's own horizon. He recounts how a shepherd named Melisaeus met Corydon in a sacred grove (69–71). Figuratively this event refers to Pontano's assumption of pastoral poetry, since "Melisaeus" was Pontano's fictive name in his own poetry while "Corydon" designates Virgil's pastoral persona. The model in Virgil's own *Eclogue* VI is Silenus's account of the soldier Gallus's initiation as a poet (VI.64–73). Commenting on the inner world of poetry, the account now turns contemporary history into timeless myth. Sannazaro's adaptation is more limited than Virgil's original. Its focus is exclusively literary. By recording Pontano's commitment to poetry, Sannazaro also recalls his mentor's endorsement of him when he was young. At the same time, by depicting the pastoral landscape of Corydon's cove, he transports his audience from the remote mythic world to a proximate literary one. This world has its own culture and refinement, as Melisaeus's song about the starry sphere (referring to his *Urania*) suggests (72–74), but it also has its disappointments and dangers. Indeed, for both the speaker and his audience its Arcadian innocence now no longer exists. In the world of human affairs, disasters often occur. Proteus's references to ships trapped in the bay's rocks, to the Roman town of Stabiae and the eruptions of mighty Vesuvius that buried it, drive the point home (77–78).

The death of Ferdinand's father, the late King Federigo, in his exile at Tours, enforces the point more sharply. The tone shifts abruptly with a dramatic intrusion of the second-person pronoun announcing Federigo's death: "Addit tristia fata, et te quem luget ademptum / Italia infelix" (81–82; "He adds the sorrowful fates, and you whose removal hapless Italy weeps"). Proteus is, after all, the figure of change, and it is fitting that he draw to the end of his account with a stress on the mutability of things. The god and seer of change begins to enumerate the kings of Naples and the battles they fought. Among the unfortunate ones he addresses Federigo a second time when he plaintively asks whether the little stretch of land in France was reserved for his grave after so many labors (87–88). The evocation of Federigo's burial on foreign soil has a curious double potential. On the one hand it might fire Ferdinand's will to return to his homeland. On the other, it might do the opposite, because in the final lines Proteus seems to urge a tempering of one's ambitions. All the earth is a grave and any one part of it suffices as well as another: "Grata quies patriae, sed est omnis terra sepulcrum" (91; "Rest in the homeland is welcome, but all the earth is a grave"). Mutability, taken on its own terms, leads to this negative vision.

The speaker, however, in his own conclusion suggests a wider, more optimistic view when he shifts from Proteus's voice to his own. He knows that, as time passes and memories of heroic acts in the outer world fade, the poet can rescue bits and pieces from oblivion (94). All the while history sets the stage for its own continuation. It constitutes an on-going process with possibilities for repetition and renewal at each change of the moon. Heaven's deities proceed in a steady ascent to their shining thrones (95–96). A recollection of the past does indeed offer good reason to pursue one's ambitions, and thus the speaker answers Proteus's (and possibly Ferdinand's) melancholy defeatism with a positive response. By taking up his burden in the outer world, Ferdinand will join a long line of heroic figures in the history of Naples, from the Giants, Hercules, and Parthenope in the distant past to others yet unknown in the future. And by providing new matter for high song, Ferdinand's deeds will enable the speaker to find his own place in the nostalgic inner world of poets who have cultivated the tradition before him, as far back as Proteus, perhaps, and including such countrymen as Virgil and Pontano. The speaker's poem transforms this exhortation into a statement with powerful emotional undercurrents. It is both personal and political at once, while its focus remains sharply centered on the inner literary world.

In *Piscatoria* V the speaker records the amatory laments of two fishermen in a poetic contest. He dedicated the eclogue to Cassandra Marchese Castriota and probably wrote it while he was championing her in her husband Alfonso's divorce suit. In the laments, each fisherman complains of his beloved's absence. It records a pair of laments by shepherds frustrated in love. Damon sings of a shepherd who contemplates suicide because his beloved Nisa was betrothed to another shepherd, Mopsus; while Amphesiboeus, vexed by the absence of his beloved Daphnis, concocts charms to summon Daphnis to him.

Sannazaro's sense of absence is less dramatically consistent, but perhaps more haunting. From the beginning, his own primary audience, Cassandra Marchese Castriota, is absent, too. In the prologue the speaker summons her from whatever activities may detain her—the learned arts of Athene, which imply her intellectual pursuits (7), the Dryads' chorus and Diana's band, which imply her gracious, convivial interests (9), and her meditations upon the sportive Nereids, which imply her contemplative interests (13). The speaker promises compensation if she comes to him. He urges her to "look upon his own sportings" (14). The *lusus* that he offers ought to appeal to her more than the Nereids, and with their intellectual values and active purpose they ought to complement her other affairs.

The speaker's own reason for presenting these songs is both to please Cassandra and to avoid the accusation that he has excluded her from his poetry. And yet he mentions her name only in the prologue. Covertly he may be projecting her into his fishermen's laments. If so his strategy has become oddly complex. The two laments contrast sharply with each other. The first, that of Dorylas, is flamboyantly imaginative, while the second, Thelgon's, is rhetorically rich but thematically conventional.

Curiosities abound in the first lament. As Dorylas narrates it, its fictive speaker, the witch Herpylis, complains about male lovers. The inversion of sexual roles whereby Dorylas assumes the feminine voice of Herpylis lends an extra resonance to the witch's denunciation of her former lover, Maeon. Cursing him for his infidelity to her, she prepares a poison potion to kill him. The model for this lament is Theocritus's *Idyll* II, where Simaetha curses her own unfaithful lover. Dorylas embellishes the model with colorful touches. Herpylis burns seaweed so that her lover may literally burn to the marrow (39); she soaks up her tears with a sponge so that he may lose all sensation (47), grow fat (50), and be battered, halted, and restrained (58) before succumbing to her poison (62). And for each part of her curse she repeats a menacing refrain, eight times in all: "Volvite praecipitem jam nunc, mea licia, rhombum: (32; "Now, now, my thread, revolve the spinning reel").

Thelgon's lament (76–121) is different. The speaker knits it tightly and purposively with a sharper rhetorical impact, part of which comes from its concrete setting. Thelgon's first words evoke the cliff where he sat with Galatea, viewing Capri on one side, Vesuvius on the other (76). In contrast to the strong visual image elaborated in the following lines, Galatea, the object of the poem, is absent. Her absence generates a dramatic tension as the speaker seeks to recover her traces in the places she no longer inhabits: "saepe ipsa pedum vestiga quaero" (94; "Often I see the very traces of your feet"). The verse's spillage over these lines dramatizes the speaker's own lack of inner containment.

The reason for Galatea's absence soon emerges. A rival lover claims her attention, and he differs from the speaker by being a woodland shepherd rather than a seaside fisherman (97–98). The speaker nonetheless protests that his own artistic talents equal his rival's (99–100). At this point the biographical resemblances between him and the controlling poet, Sannazaro, become powerful ones. Like Sannazaro, he has spent time in France; he has fished in the Varus, the Arar, and the British Sea (113–15). In the final lines, however, he resigns himself to Galatea's absence, and hence to her preference for someone else. He urges her to accept the poem as his final offering, drawn from his own inner world: "Sed accipe munus, / Accipe" (118–19; "But take this offering, take it").

Sannazaro's *Piscatoriae*, then, succeed in moving between the outer and inner worlds of the pastoral with an ease reminiscent of the best classical models. Unlike Mantuan's eclogues, which epitomize the didactic, sententious tones of the early renaissance pastoral, these eclogues create an "other" world whose poetic speakers have the leisure to resolve tensions between their outer and inner selves. Unlike contemporary eclogues by Pontano, Castiglione, Vida, and Navagero that established the mode as the premier vehicle for dirge, Sannazaro's eclogues treat the motifs of presence and absence, hope and despair, memory and desire in rich and satisfying ways. Unlike eclogues by Strozzi and Boiardo that appropriate the technical form with minimal feeling for its subtler conventions, Sannazaro's poems achieve a balance of form and idea where the two are suffused into one. Sannazaro's merit in the *Piscatoriae* was to have realized the topical potentials of the classical pastoral in Latin hexameters of charm and polish. No other collection of Latin eclogues in the Renaissance duplicated them.

DE PARTU VIRGINIS: PASTORAL AND THE SHORT EPIC

Two modes of verse narrative were common in the early Renaissance. One was the erotic-mythological tale with roots in classical poetry and particularly in Ovid's *Metamorphoses*; the other was a composition on some aspect of the life of Christ or the saints with roots in medieval devotional verse. Both employed pastoral settings, themes, and motifs, and Sannazaro produced an example of each. His *Salices*, as we have seen, demonstrates the Renaissance's attraction to Ovidian narrative purged of the moralizing, allegorizing commentary attached to medieval renditions. His *Lamentatio de Morte Christi* (Lamentation on Christ's Death) reveals an aspect of Renaissance religiosity often forgotten in the work of the great humanists. The dates for their compositions are uncertain, but both were first published together with the *Piscatoriae* and the *De Partu Virginis* in the 1526 edition of Sannazaro's major Latin works.

The *Lamentatio de Morte Christi* is a lesser poetic accomplishment than *De Partu Virginis*, but it is a precursor of the better poem. Sannazaro initially printed it along with *Salices* in the first edition of the *Piscatoriae* and *De Partu Virginis* (1526), but he had composed it probably in 1502 during his exile in France. In the form of an epyllionic lament, it represents Christ's crucifixion and descent into hell in graphic visual terms. It also functions as a hortatory appeal to the audience to renounce sin. Vocatives, imperatives, and interrogatives abound throughout the poem's 118 lines, and the audience that they address undergoes a shift from weary mankind in general, "aegri / Mortales" (9–10) at the beginning, to obdurate sinners, "Infelix genus" (85), awaiting punishment at the end.[16] The moralistic tone is pervasive and oppressive.

The poem's vitality derives from its vivid pictorial composition on Christ's suffering. The first command addressed to weak mortals urges them to direct their minds to the sight of Christ pierced with cruel iron (11). The speaker stresses the immediacy of the situation when he addresses the moon as it grows dark and deformed while Christ hangs on the cross (25–26). In a series of desperate questions he next depicts the natural disorders that accompanied Christ's death: turbulence, floods, earthquakes—"Quid? non et pelagi rabies attollere fluctus / Immaneis visa est?" (33–34; "What? don't you see savage rage stir up great waves on the beach?"). Invoking the audience, he asks whether they can visualize the underworld and Christ's descent there to reclaim the expectant souls (57–58). This descent moves the speaker to exhort: "Quare agite, ex animis mortales pellite vestris" (70; "Why be troubled: drive mortal concerns from your hearts"). The speaker nonetheless knows that a certain segment of the audience will never prepare itself for God: "At vos obtusas ignari avertitis aureis, / Infelix genus, et saevae ludibria mortis" (82–83; "But you ignorant ones, unhappy class of people, and plaything of cruel death, you divert your obtuse ears"). God will punish them. The speaker makes a final earnest appeal to them to mend their ways, "Ergo vitaleis miseri dum carpitis auras" (104; "While you wretches are still breathing the air of life"). In the poem's closing lines he presents a vision of God as almighty judge assigning rewards in the heavenly spheres, allowing some to sit at His feet and see the starry fortress of heaven: "Sub pedibusque dabit stellantia cernere claustra" (118).

As a preparation for *De Partu Virginis*, the poem gives little indication of what would follow. Its overt moralism suggests none of the subtle sophistication of Sannazaro's later epic. Its hortatory appeals, however, its sense of an audience's presence, and its emphasis on visual rendition of the events narrated all confirm the direction of Sannazaro's art at the time. In the diversity of its rhetorical techniques, its narrative sustains analogies with the pastoral mode. Just as ancient pastoral in some respects represented a miniaturization of epic, so does the *La-*

mentatio. The topic of the crucifixion, however, is less apt for pastoral purposes than the topic of Christ's birth. Sannazaro would focus on that topic in *De Partu Virginis.*

As Petrarch did his Latin epic, *Africa,* Sannazaro viewed *De Partu Virginis* (On the Virgin Birth, 1526) as his greatest project. He spent more than twenty years polishing its 1,443 hexameters, having begun its composition upon his return from exile in 1506, publishing it in 1526. By 1513 he had completed at least a sketch for the entire poem. Between 1520 and 1523 a Venetian literary pirate acquired and published 356 lines of Book I. In the years that followed, Sannazaro distributed seven manuscript versions among trusted friends, seeking commentary and pointed criticism for final revisions. His respondents included the respected Ferrarese poet, Antonio Tebaldeo (1463–1537); the pious Cardinal Egidio da Viterbo (1465–1532); the learned humanist churchmen, Pietro Bembo and Jacopo Sadoleto (1477–1547); the Curial secretary Antonio Seripando; and the humanist academician Aulo Giano Parrasio (1470–1522).[17]

One reason for Sannazaro's hesitations was that the religious ferment of the times had sharpened his scruples about the doctrinal implications of his poem. Luther broke with Rome in 1517. The full consequences of that act along with other reform movements in the north seem to have eluded Sannazaro, but they did sharpen his sensitivity to the ways audiences would receive his sacred epic. On 6 August 1521, Pope Leo X issued a *motu proprio* encouraging Sannazaro to publish *De Partu Virginis* as a counterstatement against the German heretics. In a letter to Antonio Seripando dated 13 April of that year, the poet had expressed doubts about his own theological accuracy.[18] His appropriation of Virgilian diction might have led him to adopt such terms as "nymph" for the Virgin and "Son of Jove" for Christ, but he has resisted them. More problematic have been the prophetic passages, where he incorporates the pagan deity Proteus and borrows from Virgil's *Eclogue* IV and Ovid's *Metamorphoses* to foretell Christ's ministry. He worried that the pagan fiction might distort sacred truth and sabotage his pious intent. He even worried that his poetic invention of David's prophecy about the crucifixion might disturb readers because it has no basis in Scripture. His sole concern in revising the text was to temper poetic fiction and mitigate the confusion be-tween sacred and profane.

Another reason for its prolonged composition was that as a Latin stylist Sannazaro remained infinitely sensitive to the finest nuances of diction, syntax, rhythm, voice, and address. In a long, undated letter to Antonio Seripando (LIII), he expressed the difficulties of following Virgil's model for the high style. For his catalogue of nations in the Roman Empire at the time of Christ's birth, for example, he found that the best source, Pliny, used different forms for place names from those that Vir-gil had used, so that for places Virgil did not cite there could be no way of knowing which form he would have preferred. In a detailed examination of other elocutionary choices, however, Sannazaro argues against invariably following the Virgilian model. He assails ignorant pedants who claim that if Virgil hadn't used a particular word, then it cannot be good Latin: "there are many words that Virgil does not use, but others do, and they are among the most beautiful ones in the language. . . . I yield to no one in liking, admiring, even adoring Virgil, but it seems to me to be pure madness to validate only what Virgil has said" (Mauro, ed., *Opere*, p. 381). Accordingly he defends his use of unusual constructions found in Ovid, Horace, Juvenal, Martial, Propertius, Lucan, Statius, Claudian, Pliny, and Strabo. The good Latin stylist will come to sound like Vir-gil without always echoing him.

Sannazaro's stylistic heterodoxy brought him into close con-tact with modern texts as well as older ones. There were already many Neo-Latin epics on various topics. Though none of them was very good, they nonetheless presented Sannazaro with a variety of structural models. From Petrarch's *Africa* (1338–41 ff.) onwards, poets had struggled to combine Christian with pagan elements in an epic framework with little success. They produced stiff, invariable, unyielding hexameters constricted by a flat-footed sense of imitating the ancient classics. They lacked variety and suppleness, the fluid integration of different modes and changing styles into the generic form of the epic.

Sannazaro's skill was precisely to integrate those modes with elevated, middle, and humble styles into the epic. For this achievement, not reached in the Latin epic since antiquity, he had no contemporary precedent. Indeed the Neo-Latin epics at hand tended towards modal and stylistic monotony. For panegyrical and encomiastic models there were Basinio Basini's *Hesperis* (1455) about the Malatesta family, Tito Vespasiano Strozzi's *Borsias* (1471) about Borso d'Este, and Francesco Filelfo's *Sphortias* (1473) about the Sforzas. For mythic epics there were Maffeo Veggio's *Vellus Aureum* (1458) about the Argonauts and Pontano's *Urania* (1481) about the plan of the starry spheres according to the tales of the ancients. For Christian epics there were Ugolino Varino's *Paradisus* (1468–69) and Mantuan's seven *Parthenicae* (1481) about the lives of female saints. The humanists' discovery of two early Christian poetic narratives, the *Evangelii* of Gaius Juvencus (d. 337) and five *Carmina Paschalia* of Caelius Sedulius (published 494) stirred interest in religious topics. Sannazaro mentions them with enthusiasm in a letter to Antonio Seripando (XXXVII, 23 March 1521), along with the better known *Historia Apostolica* of Aratore (544) and Prudentius's *Psychomachia* (400). None of these examples, however, revealed all the possible varieties of mode or style available to the epic poet.

Early in composing *De Partu Virginis*, Sannazaro decided to forge his own structure. A brief summary of its contents points to the flexibility and suppleness that he would attain in its execution. At the beginning the speaker invokes the aid of God, the muses, and the Virgin to tell his story (I.1–32). From His vantage point in heaven, God plans the Savior's birth (I.33–81). He sends the Angel Gabriel to announce the news to Mary, and she becomes filled with the Spirit (I.82–224). Hearing about the event in Limbo, King David bursts into song

prophesying Christ's infancy and Good Friday Passion and forecasting the opening of heaven for all the souls in Limbo (I.225–
462). In Book II Mary journeys to her aged cousin, Elizabeth,
now pregnant with John the Baptist; Elizabeth defers to her and
Mary sings God's praise (II.1–115). Three months later Mary
returns home; the emperor has ordered a census of the whole
empire, whose various place-names the speaker cites in a long
roll call (II.116–234). Joseph travels with Mary to Bethlehem;
inside a shepherd's cave at the edge of the city, Mary gives birth
to the Savior; Joseph marvels to hear a choir of angels sing
(II.235–468). Book III opens with God's reminiscence among
His good angels about the fall of Satan and the sin of Adam and
Eve; He sends one of them to announce Christ's birth to the
shepherds (III.1–168). The shepherds rejoice; two of them
greet the Child with a prophetic song, and a choir of angels
sings hymns of praise (III.169–280). In the poem's long concluding episode, the tutelary deity of the river Jordan recounts
Proteus's prediction of later events in Christ's life (III.281–
504). Finally, in his own personal voice Sannazaro ends the
poem by announcing his retirement to Mergellina, where he
will continue to devote himself to poetic production (III.
505–13).

The emergence of this personal voice is unusual for an early
Renaissance epic, and doubly so for its lack of reference to the
speaker's wider milieu, his patrons or protectors, and his social
and political environment. When Renaissance epic speakers
interrupted the flow of their narratives, they generally did so to
acknowledge their benefactors, praise their lords, or disparage
their enemies. Sannazaro's sole concern, however, is to infuse
the epic genre with a new stylistic register. He recognizes how
much the epic can accommodate within its amplitude, and almost programmatically he sets out to endow it with lyric, dramatic, descriptive, visionary, pastoral, hymnic, oratorical, and
even satiric episodes.

In this diversification *De Partu Virginis* resembles what is
surely the best brief epic in English, Milton's *Paradise Regained*

(published in 1671, but written perhaps as early as 1646). Milton himself provided a theoretical clue to understanding the genre when in his tract, *The Reason of Church Government* (1642), he distinguished between "that epic form whereof the two poems of Homer and those other two of Virgil and Tasso are a diffuse, and the book of Job a brief model."[19] His distinction between "diffuse" and "brief" epics points to the wide range of modes and styles encompassed by the long poems of Homer, Virgil, and Tasso, and the compressed unity of character, tone, and action achieved in the Book of Job. Unity, however, does not preclude diversity. By exploiting that diversity in *Paradise Regained*, Milton acknowledged his brief epic to be a no less diffuse genre than the longer one. The framework of *Paradise Regained* includes hymns (I.173–81 and IV.596–635), lyric meditations bordering on dramatic soliloquy (Christ's monologue in I.196–293), elegiac complaints (the apostles in II. 30–57 and Mary in II.66–104), debates (Belial vs. Satan in II.120–234), pastorals (Jesus in the grove, II.285 ff.), and anti-pastorals (Jesus in the city and the roll call of kingdoms, III.260 ff.). Thus Louis Martz has aptly described the poem as "a contest of styles," and, one could add, a medley of modes and generic forms.[20]

Sannazaro's *De Partu Virginis* achieved this quality a century and a half earlier than Milton's poem. And, as Milton's poem would find its source for the order of Christ's temptations in St. Luke's Gospel, so Sannazaro's found its source for the story of Christ's nativity there. Of all the Gospels, Luke's sustains the greatest variety of modal and stylistic properties. Its diversity, however, is one that not all creative poets recognized or emulated. Marco Girolamo Vida (1485–1566), for example, composed his *Christias* (1535) from the same materials, but that long poem (6,012 hexameters) lacks the finer tones and emotional shadings of either Sannazaro's (1,443 hexameters) or Milton's (2,070 lines).[21] It includes the matters of both poems—Christ's birth at III.106–1010 and Satan's temptation at IV.604–55—but it narrates them through St. Joseph's straightforward third-person description in the first instance and St. John's in the second, with little dramatic enactment in either case. Vida's poem moreover abounds in long, static descriptions, as of the marble designs in the Temple of Jerusalem (I.551–724); in catalogues and roll calls, as of the towns in Israel (II.305–529); and in didactic summaries of Christ's teaching, as in the sermon on the beatitudes (IV.882–967). Still, the *Christias* incorporates much diversity. There are prayers, such as Joseph's (III.524–38) and Simeon's (III.705–15) to the Christ-child; invocations, such as the speaker's appeal to the muses for aid (I.1, V.224 ff., VI.110 ff.); laments, such as Mary's at the foot of the cross (V.850–91); and hymns of praise sung by the angels and saints (VI.165–89, 241–65, and 736–800). On the whole, however, its poetic scope remains more constricted than that of *De Partu Virginis*. It would be unfair to say that *Christias* is monotonous, but the strain to replicate Virgilian elocutionary norms attenuates its strength and vitality. Virgilianism was its downfall.   In *De Partu Virginis*, on the other hand, a remarkable fidelity to both Virgil and the Bible preserves the poem's lightness of tone. The Bible in fact contributes more variety to the poem than any other source. Just as Milton would find it to be a repository of all modes and styles, so would Sannazaro. Though Matthew's Gospel and especially Luke's are the primary scriptural models for the story of the nativity, Sannazaro would range through the whole Judeo-Christian canon for prophecies, fulfillments, and ancillary stories. Each of the four Gospels, moreover, has its own distinctive tone, and Sannazaro exploits their differences in various ways.

To a large extent their differences result from historical factors influencing their composition. Mark composed his Gospel in Rome under the guidance of St. Peter during the age of Neronian repression (A.D. 64 ff.). Addressing an audience of persecuted believers, he emphasized Christ's fiery leadership, His own suffering, and His role as a miracle worker who surmounts human obstacles. Matthew composed his Gospel probably after A.D. 80 in Syria for an audience of Hellenized Jews with a strong rabbinic background. Accordingly he emphasized links between Christ's teaching and the Old Testament, taking special pains to demonstrate how it fulfills the law of Moses. Luke addressed a more cosmopolitan audience of gentiles. Writing in Syria after A.D. 80 with particular attention to sociological, economic, and historical detail, he emphasized Christ's role as the Universal Teacher of peace, harmony, and forgiveness. Finally, John composed his Gospel under the influence of St. Paul for an audience of Greek gentiles late in the first century. He emphasized the sense of irony, ambiguity, and mystery in Christ's life along with the sacramental symbolism and theological complexity of His teaching. Together the Gospels present a composite picture of Christ in His various roles.

This diversity at the outset provided Sannazaro with varied materials for representing Christ's maturity. The story of His birth, however, posed a different sort of problem. It appears neither in Mark, who begins with Christ's baptism, nor in John, who stresses instead His preexistence as Logos. It acquired only gradual importance in the composition of the Gospels, and it appears in Matthew and Luke with no pretense of factual accuracy. Because their accounts differ widely and are even incompatible in several respects, they are more probably fictive than historical, though fictive in a very special way. They function primarily as vehicles of their authors' religious insight.

The marked differences in their narratives serve theological purposes. Matthew emphasizes Christ's connection with the royal sons of Jacob and with Moses' deliverance. Luke emphasizes His descent from David and His humble beginnings. In Matthew the Annunciation comes to Joseph, who after the visit of the Magi leads his family into Egypt to escape Herod's wrath. This model husband thus fulfills the figure of his namesake, Joseph, who in Genesis brought his brothers to Egypt to escape the famine in Canaan. Here the focus on patriarchal leadership is outstanding. Luke, on the other hand, tells neither of the Magi nor of the Egyptian journey, but he instead emphasizes Christ's descent from David and His birth among the shepherds. In his account, the Annunciation comes to Mary, and the birth occurs in Bethlehem to comply with an improbably contrived method of taking the census. Its location in the city of David reinforces Christ's Davidic inheritance as priest, prophet, and king, while its location in a shepherd's stable reinforces His link with the Shepherd King.

Modern scholarship has shown that the style and intent of these narratives relate closely to methods used by contemporary Jewish commentators in accommodating ancient texts to newer understandings. This mode of writing is called *midrash,* and it often entailed the rewriting of existing narratives in the light of allusions and cross-references to older texts. Much of the New Testament that alludes to the scriptural fulfillment of Old Testament prophecies is midrashic. The birth narratives constitute an especially heightened and concentrated example of *midrash.*[22]

Sannazaro would not have known about the intricacies of midrashic composition, but he would have appreciated its highly allusive character. The birth narratives with their references to Old Testament prophecies, their replication of Old Testament motifs, and their extension of Old Testament figures would have struck him as evident examples of how the New Testament writers used the Old in constructing their accounts. Luke's particular narrative would have had further appeal for him with its incorporation of various poetic forms to develop its own motifs. Three poetic interpolations punctuate Luke's story of the nativity: Mary's Magnificat, Zachariah's Benedictus, and Simeon's Nunc Dimitis. Thus, beyond its merely contingent status as the Gospel that offers the longest account of Christ's birth, Luke's offers a spectrum of modes and styles that would have appealed to Sannazaro as an epic poet. Sannazaro's appreciation of the pastoral mode in biblical literature led him to find there much that would enhance his own project.

Above all Sannazaro imposed upon it a Virgilian tone that aims to replicate Virgil's hexameters. One instance of this imitation deserves special mention. It occurs in the middle of the

third book when a group of shepherds visits the Christ-child.
Sannazaro's hexameters attain a majestic effect with their
smoothly rolling rhythms and their evocation of exotic place-
names, but at the same time they are rooted in the simplicity of
the pastoral style with their limpid designation of the shepherds' names and their activities:

> Tum puero adstantes Lycidas et maximus Aegon,
> Aegon, Getulis centum cui pascua campis,
> centeni per rura greges Massyla vagantur;
> ipse caput late qua Bagrada, qua vagus errat
> Triton, Cinyphiae qua devolvuntur arenae,
> ingens agricolis, ingens pastoribus Aegon.
> At Lycidas vix urbe sua, vix colle propinquo
> cognitus, aequoreas carmen deflexit ad undas,
> et tamen hi non voce pares, non viribus aequis,
> inter adorantum choreas, plaususque decorum
> rustica septena modulantur carmina canna.
>
> (III. 186–96)[23]

Then standing before the Child are Lycidas and powerful
Aegon, who owned a hundred acres of pasture in Getulia
and led his flocks by hundreds through the Massylian fields;
where the Bagrada river, where Triton wanders aimlessly,
where the sands of Cinyps sink back. Aegon is a mighty
leader among farmers, mighty among shepherds. But Lycidas, hardly known in his own city, hardly known on the
neighboring hill, turned his song to the sea-swept waves.
And unequal in voice, with unequal strength, amidst the
circle of worshipers and the applause of angels, they nonetheless played rustic songs on their seven-reed instrument.

The shepherds' names resound from Virgil's *Eclogues*, and they
bring with them the context of Virgilian pastoral. In Virgil's
Eclogue III Aegon is the owner of Damoetas's vast flock, "nuper
mihi traditit Aegon" (2; "Aegon the other day turned it over to
me"). In *Eclogue* V Menalcas pledges Aegon's pious singing to
commemorate the dead Daphnis: "cantabunt mihi Damoetas et
Lyctius Aegon" (72; "Damoetas and Lyctian Aegon shall sing

for me"). In *Eclogue* VII Lycidas is Thyrsis's handsome beloved: "saepus at si me, Lycida formose, revisas" (67; "but if thou, lovely Lycidas, shouldst often visit me"). In *Eclogue* IX Lycidas is a generous young shepherd whose song helps to comfort Moeris: "cantantes ut eamus, ego hoc te fasce levabo" (65; "that we may go singing on our way, I will relieve you of this burden"). Sannazaro fuses the richness, piety, beauty, and gen-erosity of Virgil's shepherds in his representation of the Christ-child's first visitors. They soon pay the Child the ultimate honor of singing to Him a recasting of Virgil's *Eclogue* IV. That event at the climax of Sannazaro's narrative fully integrates the claims of epic with those of pastoral.

Sannazaro's hexameters quoted above also carry echoes from Virgil's *Georgic* III. The Virgilian model evokes agrarian wood-lands where herdsmen shear the Cinyphian goats that feed on the hills of Lycaeus:

> nec minus interea barbas incanaque menta
> Cinyphii tondent hirci saetasque comantis
> usum in castrorum et miseris velamina nautis.
> pascuntur vero silvas et summa Lycaei.
>
> (III.311–15)

Nor less, meanwhile, do herdsmen clip the beard on the hoary chin of the Cinyphian goat, and shear his hairy bristles, for the need of camps, and as coverings for hapless sailors. Again, they feed in the woods and on the summits of Lycaeus.

Servius's note on Lycaeus identifying it as a mountain in Ar-cadia may have prompted Sannazaro to consider the pastoral usefulness of these lines, but in a larger sense one can read Sannazaro's turn to Virgil's *Georgics* as an indication of his in-tent to achieve a higher style and more complex structure than those of the *Eclogues*. Sannazaro's aim in *De Partu Virginis* was to create epic hexameters in the manner of Virgil. In that aim he succeeded.

DE PARTU VIRGINIS: PASTORAL ACTION

Sannazaro's project is an epic, and like every epic, *De Partu Virginis* begins with an invocation. Its first lines establish Christ as the poem's hero and call attention to His virgin birth and coequal parentage as its central paradox: "Virginei partus magnoque aequaeva parenti / progenies" (I. 1 – 2; "Offspring of a virgin birth and equal to His great Parent"). The poem's first word, however, *Virginei*, manages to deflect the emphasis from Christ to his mother. Even after the birth Mary will play a dominant role in the poem's action. The next four lines explore the theological significance of that birth when they invoke the angels and the saints as the speaker's source of inspiration: "Sit mihi, coelicolae, primus labor" (I.5; "The deeds of that Offspring should be my first labor, o dwellers of heaven").

The lines accomplish still more. They indicate the speaker's relationship to the action both overtly and covertly. Overtly they designate this poem as his most important one: "Hoc mihi primum / surgat opus" (I.5–6; "My foremost work will arise from this"). Covertly they help the audience to judge the speaker's performance by providing an external standard of reference for it. That standard is nothing less than Christ's opening the way to closed Olympus, "Obstructique viam patefecit Olympi" (I.4; "He opened the way to closed Olympus"). Like Christ, the speaker is laboring to open a way.

Line 13 makes that analogy explicit when he calls upon still other muses: "Monstrate viam, qua nubila vincam" (I.13; "Point out the way by which I will fly over the clouds). The specific repetition of *viam* from line 4 links the speaker's road of poetic composition, the *viam poeticam*, to Christ's road of salvation, the *viam theologicam*. The speaker will travel the one through the other, leading to greater insight and understanding about divine things. He will earn his own salvation through poetry, and at the same time his poetry will honor and illuminate Christ's work of salvation.

These muses, secular witnesses of Christ's original action,

can in turn pass that witness on to the speaker. Though on line 15 they are Boeotian muses, *Aonides*, they nonetheless have a heavenly lineage and they rejoice in the sacred story: "Etenim potuistis et antrum / aspicere, et choreas" (I. 16–17; "For you could see the cave and the choir of angels"). The speaker's chief problem is his distance from the original event. Temporally and spatially it occurred long ago and far away. Still, he can over-come that distance if both the sacred *coelicolae* and the secular *Aonides* inspire him. Through their inspiration he will achieve a kind of first-hand witness, if not the real thing.

The speaker can overcome the distance in yet another way. One of the agents in the action, Mary, makes herself available to mankind as mediatrix of grace, "Tuque adeo, spes fida homi-num, spes fida deorum" (I. 19; "You are the faithful hope of men and gods"). This third address enables the speaker to cross the barrier separating him from the action, since Mary was a direct participant in the event and the speaker's reverence for her brings him closer to it. Four elaborately ordered *si* clauses de-scribing the chapel in her honor built by Sannazaro at Mer-gellina underscore the majesty of this address, and a pointed repetition of *viae* at its climax indicates the speaker's serious-ness about his poetic vocation: "Niveis tibi si solemnia templis / serta damus, si mansuras tibi ponimus aras / . . . Si laudes de more tuas, si sacra, diemque, / ac coetus late insignes ritusque dicamus, / . . . tu vatem ignarumque viae insuetumque labori, / diva, mone, et pavidis jam laeta allabere coeptis" (I. 23–32; "If we give you festive garlands in our gleaming temples, if we set up enduring altars for you . . . if we sing your praises by custom and if we declare widely your holy day, . . . then, goddess, in-struct this seer ignorant of the way and unused to the task, and come joyfully to his timorous undertakings").

The prominence of the Virgilian formula "Tu vatem . . . diva, mone" in the last two lines of the invocation indicates the speaker's final solution to a difficult artistic problem. The speaker needs on the one hand to mitigate the distance be-tween himself and the action, and on the other to maintain narrative dignity in as high a style as possible. The Virgilian echo can achieve both ends at once. The speaker repeats this strategy in the lines that follow when he begins a direct report of the action. Indeed he starts on a high note *in medias res* by rendering the scene from God's point of view:

> Viderat aetera superum regnator ab arce
> undique collectas vectari in Tartara praedas
> Tisiphonenque imo conantem cuncta profundo
> vertere, et immanes stimulantem ad dira sorores.
>
> (I.33–36)

From His heavely citadel the ruler of the celestial ones had seen spoils collected from everywhere, drawn into Tartary, and Tisiphone in hell attempting to overturn everything and inciting her horrible sisters to frightful acts.

This diction is replete with Virgilian turns: the past perfect tense of *viderat* conveying the sense of action having occurred in the remote past; the neutral nonbiblical term for God, *superum regnator*; the classical mythic term for hell, *Tartara*, and the classical mythic figures of Tisiphone and the fates; and above all the Virgilian tag, *imo vertere*. Its familiarity as part of the established classical canon, coupled with its high epic associations, pulls in the opposing directions of the ordinary and the exalted at once. Miraculously it foreshortens the very remoteness it implies.[24]

One way that the speaker continues to overcome distance throughout the work is to find analogies between higher beings and himself. He continually casts angels, saints, and even God in roles compatible with his, thereby locating them on his level without sacrificing their special qualities. God, for example, enters the poem brooding like an Old Testament patriarch on the fall of man; but when He urges Gabriel to deliver the Annunciation to Mary with all the elocutionary arts at his disposal, He begins to sound like a modern teacher of rhetoric: "Ergo age, . . . castas haec jussus ad aures / effare, et pulchris cunctantem hortatibus imple" (I.77–79; "Therefore go, . . .

announce these commands to just ears and blandish her hesitation with sweet encouragement"). Gabriel, in turn, proves
more than adequate to the task: "Cui latea fandi / copia divini-
que fluunt e pectore rores / ambrosiae, quibus ille acres mulcere
procellas / possit; et iratos pelago depellere ventos" (I.135–38;
"From whose breast flow milky streams of language and divine
ambrosial dew, by which he could calm rough storms and dispel
raging winds from the sea"). Like God's, moreover, his rhetoric
equals truth; he uses it not to deceive but to enlighten and
uplift. He prefaces his subsequent speech to Mary by declaring
his inability to mislead: "Vaticinor non insidias, non nectere
fraudes / edoctus: longe a nostris fraus exulat oris" (I.144–45; "I
make this prophecy well taught not to weave deceits and deceptions: fraud is far in exile from our shores"). Among God and
His angels, rhetorical skill constitutes proof of honest intent.

Mary plays the role of perfect audience. She is an accomplished interpreter of God's word, partly through her innate
goodness and partly through patient practice in deciphering
texts of the old prophets. When Gabriel first approaches, he
finds her reading and meditating about the promised birth:
"Atque illi veteres de more Sibyllae / in manibus, tum si qua
aevo reseranda nepotum / faticidi casto cencinerunt pectore
vates" (I.93–95; "As usual, ancient sybils' writings were in her
hands, and whatever else prophetic seers composed as revela-
tions for their descendants"). These prophecies have an exem-
plary effect on her. Unaware that she is the very virgin destined
to bear the Son of God, she pays honor and reverence to the
chosen one. The process of understanding God's revelation is
circular, but Mary does not yet grasp the whole because she remains unaware of one link in the chain: her own role in the
Incarnation. After Gabriel's disclosure, the words that she
reads in the Sybilline books will bear different meanings.

A later action dramatizes Mary's response to Scripture.
Zachariah, Elizabeth's husband, who has been struck dumb
since her pregnancy, shows Mary the Book of Scripture and
points to certain key passages: "Ostenditque manu vatum tot

scripta priorum" (II.81; "With his hand he showed her the writing of earlier prophets"). God's word reaches out silently from the past and the reader of Scripture comprehends it in an instant. Mary's comprehension differs from the others', however, and it prefigures what the others' comprehension ought to be. Silently she applies Scripture's words to herself: "Seque rubum virgamque, alto se denique missam / sidus grande mari prorsum agnoscitque, videtque" (II.93–94; "She recognizes and sees that the bramble and twig sent finally from above, and the star straight over the sea, figure forth herself"). Mary's response is a paradigm for the entire audience. The text invites each reader to respond by seeing it as a mirror of his or her own individual reality.

Mary's hermeneutic act has a concrete stylistic analogy in the speaker's very choice of diction. He fashions his poem in the ancient Latin language and he embellishes it with Virgilian elocutionary devices. That language antedates the Christian message, and those devices have served as vehicles for a quite different world view. The audience's understanding of them now depends not just on comprehending their ancient meanings but on realizing their possible extensions to a new Christian meaning as well. It comes as a small challenge for the audience in the poem's first hundred-fifty lines to adjust its classical diction to the biblical reference. Eschewing familiar proper names, for example, the speaker uses such unexpected forms as the plural *deorum* (I.19), "gods," and *numina* (I.153), "deities," for the trinitarian God; *superum regnator* (I.33), "ruler of heaven," for the Father; *numen* (I.75, 140), "deity," for the Son; *coelicolae* (I.5), "heaven dwellers," and *superis* (I.43), "heavenly beings," for the angels; *diva* (I.32), "goddess," *reginam* (I.91), "queen," and *dia* (I.139), "goddess," for Mary; Olympus (I.4, 105), *arce aethera* (I.33), "citadel of heaven," and *oras divum* (I.46), "regions of the gods," for heaven; and *veteres Sibyllae* (I.93), "ancient Sibyls," for the prophets. Their meanings are clear, but the application is sometimes startling. The description, for example, of "that ancient known for his slingshot, graceful with his harp, distinguished in his rule" (I.236–37) indicates the Judaic King David, but it could equally indicate the classical figure of the pastoral poet.

In most cases the speaker helps the audience towards a proper recognition. Nowhere is he deliberately arcane or perversely mystifying. In an epic simile describing Mary's astonishment at the Annunciation, he compares her to a girl at the seashore frightened by the appearance of an armed merchant ship returning from Arabia: "Dona ferens, nullis bellum mortalibus infert, / sed pelago innocuis circumnitet armamentis" (I.133–34; "Bearing gifts, it makes war on no one, but with its harmless armaments it gleams on the open sea"). The modernity of the reference is striking. The speaker seems deliberately to be using it to bridge the distance between himself and his high material. It describes the action in elegant, decorative fashion while it reinforces the witness of the speaker who approaches it from his own current perspective addressing an audience likewise bound to its own perspective. Like all successful epic similes it achieves a contrapuntal effect.

Elsewhere the speaker aids the audience's understanding through a careful registering of different stylistic levels integrating the classical, modern, and biblical materials. Sometimes he conflates all three styles. The episode narrating David's prophecy of Christ's birth is a good example. David, the pastoral poet-king of the Old Testament, resides in Limbo and passes his time so that "per opaca locorum / dum graditur, nectitque sacros diademate crines" (I.237–38, "as he wanders through the shade of that region, he binds together sacred strands into a diadem"). The act of weaving diverse strands into a textured whole typifies the pastoral poet's task, just as it typifies the work of a ruler who brings his people together. David is an ideal pastoral figure to extol Christ's birth among the ancients. He wedded art and politics into a meaningful synthesis, but he also began his career as a humble shepherd by wielding his mighty slingshot against Goliath. Now he proclaims the coming of Christ, who will fulfill the typological pastoral pattern with His own birth in a shepherds' cave near the city of David. David's art reaches new heights as he celebrates the proclamation. Famous for his Psalms joined in a lyric sequence, he now attempts a sturdier composition that moves from a hymn (I.245–58) through a narrative about Christ's birth (I.259–304) and a dramatic representation of His passion (I.305–67) to an apocalyptic vision of the souls' entry into heaven (I.368–452).

Inspiration strikes David with unusual violence: "Attonita subitos concepit mente furores / divinamque animam et consueto numine plenus / intorquens oculos venientia fata recenset" (I.242–44; "He began to feel in his stunned brain a sudden furor and divine spirit, and filled with the deity's accustomed might, rolling his eyes, he recounted the will of God to come"). The strands that he wove earlier in the shades of Limbo now prefigure the bonds that have shackled mankind before Christ's coming. Thus in his hymn David exhorts Christ, "Nascere, magne puer, nostros quem solvere nexus / et tantos genitor voluit perferre labores" (I.245–46; "Be born, mighty Son, whom the Maker willed to loosen those bonds and endure so many pains"). The abstract prophecy turns into concrete reality as a vision of the Child takes hold in David's mind. He sees three kings on a journey to honor Christ, and he addresses them as witnesses of a miraculous event: "Salvete, beati / Aethiopes, hominum sanctum genus, astra secuti" (I.256–57; "Hail, holy Ethiopians, blessed race of men, following the star"). Soon all the world will join in the hymn of divine praise.

The concreteness of the vision affords David a brilliant entry into his narrative about Christ's life. As speaker, David begins by addressing the child and mother directly: "Accipe dona, puer, tuque, o sanctissima mater, / sume animos: iam te populique, ducesque frequentant / littore ab extremo, et odoriferis Nabathaeis" (I.259–61; "Receive these gifts, Son; and you, o holiest of mothers, take heart; for people and leaders from far shores and perfumed Arabia are gathering together to visit you"). He then advances quickly through an account of the circumcision and Simeon's wonder at seeing the Child to an account of the slaughter of the innocents. Horror at the latter impels him to address Herod: "Crudelis, quid agis? nihil hi meruere neque illum, / quem petis, insano dabitur tibi perdere ferro" (I.276–77; "Cruel one, what are you doing? They deserved none of this; nor will you be allowed with your blind sword to kill him whom you seek"). With great urgency he exhorts all mothers to abscond with their children, and with special urgency he urges Mary to flee to Egypt: "Tuta domus, tutique illic tibi, Dia, recessus" (I.282; "A safe home, safe places of retreat await you there, goddess").

David renders the next event, the finding of Jesus in the temple, at somewhat greater length than the earlier ones, and in it he focuses on Mary's emotions as she seeks her lost child. Addressing her as a goddess, *dia*, he emphasizes her sense of loss: "Perquires nequicquam amens" (I.289; "Worried, you search in vain for your Son"). The poignant moment foretells Mary's grief at the crucifixion. David establishes the mood with great care before passing on to the dramatic account of Christ's Passion.

That account fully exemplifies the technique of pastoral. It relates passages of dramatic intensity to others of lyric expression, and with quicksilver speed it shifts from visual description to reported speech to meditative profundity. Up to this point David's narrative had fused typological significance with hymnic inspiration and abstract prophecy with concrete vision. Turning now to the crucifixion, David employs direct addresses to Christ, His persecutors, Mary, and other bystanders; he integrates his own exclamations with Mary's monologue and the angels' hymn welcoming Christ into heaven; he shifts from an account of torment to an account of splendor; and he unites allusions to scriptural prose with allusions to classical poetry . To represent the life of Christ requires the full range of generic, modal, and stylistic resources available to the poet. Sannazaro's success at the end of *De Partu Virginis*, Book I, owes to his earlier mastery of pastoral technique, which above all entails the harmonious appropriation, accommodation, and fusion of every available resource. It is moreover fitting that in this instance the articulation issues from David, the foremost pastoral poet of the Old Testament.

David begins with an address to Christ's tormentors after they have captured Him in the garden: "Tu vero quid in arma ruis scelerata juventus?" (I.305; "O wicked band of young men, why do you rush to arms?"). As if he were actually present, David watches in horror while they bind Christ, who, he remarks, only a few days earlier had received accolades of palms upon entering the city. With increasing turbulence David describes the crucifixion, summoning the rhetorical power of exclamations, interjections, and apostrophes to various participants. He addresses the cross that Christ carried to Mount Calvary: "Infelix opus, unde hominum lux illa, decorque / Pendeat" (I.327–28; "Unhappy labor, whereon the light and ornament of mankind hung"). The intensity rises to a high pitch as Christ stretches out His arms on the cross and dies.

When David represents Mary's monológue at the foot of the cross, the account achieves its full dramatic climax. Introspectively at first, and in language that echoes Dido's complaints in *Aeneid* IV, she asks who has willed such a harsh fate for her. Addressing her dead Son, she directs the question to herself in an attempt to comprehend the situation: "Exclamans: 'Quis me miseram, quis culmine tanto / dejectam subitis involuit, nate, procellis?'" (I.344–45; "Exclaiming, 'Who has wished me to be miserable, to have been hurled from such a height, my Son, in such a sudden storm?'"). As she comes to realize the enormity of her grief, she turns outwardly to her Son and recognizes that His death means the death of her God. Others can prevail upon God at the death of their loved ones, but her beloved is God Himself: "Ast ego pro nato, pro te dominoque deoque / quem misera exorem? quo tristia pectora vertam?" (I.357–58; "But miserable me, for you my Son, my Lord, my God, whom can I implore?"). She offers herself to the executioners in place of her Son: "In me omnes effundite pectoris iras" (I.361; "Pour out all your wrath on me"). Finally she turns to the dead Christ and petitions Him to take her into the shades of death: "Vel tu, si tanti est hominum genus, eripe matrem / quae rogat, et Stylgias tecum duc, nate, sub umbras" (I.362–63; "Or, if the human race is so depraved, take your mother, who entreats you, o Son, to the Stygian shades").

David represents Mary's grief so that it contrasts with her youthfulness earlier in the poem and thus deepens her character immeasurably. What follows, however, is more descriptive than dramatic. David foretells the convulsions that will occur upon Christ's death, and with a touch of Virgilian melancholy from *Aeneid* VI he addresses the spirits of the dead, who will rise from their graves: "Quid, o, quid abire paratis, / illustres animae? Non omnibus haec data rerum / conditio, paucis remeare ad lumina vitae / concessum" (I.381–84; "Why are you preparing to depart, o illustrious spirits? This power is not given to everyone; few are allowed to return to the light of life"). The description evokes St. John's Revelation as David renders it from his own apocalyptic point of view. The souls in Limbo now rise with Christ to heaven, honoring Him with hymns of praise: "Victor, io; bellator, io: tu regna profunda" (I.404; "Victor, warrior, you restrain the lower kingdom").

The entry of the blessed into heaven introduces a description of the triumphal march carrying the Son to His Father's throne. He will sit on a high wagon drawn by conventional figures for the four Evangelists: the ox (Luke), lion (Mark), eagle (John), and a man in rich robes (Matthew). The tradition animating these images extends from Old Testament figures in Ezekiel 1.5–27 and New Testament ones in Revelation 4.6–8 to their triumphal representation in Dante's *Purgatorio* XXXI. Here David's Latin poetry preserves its own reminiscences from Virgil's *Georgics* and Ovid's *Metamorphoses,* and it encompasses the scriptural archetypes in a perfectly seamless synthesis.

This synthesis moreover achieves the fusion of horizons so ardently sought by the humanist poet. It brings together references to Old Testament Scriptures, the New Testament, classical poetry, and medieval tradition. Again the fusion exemplifies the poet's mastery of pastoral hybridization, with the added benefit of realizing the humanists' goal to transcend historical differences. In its blend of Hebrew and Christian, classical and modern, the text recognizes their differences, but it also proclaims the possibility of relating them one to another. David's evocation of the evangelical ox, for example, refers to Revelation 4.6–8 where St. John names the four animals who praise God in song. Though in the Vulgate the second animal is likened to a calf, "et secundum animal simile vitulo" (Revelation 4.7: "and the second animal was like a bull-calf"), an apt translation of the Greek *kai to deuteron zōon homoion moschō*, Sannazaro designates the animal as a bull:

> Stellatus minio taurus, cui cornua fronti
> aurea, et auratis horrent palearia setis,
> perque pedes bifidae radiant nova sidera gemmae.
>
> (I.413–15)

The bull is speckled with cinnabar and has a horn of gold on its forehead, and its dewlaps are rough with golden bristles, and at its feet like new stars shine jewels split into two parts.

These lines draw upon two classical texts. From Virgil's *Georgic* I comes a representation of the astrological Taurus as a white bull with gilded horns, "candidus auratis aperit quum cornibus annum / Taurus" (*Georgic* I.217–18; "when the snow-white Bull with gilded horns ushers in the year"). From Ovid's *Metamorphoses* comes a representation of Jupiter as a bull preparing to seduce Europa:

> colla toris exstant, armis palearia pendent,
> cornua parva quidem, sed quae contendere possis
> facta manu, puraque magis perlucida gemma.
>
> (*Metamorphoses* II.854–56)

Muscles bulge on his neck, and dewlaps hang down in front; his horns are indeed small, but you could swear that they were made by hand, more polished and shining than a jewel.

Beyond the evident verbal reminiscences, Sannazaro evokes the contexts of the biblical and Roman sources. The reader aware of them discovers a powerful subtext. The passage in Virgil occurs amid instructions for planting beans in early spring; it proclaims the renewal of the year and the fertility of nature. The passage in Ovid precedes an epoch-making journey of exploration and discovery. Sannazaro fuses the horizons of these different texts with an aptness that dissolves their historical anachronisms. By developing St. John's visionary motif through references to Virgil and Ovid, Sannazaro enables his modern audiences to share something of the experiences and expectations that earlier audiences shared with the classical texts.

As David finishes his prophecy, the souls of the blessed burst into high applause. The pagan demons of classical antiquity react differently: "Commotisque niger Cocytus inhorruit antris: / et vaga Sisyphiis haeserunt saxa lacertis" (I.461–62; "And black Cocytus quivered in its shaking caves, and falling rocks came to a standstill at the arms of Sisyphus"). After such a massive upheaval in hell, the stasis achieved in these last lines of Book I is noteworthy. The opening of Book II contrasts markedly: "Regina ut subitos imo sub pectore motus / sensit et afflatu divini numinis aucta est" (II.1–2; "The queen felt a sudden tremor within her breast and was enlarged by the breath of divine majesty"). The rapid shift from tremulous agitation in the underworld to the delicate palpitation within Mary's body announces a dramatic change of tone.

The poetic speaker now assumes a quieter, more intimate voice as he narrates Mary's journey to Elizabeth.[25] In a series of subdued heroic similes echoing the high style but not exploiting it, he describes her appearance: "Qualis stella nitet, tardum quae circuit Arcton / hyberna sub nocte" (II.14–15; "As a star shines that circles the slow northern sky under the Hibernian night"). All nature pours forth a stream of colors while trees and flowers smile on her passage. The speaker allows his style to reach its most personal level when he sings of nature's joy: "Quaque datur gradientem voce salutant" (II.29; "And with whatever voice is given them, the winds salute her as she passes"). The light but sure touch of classical allusiveness enters into the larger descriptive synthesis of Boreas and Zephyr.

When Mary arrives at Elizabeth's house, the speaker renders a classical version of biblical style by recasting St. Luke's Gospel in Virgilian tones. Mary's response to Elizabeth's greeting is a most striking example. In Luke 1.46–55 the response is a self-contained hymn proclaiming the Lord's greatness. It is known as the Magnificat, from the first word of its Latin version in the Vulgate: "Magnificat anima mea Dominum; et exultavit spiritus meus in Deo salutari meo" ("My soul doth magnify the Lord, And my spirit hath rejoiced in God my Savior").[26] Luke's original Greek style echoes and reechoes Old Testament prophecies and lamentations from the Septuagint, especially Isaiah 61.10, 1 Samuel 2.1, and Habakkuk 3.18. Sannazaro's rendering expands the Vulgate version of Luke without losing sight of its tone or basic structure. In the Vulgate, for example, Mary rejoices "Quia respexit humilitatem ancillae suae" (I.48; "For he hath regarded the low estate of his handmaiden"). Here God "me ima tenentem / indignamque humilemque suis respexit ab astris" (II.52–53; "regarded me from his great heights, persevering and lowly and humble"). In the Vulage Mary exclaims: "Ecce! enim ex hoc beatam me dicent omnes generationes" (I.48; "From henceforth all generations shall call me blessed"). Here the poet uses the classical *felix* rather than the Christian *beatam* and the classical *gentes* rather than the biblical *generationes*: "gentes felix ecce una per omnes / iam dicar" (II.54–55; "I will be called happy by all races"). In the Vulgate: "Et misericordia ejus a progenie in progenies timentibus eum" (I.50; "And his mercy is on them that fear him from generation to generation"). Here: "Et quae per magnas clementia dedita terras / exundat" (II.58–59; "His devoted mildness overflows throughout the whole world"). *Clementia*, a deliberate departure from the Vulgate's *misericordia*, renders the original Greek *eleos* less well than the latter, but succeeds in establishing God's beneficent mildness to a greater degree. Indeed, Sannazaro's

"Magnificat" emphasizes God's favor towards the weak at a greater length (II.61–68 elaborates that topos) than Luke's, and it prepares pointedly for the ensuing narrative of the birth.

That narrative recounts nothing less than history's greatest manifestation of God's favor towards the lowly. The speaker delivers it in the most sustained use of his personal style. It is by turns lyric, dramatic, rhetorically straightforward, rhythmically complex, and verbally ornamented with carefully chosen classical figures. The long episode (II.235–468) begins and ends from the viewpoint of Joseph, who first leads his expectant wife to Bethlehem (II.235–83) and then gazes with wonder at her newborn Child (II.409–68). Several hortatory appeals directed by the speaker towards his muses, to Mary and the Christ-child, and finally to God (II.301–08, 342–47, 397–408) punctuate the narration. Its central action, meanwhile, echoes Virgil and Scripture, with dramatic speeches, interpolated songs, and several deftly extended similes.

Joseph's introduction to the action is particularly effective. His awareness of his descent from the line of David, of David's example and the examples of his forefathers, of his people's hard-fought history and their covenant with God, provides a fine Hebraic counterpoint to the poem's otherwise Christian emphases. Joseph's first glimpse of Bethlehem provokes his introspective meditation on the city's historical significance for his people: "Secum proavos ex ordine reges / claraque facta ducum pulcramque ab origine gentem / mente recensebat tacita" (II.240–42; "He recounted privately in his quiet mind his royal ancestors in regular seccession, and the famous deeds of leaders and a race admirable from the outset"). As Joseph leads Mary to Bethlehem, his sense of heritage weighs heavily upon him.

Joesph remains unsure, however, of precisely what awaits him with the birth of Mary's child. His faith is that of the Old Testament prophets in vague, unspecified promises made to them by the Lord. He knows that one day his nation will surpass Rome in glory, but he does not know exactly how it will do so. In an impassioned address to the city of Bethlehem—"Bethlemiae

turres et non obscura meorum / regna patrum magnique olim
salvete, Penates" (II.252–53; "Towers of Bethlehem, and not
uncelebrated kingdom of my fathers, and great Penates, hail!")
—Joseph envisions the day when Rome will bow to it: "Parva
loquor: prono veniet diademate supplex / illa potens rerum
terrarumque inclita Roma, / et septem geminos submittet ad
oscula monteis" (II.260–62; "I say little: all-powerful Rome,
renowned throughout the world, will come as a suppliant with
bowed diadem, and will command her seven hills to kiss you").
Joseph's blind faith becomes all the more poignant against the
scene pressing in on him, as the inhabitants of Bethlehem pursue their urban routines unaware of the great event unfolding in
their midst (II.270–73).

The speaker's own direct intrusion into the action next
heightens several key passages. Following an established epic
convention, the speaker invokes heavenly spirits to aid him at
the climactic part of his narrative. The topic of Christ's birth
had precedent neither in the Old Testament nor in classical literature, so that the speaker feels the need for divine assistance
as he composes the sequence. Thus he turns not to the pagan
muses but to the sacred *coelicolae*, whom he had addressed at
the beginning of the poem: "Vos secretos per devia calleis, /
coelicolae, vos, si merui monstrate recessus / intactos" (II.303–
05; "Show me, o heaven dwellers, your secret paths off the
beaten track, your untouched recesses"). In a series of metono-
mies the speaker announces that he has come to the high point
of his sublime story, paradoxically involving such lowly topics
as an infant's cradle and a baby's crying: "Ventum ad cunas et
gaudia coeli" (II.305; "I have arrived at the cradle and joy of
heaven"). He seems seized by a power beyond himself, at once
borne up to his divine subject matter and likewise witnessing
divinity descend to earth.

Moments before the birth, the speaker addresses Mary. Ob-
jectifying himself as *vatem* in the third person, he begs protection and guidance from the Virgin, who has experienced these

same sensations in her own private way: "Accipe vatem, / diva, tuum; rege, diva, tuum" (II.342–43; "Receive your poet, goddess; guide him, goddess"). Within himself a conflict rages between completing the narration as he wishes and attending to banal matters that impinge upon his efforts. The challenge in narrating the action is to expand the brief material that Scripture offers him, stretching it to the length of an epic poem. The verb he uses is *pandere,* "to spread out, lay open." "Da pandere factum / mirum, indictum, insuetum, ingens" (II.345–46; "Allow me to unfold the marvelous, untold, extraordinary, far-reaching event"). Only with Mary's assistance can he maintain the middle road between absolute awe and the competing claims that subvert his intentions.

Still, despite the proximity that he wishes for and even feels, he cannot fully fathom the Virgin's emotions. He must keep his distance as a mediator between the action and his own audience. Addressing Mary, he explicitly asks her how she reacted to the animals at the crib (II.397–98). The beasts have attended to Christ, while mankind, whom Christ has come to save, ironically ignores Him. The irony impels the speaker to question the Father Himself about the power that inspired the animals (II.402–04). His questions, moreover, are not without satiric implications about the foibles of mankind, busy with its mundane affairs.[27]

The speaker's intrusions thus provide an Archimedean reference point for the audience to gauge its own distance from the event. As intermediary between the action and his own audience, the speaker enjoys a special vision of history. As close as he comes to the action and its participants, however, he still preserves his separate identity in time and space. Much of the interior action, the participants' emotions, and the final significance of the event remain impenetrable to his understanding. He is, after all, a limited human being, however much divine inspiration has aided his intelligence. The pastoral stance of feigning a humble style defines this attitude. Moreover, many of the verbal techniques that he uses to communicate with his wider audience invoke the ineffability of the action. Mere words cannot convey what really has happened.

From this perspective the classical conventions become a form of insulation acknowledging the narrative's remoteness while yet conveying it clearly and comprehensibly. At every turn the speaker endows those conventions with his own characteristic insight. In describing the cave where the birth occurs, for example, he lightly acknowledges from the *Aeneid* Virgil's description of the cave where Aeneas and Dido pledged their love (*Aeneid* IV.160) and of the cave where Aeneas began his journey to the underworld (*Aeneid* VI.42–43): "Est specus haud ingens parvae sub moenibus urbis, / incertum manibusne hominum genione potentis / naturae formatus" (II.284–86; "There is a not very large cave close to the city's walls, unknown whether formed by human hands or potent nature's skill"). The speaker thereby recognizes the irony that the Savior makes His first appearance on earth in a cave suited for diverse functions. Likewise he dramatizes Mary's feelings about the birth by implicitly evoking Venus's affection for Aeneas from the prelude to the shield episode of the *Aeneid* (VIII.388). Here Mary addresses the Christ-child in language reminiscent of Venus's warmth and concern in the classical epic: "Ergo ego te gremio reptantem et nota potentem / ubera, care puer, molli studiosa fovebo / amplexu?" (II.334–36; "Will I caress you with delight in soft embraces, dear Boy, as you bounce on my lap, seeking my familiar breast?").

The moment of the birth itself motivates several figures in the high style. The conventional epic device to render such miraculous action is the long simile. One that the speaker uses has its intertextual roots in shorter comparisons from Virgil's *Eclogue* VIII.14–15 and *Georgics* II.202 and III.325–26. Its properties thus belong to the pastoral middle style rather than to the epic high style, and its tone renders just the right hominess, ease, and familiarity at such a delicate moment. The angel had told Mary that she would experience the birth without pain or discomfort. Appropriately the vehicle of the simile compares such a birth to the sensation of seeing a spring shower without feeling it: "Qualis rorem, cum vere tepenti / per tacitum matutinus desudat Eous" (II. 360–61; "As when the morning star silently exudes dew on a warm day and everywhere round drops glisten on the grass"). The surprise elicits an exclamation from the speaker, "Mira fides" (II. 366; "Wonderful faith") and the interpenetration of his surprise with Mary's is complete.

Book II ends with a hymn that Joseph sings at the Baby's crib after the host of angels has descended from heaven. There is a gentle comic irony in his recognition that he has just slept through the event. Now, in a deeply meditative tone Joseph contrasts the humility of Christ's birth with the magnificence of His destiny, groping towards a fuller comprehension of the event as he adds phrase after phrase to his song. He begins with the absence of material greatness attending Christ's birth. There is no regal splendor in the cave (II. 444–46). Instead, signs of greatness have proceeded from heaven (II. 452–53). Bursting with inspiration, he foresees other signs in the near future: "Et tamen hanc sedem reges, haec undique magni / antra petent populi" (II. 454–55; "For all that, kings will seek out this abode, as well as people from all over").

The composition of these events leads Joseph to perceive Christ's role in more analytic terms. Advancing to a pastoral vision of the distant future, he portrays Christ as the Good Shepherd in fulfillment of the Word. In a final application of his own awareness as a beneficiary of Christ's coming, Joseph celebrates his privilege of being among the first to honor God's Son (II. 466–69).

God the the Father's speech at the opening of Book III balances Joseph's prayer at the closing of Book II. Whereas Joseph's setpiece is meditative in tone, a Christian hymn adapting the pastoral topos of the Good Shepherd from the Old Testament Psalms to the New Testament life of Christ, God's is more dramatic. Apocalyptic in tone, it draws at the outset upon the terminal books of Scripture, Genesis and the Book of Revelation,

to record events prior to man's fall. Before His audience of
angels in heaven, God reminisces about the act of creation, the
revolt of the fallen, and the victory of the good (III.36–39).
Because His audience knows the details, God can recount the
story in its barest, most impressionistic outlines. The open-
endedness recalls the vague symbolic account in the Book of
Revelation 12.4–11, which itself draws upon Old Testament
apocalypses, particularly Daniel, to represent its vision of God's
people in trouble: "Fida manus mecum mansistis et ultima tan-
dem / experti coelo victricia signa tulistis / aeternumque alta
fixistis in arce trophaeum" (III.43–45; "You stayed with me as a
faithful band, and, sorely tested to the limit, you bore victori-
ous insignia to heaven and established an eternal trophy on its
high citadel"). The voice of the wrathful God echoes Genesis 3, when He recalls how He exiled Adam and Eve for eating
the forbidden fruit. Again He addresses His audience of angels
as intermediaries who visited those punishments upon the first
pair (III.55–56).

But this God is also a merciful one. His voice mellows as He
proposes reconciliation with man, and He announces to His
angels the beginning of a new dispensation (III.67–70). The
variation of tones characterizing God's speech is subtle and
secure. Ranging from eschatological to patriarchal, from aveng-
ing to conciliatory, and from judgmental to merciful, it demonstrates the pastoral style's full flexibility in accommodating such
epic extremes to its central Latinate norm.

DE PARTU VIRGINIS: PASTORAL RESOLUTION

If the scene in heaven provides a grandiloquent contrast to
the preceding one of Christ's birth in a humble cave, the return
to earth and the pastoral landscape in the lines that follow provide yet another contrast. The angel's announcement to the
shepherds and their subsequent visit to Christ's manger unfold
in a series of set speeches balanced on a deliciate axis. At the
center is the shepherds' reaction. Stylistically it transposes the

text of Virgil's celebrated *Eclogue* IV to its own needs. Before it is the angel's announcement; and after it, an elaborate canticle in praise of God the Father. The speaker's description of the characters' accompanying gestures links the monologues: they include the angel's splendid appearance, the shepherds' dance of joy, and a triumphant pageant enacted by the angels outside Christ's cave. The poem's stylistic accomplishment rises to its height of perfection in these lines. They are at once allusive and original, jubilant and controlled.

The angel's opening address is gentle and ingratiating: "Tunc ait: 'O parvi vigiles gregis, o bona pubes / sylvarum, superis gratum genus, ite, beati / pastores, ite, antra novis intendite sertis'" (III.135–37; "Then he said, 'O guardians of a small flock, kind youths of the woods, a race pleasing to the gods, go, blessed shepherds, go, hang new garlands around the cave'"). He tells them that God—"moderator Olympi" (III.139)—has chosen them to view "reginam ad cunas positumque in stramine regem" (III.138; "the queen of heaven and, placed into a cradle amid straw, the King of creation"). He stresses the sheer joy of the event, its unusual nature, its unparalleled occurrence as he exhorts them: "Insuetum et silvis stipula deducite carmen" (III.142; "Summon forth on your pipe a song unprecedented in these woods").

The angel's rhetoric proves highly effective. The shepherds respond with eagerness to follow his command. They hold animated discussions about how to find the cave. At this point the poem's language becomes particularly translucent as the angel's words generate such ready activity: "Olli inter sese vario sermone volutant / quid superum mandata velint, quas quaerere cunas" (III.145–46; "They occupy themselves with lively talk about the meaning of God's commands and what cradle they should seek"). Through simplicity and directness God's creatures now acquire a firm hold on the universe of discourse.

Soon the shepherds break into song and dance. Their festivities occur as a tangible sign of the profound impact made by the angel's words. In accord with this impact, the poetry evokes sensations that encompass visual, aural, tactile, and olfactory powers: "Perque intervalla canentes / cum plausu choreisque et multisono modulatu / vestibuli ante aditum statuunt; . . . / longisque advelant limina sertis / et late Idaliam spargunt cum baccare myrtum" (III.163–68; "And singing rhythmically with clapping and dancing and harmonious modulation, they stood in front of the entrance; . . . and they covered the threshold with long garlands and scattered Idalian myrtle with sweet-smelling herbs"). The enumeration of their simple gifts—the fruits of the earth and the products of their labors—imparts a wonderful dignity to the episode.

When they arrive at the cave, two shepherds step forth to sing a song to the Christ-child. As we have seen above, they perform a very special function. One is Aegon, older and well known in the community, "ingens pastoribus" (III.191; "a leader among the shepherds"). The other is Lycidas, young and "vix urbe sua, vix colle propinquo / cognitus" (III.192–93; "hardly known in his own town or on the nearby hill). Together they represent a microcosmic hierarchy of any society, from old, famous, and powerful to young, humble, and lowly. As they begin to sing, however, their differences of age and rank blend into perfect harmony. One complements the other, and together "rustica septena modulantur carmina canna" (III.196; "they modulate their rustic songs on a seven-piped flute"). Moreover, their musical tribute reflects the contribution of yet another shepherd, the far distant Tityrus. They claim, with a verbal echo of Virgil's fourth eclogue, to be singing his songs, "dignas Romano consule" (III.199; "worthy of a Roman consul"). With his physical distance Tityrus becomes a figure of the controlling poet. Despite his absence, the whole company comes to feel his presence in the strongest possible way. His song amounts to a nearly verbatim transposition of words, phrases, and whole lines from Virgil's *Eclogue* IV, the prophetic encomium honoring Pollio, the father of an anticipated hero. It invades their precincts and, though composed long ago, makes itself felt here and now. The gift of Tityrus-Virgil is the most substantial gift that the Child receives, and it is one that more-over remains just as available in the current age to contemporary audiences as it was then to the shepherds and the Infant Jesus.

Its availability is particularly significant in a philological sense. The preservation of Virgil's *Eclogue* IV since antiquity, its evocation here in a new context, and the singers' pious fidelity to the original, constitute a remarkable gesture of poetic humility. Generations of medieval commentators thought that Virgil's poem prophesied the birth of Christ. By reproducing that poem to honor Christ, the shepherds—and the controlling poet—honor not only God, but also Virgil. In fact, the passage represents the poem's most sustained and concentrated debt to Virgil, and possibly the most self-conscious homage to Virgil by any major poet in the entire Renaissance. The boldness of its direct transcription from *Eclogue* IV gives the passage the quality of a jewelled inset. The few additions to the original and certain minor changes (as in III.211–12, where Virgil's third person verbs become second person ones to conform with Tityrus's direct address) heighten that quality. At the same time the lines surrounding it do not suffer by comparison. Because it accords so perfectly with the rest of the poem, the transcription from Virgil's eclogue demonstrates to what extent Sannazaro's entire epic captures the essence of Virgil's pastoral art.

If the humanist movement in its embrace of the vernacular during the late fifteenth and early sixteenth centuries were experiencing a form of hermeneutic pessimism, a sense that the meaning and nuances of the past were forever inaccessible to modern ears, Sannazaro's cento of Virgil's *Eclogue* IV exemplifies a radical response to the problem. Some might argue that one can only repeat the words of antiquity without improving upon them, and possibly even without fully understanding them. Sannazaro, however, would argue that one can repeat them in new contexts that illuminate other, unsuspected meanings issuing from them. Such an understanding requires not the overcoming of a sense of temporality separating the past from the present, but rather the acceptance of that sense of temporality. By acknowledging the differences between past and present and by anticipating their consequences, one turns time into a supportive ground that links events in history instead of separating them. What is important beyond the verbal signs themselves and their actual or intended meanings, is the sharing of attitudes toward those signs by author and audience. This sharing unlocks their potential, so that what is left unsaid in words becomes understood in the act of interpretation.

Nor do the Virgilian words, phrases, and lines sound inappropriate in the shepherds' voices. Thus they proclaim, "Scilicet haec virgo est, haec sunt Saturnia regna, / haec nova progenies coelo descensit ab alto" (III.202–03, echoing Virgil's *Eclogue* IV.6–7; "Here is the virgin, here Saturn's kingdoms; here descends a new race from high heaven"). The most famous line of the Virgilian prophecy remains intact: "toto gens aurea mundo/ surget" (III.204–05, repeating Virgil's *Eclogue* IV.9; "a golden age shall spring up throughout the whole world"). The Virgilian *sceleris* lends itself perfectly to the Christian concept of sin, for with Christ "qua duce, si qua manent sceleris vestigia nostri, / irrita perpetua solvent formidine terras" (III.206–07, repeating Virgil's *Eclogue* IV.13–14; "as leader, if any traces of our sin remain, rendered void they shall release the earth from perpetual fear"). The topos of the serpent in Virgil's poem recalls the one from St. John's Revelation that God pronounced earlier: "Occidet et serpens" (III.209, repeating Virgil's *Eclogue* IV.24; "And the serpent shall die").

Expanding their song, the speakers address the Child directly, turning Virgil's third-person prophecy into an immediate fulfillment: "Tune deum vitam accipies, divisque videbis / permistos heroas et ipse videberis illis, / pacatumque reges patriis virtutibus orbem" (III.211–13, repeating Virgil's *Eclogue* IV.15–17; "You shall accept the life of the gods, and shall behold heroes consorting with gods; and you shall be seen by them, and shall rule the peaceful orb with your father's virtues"). One of the passage's rare allusions beyond Virgil occurs in the next line. It evokes Lucretius's *De rerum natura* I.9, where Lucretius addresses Venus as the spirit of love and the prime force behind the movements of the universe: "Pacatumque nitet diffuso lumine caelum" (I.9; "The sky, made peaceful, glows with diffused radiance"). Here Tityrus exclaims upon the power of Christian love: "Adspice felici diffusum lumine coelum / camposque, fluviosque, ipsasque in montibus herbas" (III.214–15; "Behold heaven, diffused with happy light, and fields and streams and vegetation on the mountains"). The shift in reference from Venus to Christian love is powerful. It exemplifies the way Christianity has transformed all ancient thought and feeling, drawing strength from analogical resemblances, confirming them in the Christian vision and the Christian vision in them.

Another example of transposition occurs in the next lines: "Ipsae lacte domum referent distenta capellae / ubera: nec magnos metuent armenta leones" (III.217–18, repeating Virgil's *Eclogue* IV.21–22; "The goats themselves shall bring home their udders swollen with milk; nor shall the herds fear the mightly lions"). Again the diction comes verbatim from Virgil's *Eclogue* IV, and again it sustains a yet wider reference to the word of God. This time it evokes the Gospels' accounts foretelling the apostles' preaching, teaching, and resistance to persecution (cf. Mark 6.8–11, Matthew 10.6–39, and Luke 10.2–12).

Still other prophecies emerge as direct quotations from Virgil in more general ways: "Ipsa tibi blandos fundent cunabula flores" (III.223, repeating Virgil's *Eclogue* IV.23; "Your birthplace itself shall pour forth pleasant flowers for you"); "et durae quercus sudabunt roscida mella" (III.224, from Virgil's *Eclogue* IV.30; "and the hardy oaks shall perspire dewy honey"); "omnis feret omnia tellus" (III.25, from Virgil's *Eclogue* IV.39; "every land shall produce everything"). For the distant future, after "firmata virum te fecerit aetas" (III.226, from Virgil's *Eclogue* IV.37; "time has given you the strength of manhood"), the speaker foresees a period of wars and explorations leading directly to contemporary times: "Alter erit tum tiphys et altera

quae vehat Argo / delectos heroas; erunt etiam altera bella"
(III.228–29, repeating Virgil's *Eclogue* IV.34–35; "Then there
shall be another Tiphys and another Argo who shall transport
chosen heroes; there shall also be other wars"). Of course, Virgil's prophecy could not have foretold the voyages and wars of
the fifteenth and sixteenth centuries, but his poem accommodates those events and the shepherds' quotation of it reinforces
the accommodation. Finally, the last lines return to the event
of Christ's birth and they encourage the Child: "Incipe, parve
puer, risu cognoscere matrem" (III.231, repeating Virgil's *Eclogue* IV.60; "Little boy, begin to know your mother by her
smile"). The song thus ends as it began, with the shepherds re-
joicing in the presence of the Lord.

Balancing Lycidas's and Aegon's pastoral song is another
angelic appearance, this time of a whole heavenly host. The
angels' radiant splendor and their lofty song in praise of God the
Father contrast with the shepherds' rustic dance and their humble strewing of garlands. The angels appear as "terna agmina
ternis / instructa ordinibus belli simulacra ciebant" (III.241–
42; "a battle line divided into three colums that performs a simulacrum of war drawn up into three ranks"). Each of the three
divisions enacts a separate event. The first stages a pageant in
honor of Christ's Passion, displaying His thorns and nails as
proof of mankind's salvation, "sublimemque crucem immanem-
que collumnam" (III.254; "and the high cross and the towering
column"). Another group sings a hymn in praise of God the
Father, and that hymn itself blends imperceptibly with a hymn
sung by the third group in praise of the Triune God: "Tibi
nomina mille, / mille potestatum, regnorum insignia mille"
(III.275–76; "You have a thousand names, a thousand powers,
a thousand royal distinctions"). These military trappings mark
a gesture towards the epic convention of the heroic games in
Iliad XXIII and *Aeneid* V.

The angels' hymn leads to the poem's long, final section. It
introduces the tutelary deity of the river Jordan, who recounts
Proteus's extensive prediction of events in the later life of Christ.

The river Jordan aptly figures the start of Christ's public career. In ages to come, His baptism there by St. John would itself prefigure the initiation of every Christian into the life of Christ. The baptism therefore functions as a central event in Jordan's narration of Christ's later ministry. References to it occur twice within a hundred lines, though Jordan, a pagan god, seems only dimly to understand its significance. The tutelary deity plays the role of mediator and contemplator, to whom just a partial vision of Christ's future magnitude has been granted.

Jordan resides in a cave of water surrounded by his daughters, minor tributaries. The setting draws upon Virgil's account of Proteus's cave in *Georgic* IV.418–529. It also recalls the final chapter of *Arcadia,* when the speaker descends into the source of all the earth's rivers in preparation for his restoration of ancient poetry. Finally it evokes the watery setting of *Piscatoria* IV, where Proteus demonstrated the poet's own powers of multiform variability. Jordan's cave fulfills those passages from *Arcadia* and the *Piscatoria* as much as it concludes *De Partu Virginis.* There Jordan lives in quiet meditation (III.282). He guards an urn from which the river's waters pour forth. The urn itself is decorated with figures and engravings depicting events in the river's history (III.299–301). Its centerpiece is Christ's baptism by St. John, attended by His disciples, approved by the Father, and watched over by the Holy Spirit in the form of a dove (III.307–09). Jordan's response to this scene is sustained wonder. He gazes fixedly at the urn, rapt in marvelous contemplation as he lets the waters issue forth.

At the moment of Christ's birth, a disruption shakes the foundations of Jordan's cave. Huge waves roll in and they portend for the deity the fulfillment of a prophecy once told him by Proteus.[28] Jordan now addresses his daughters with an account of that prophecy. He claims to reproduce Proteus's own words, though he warns that their original speaker is notoriously elusive and difficult to grasp. Nonetheless, "mendax si caetera Proteus, / non tamen hoc vanas effudit carmine voces" (III.336–37; "if Proteus is a liar about certain things, in the case of this song

he did not utter vain words"). Proteus's veracity raises a problematic issue. As *Piscatoria* IV showed, his ever mutable nature
mirrors the changing history of the world. His talent for assum-
ing various shapes casts him in the role of the archetypal artificer, and, as artificer, a figure of the poet with special reference
to the poet's gift of invention. Moreover, his ever transforming
powers complement the poet's obligation to record change, human history, and man's destiny. For all these reasons, Proteus is
an appropriate bearer of truth despite his reputation for lying.
He had thus related to Jordan the news of Christ's life, its effect
on the lives of others, and the decisive impact that it will make
on the world's history. It represents the culmination of this
poem's endeavors, since the primary topic of this poem, the
birth of Christ, is but a prelude to His life and its importance in
history.

As Jordan quotes it, Proteus's account of Christ's Life (III. 338–
485) emphasizes the miracles that He will perform. Proteus
praises the river, declaring that its fame will surpass the glory of
the Nile, the Indus, the Ganges, the Tiber, the Danube, and
the Po. In its waters Christ will launch His career of caring for
the afflicted bodies of men in His time and for the souls of men
ever after: "Cedet et infestae violentior ira Dianae" (III. 352;
"The violent wrath of hostile Diana—the patroness of unfore-
seen death—will come to nothing"). The curing of lepers, pa-
ralytics, the blind, the deaf, and the raising of the dead furnish
signs of more penetrating wonders that Christ will achieve in
human history. All nature will proclaim His lordship: "Huic tu
nutantes quoties assurgere montes / et mirum insuetas curvare
cacumina silvas / adspicies?" (III. 395–97; "How often will you
see mountains rise nodding to Him and—o marvel!—forests
bend the tips of their trees to him in an unprecedented manner"). Virgilian echoes from *Eclogues* I. 56, VI. 28, and *Georgic*
I. 188 with their evocation of the world beyond Jordan's milieu
here reinforce the universality of Christ's effect on mankind:
He has come for Roman and Jew, pagan and believer, and He
offers his beneficence to all.

Proteus forecasts that Christ's baptism in the river Jordan will draw Him out of obscurity and into the public arena. At that time Father, Son, and Holy Spirit will declare His ministry and a new age will commence. Proteus moreover prophesies that when that act occurs, Jordan will burst into song addressing his nymphs: "Ite citae, date thura pias adolenda per aras, / Caeruleae comites" (III.408–09); "Go quickly, Caerulean companions, bring sweet-smelling incense to the holy altars"). The implications of Christ's ministry will reach far into the future. Through His disciples He will touch many people in far distant lands and future times. Proteus refers to Christ's command to His apostles to go forth to various nations, declaring that what they do on earth shall be done in Heaven. Though they clearly evoke Matthew 16.18–19, Proteus's words do not repeat any of the Vulgate's diction or grammatical construction, partly because Proteus's own diction and syntax have already established their own stylistic register throughout the elevated discourse, and partly because Proteus remains a pagan deity with no real Christian equivalent anyway (III.438–41). In his own classical remoteness from the Christian era, Proteus, like his audience Jordan, lacks full comprehension. The significance of Christ's life holds mystery for both speaker and audience, and indeed it must preserve its mystery even for the controlling poet and his own present audience. It forever eludes human understanding.

The choice, therefore, of the river Jordan and, through his voice, of Proteus, as the final speakers in the poem's action, helps to reinforce the sacred and universal meaning of Christ's birth. Earlier speakers in the poem—the angels, Mary, Elizabeth, Joseph, David, the shepherds—all expressed that meaning directly. The river's deity and Proteus express it ironically both by their very natures as superhuman beings and by their status as living remnants of ancient culture. They also express it by functioning, in their own ways, as figures of the controlling poet. Proteus's role as a type of poet is already clear from *Piscatoria* IV. Jordan's is established by acting as a mouthpiece for Proteus.

The strategy whereby Jordan recounts Proteus's words now
effectively allows the poem to end with three separate but interlocking conclusions. First Jordan represents Proteus's epilogue;
then he offers his own; and finally the controlling speaker sets
down his. Each of these epilogues moreover asserts its own
tone. Proteus's has the most conventional poetic assignment.
The mutable god confesses inadequacy in understanding and
representing the topic he is charged with. He describes his own
poetic craft, in terms reminiscent of Dante's "navicella," as one
"vectus super alta phaselo" (III.478, "conveyed on the high
seas in a mere skiff"). He acknowledges the aid of the muses,
but implies that even their most generous attention would not
confer any greater power on his voice or illuminate his mind
with any sharper insight. Nor would he achieve finer results with
any other faculties. The topic defies his attempts to continue.
At the very end of his speech Proteus denies that "Laudatos
valeam venturi principis actus / enumerare novoque amplecti
singula cantu" (III.484–85; "I will be strong enough to list the
praiseworthy deeds of the prince to come, and to embrace them
one by one in any new song"). Glory belongs to God alone. Of
the poem's three epilogues, then, this one reflects the greatest
humility.

Jordan's epilogue has a different aim. As a figure for the per-
sistence and flow of time, the river functions as an apt agency
for expressing the poem's final temporal concerns. Thus Jordan
ends his speech when he sees the first rays of dawn illuminate
the eastern sky (III.490–92). A recognition of time's passage
emphasizes once more the poem's deep concern about its own
distance from antiquity. Not only does Jordan evoke the scriptural past as Proteus evokes the classical past, but he also evokes
the present's separation from both. The call to another day signifies the moment of a new beginning as well as a recognition of
its essential continuity with the old. Dawn comes gradually,
progressively, as the profusion of present participial verbs implies, so that no really distinct break marks the new day. The

present grows out of the past without rupture or discontinuity, while the past is recuperable in the present.

And the primary vehicle of recuperation is language. Words from the past can shine as radiantly as dawn in the texts of the present. The final epilogue is the speaker's. His voice here and now takes on a concreteness heard nowwhere else in the poem. Earlier it had emerged as the omniscient, impersonal voice of an epic poet intent on communicating his muses' inspiration to his larger public audience. Now in the poem's final lines it emerges as the personal voice of Jacopo Sannazaro, a human being rooted in the world of contemporary reality. If Proteus's epilogue stressed the poet's humbling by God's infinite glory, and if Jordan's epilogue stressed time's force and its historical continuity, this one stresses the power of location and its persistent influence on the poet's endeavors to wrestle with, conquer, and subdue the intractability of language.

The location is, of course, Mergellina, the speaker's home in Posillipo, the place where the muses first inspired him, and the place where he is now completing his task of writing *De Partu Virginis*. Thus he takes leave of his poem and turns towards the Mediterranean shore that has long nourished his activity as a poet: "Hactenus, o Superi, partus tentasse verendos / sit satis: optatem poscit me dulcis ad umbram / Pausilypus" (III.505–07; "At this point, o heavenly muses, it should be enough to have attempted holy verses on Christ's birth: sweet Posillipo now calls me to its welcome shade"). The villa of Mergellina awaits him, not just as a place of retirement, but as a place where his experiments with the power of language will come into full bloom. The poem's last three lines hint, moreover, that the poet plans to continue his poetic production even into his retirement: "Mergillina, novos fundunt ubi citria flores, / citria Medorum sacros referentia luces, / et mihi non solita nectit de fronde coronam" (III.511–13; "And Mergellina, where cedar trees scatter new flowers, the cedars of Media restoring holy illumination, will weave for me a crown of unusual foliage").

The poem's final impulse, then, registered in its closing image of Mergellina, is an intensely private, personal, lyric one for Sannazaro. It is as though his epic had opened out to include all that is valuable in his world, and were now closing on a note consonant with both tradition and the individual talent. The amplitude of the pastoral mode easily accommodates this lyric voice, and it affirms once more the question of language's power to communicate over the span of time.

Indeed its presence and immediacy imply that time is no temporal chasm that separates events in history, but rather a supportive ground that links them. The speaker's distance from the past affords him a positive and productive possibility of understanding it. This understanding repudiates the naive historicism of the strict Virgilians and the Ciceronians who claimed a genuine encounter with the past only by thinking with its thoughts, words, and syntax. Instead it elevates the idea of continuity and tradition, of what in our own time Hans-Georg Gadamer has called "an effective historical consciousness" that fuses the past horizon with our own present one.[29] The solution to the problem of understanding the past and replicating its norms in the present is to seek a coherence of meaning that can transcend the horizon of both. In his life's work Sannazaro had achieved that solution, and *De Partu Virginis* concludes by recognizing it.

*   *   *

Sannazaro had settled at Mergellina in 1506, just when he began composing *De Partu Virginis* and twenty years before he published it. During those years that villa was by no means an abode for inactive retirement. After finishing *De Partu Virginis*, however, Sannazaro gave no evidence of planning another major poem, nor even of producing shorter poems in either Latin or Italian. He may or may not have written several epigrams after 1526, but we have really no idea how many he started and abandoned or deemed unworthy of publication.

Despite the fame of *Arcadia* and the *Piscatoriae* in Italy and abroad, *De Partu Virginis* resisted emulation. Among other brief epics on Christ's life, most emphasized different events. Marino's *Strage degl'innocenti* (1632) portrayed the slaughter of the innocents, while Tansillo's *Le lacrime di San Pietro* (begun in 1539, published in 1585) and Malherbe's French version, *Les Larmes de Saint Pierre* (1587), focused on the crucifixion. In England Giles Fletcher's *Christ's Victorie and Triumph* (1610) depicted the harrowing of hell, while Milton's *Paradise Regained* (1671) encapsulated Christ's whole career within the action of the temptation. It is true that Milton echoed the topic of *De Partu Virginis* in his *Ode on the Morning of Christ's Nativity*, but nonetheless Sannazaro's major Latin poem had remarkably few imitators in any language.

One reason may have been Sannazaro's very choice of Latin as a literary medium. Historically the movement to develop a Neo-Latin literature in Italy and throughout Europe reached an abrupt end within a generation after Sannazaro's death, as much for political and ecclesiastical reasons as for philological ones. As Latin came to be identified with Roman Catholic orthodoxy, its appeal as a pan-European literary language diminished. The Counter-Reformation, moreover, soon encouraged the use of the vernacular against Protestant heresy. In the north, the forces of Neo-Latin literature were just gaining a foothold with such superb stylists as Marc-Antoine Muret, Conrad Celtis, Joannes Secundus, and Maciej Sarbiewsky when the Protestants rejected the idea of *Latinitas* altogether. Even those northern Latinists sympathetic with Sannazaro's Roman orthodoxy would find fault with his poem. Erasmus, for example, felt that "he would have deserved more praise if he had treated his sacred subject somewhat more reverently."[30] It would seem then that Sannazaro's detailed attention to Latin style had reaped insufficient rewards.

Under these conditions Mergellina became more and more a place of seclusion for Sannazaro in the last four years of his life. There he supervised reprintings of his *Arcadia*, *Piscatoriae*, and *De Partu Virginis* in 1527 and 1528 and he was planning the first publication of his Italian *Rime* at the time of his death in 1530. He had already entrusted his shorter Latin poems to Antonio Garlon for posthumous publication. And he continued to make minor revisions in *De Partu Virginis*, which received its definitive printing at the Aldine Press in 1535. Meanwhile the rest of Europe went its own way through treaties, leagues, wars, and convolutions unexampled in earlier history. In 1526 the threatening Turks defeated the Hungarians at Mohacs, and in 1529 they attacked Vienna. By initiating the League of Cognac in 1526 France allied herself with Northern Italy against Spain and the empire, leading to Charles V's sack of Rome in 1527. With the Peace of Cambrai in 1529 France finally renounced her claims to Naples, which now fell fully under Spanish control. That year, Henry VIII summoned the reform parliament in England.

None of these events seems to have meant very much to Sannazaro. Nowhere in his writings or revisions does he comment on them or even refer to them. Whether by an aggressive act of the will or merely out of a resigned world-weariness, he allowed Mergellina to insulate him from religion, wars, and politics— from everything, in fact, but his pursuit of older literature. By the time he died on 6 August 1530, he was too caught up in its rarefied textuality to pay current history any mind. He had accomplished his own aims by developing the experimental, archaeological, and philological uses of pastoral to their sovereign potential.

NOTES

INTRODUCTION

1. Printed in *Le opere volgari di M. J. Sannazaro* (Padua: Giuseppe Comino, 1723), with commentaries by Tommaso Porcacchi, Francesco Sansovino, and Giovambattista Massarengo, and the 1593 biography by G. B. Crispo; Sansovino's introduction appears on pp. 321–24.

2. Preface to Book II in Eugenio Garin, ed., *Prosatori latini del Quattrocento* (Milan: Riccardo Ricciardi, 1952), p. 604. For the development of rhetoric and philology in this light, see Aldo Scaglione, *The Classical Theory of Composition* (Chapel Hill: University of North Carolina Press, 1972) and George Kennedy, *Classical Rhetoric and Its Christian and Secular Tradition* (Chapel Hill: University of North Carolina Press, 1980). For its influence on historiography and literature see Peter Burke, *The Renaissance Sense of the Past* (London: Edward Arnold, 1969) and Nancy Struever, *The Language of History in the Renaissance* (Princeton, N.J.: Princeton University Press, 1970). For its effect on literary production see Thomas M. Greene, *The Light in Troy* (New Haven, Conn.: Yale University Press, 1982), and Terence Cave, *The Cornucopian Text* (Oxford: Clarendon Press, 1979). A close study of its manifestation in France is Claude-Gilbert Dubois, *Mythe et langage au 16ᵉ siecle* (Paris: Ducros, 1970).

3. Leon Battista Alberti, *Opere volgari*, ed. Cecil Grayson (Bari: Laterza, 1960), I, 154.

4. Garin, *Prosatori*, p. 742.

5. *Ibid.*, p. 902.

6. Desiderius Erasmus, *Ciceronianus*, trans. Izora Scott (New York: Columbia University Teachers College Press, 1908), p. 121.

7. See E. J. Kenney, *The Classical Text: Aspects of Editing in the Age of the Printed Book* (Berkeley: University of California Press, 1974) and Elizabeth Eisenstein, *The Printing Press as an Agent of Change*, 2 vols. (Cambridge: Cambridge University Press, 1979), I, 72–74. The work of Walter Ong, S.J., is central to this issue, especially *Rhetoric, Romance, and Technology* (Ithaca, N.Y.: Cornell University Press, 1971) and *Interfaces of the Word* (Ithaca, N.Y.: Cornell University Press, 1977).

8. For critical commentary on the pastoral see Ellen Zetzel Lambert, *Placing Sorrow* (Chapel Hill: University of North Carolina Press, 1976); for its Theocritan conventions, see Thomas Rosenmeyer, *The Green Cabinet* (Berkeley: University of California Press, 1969); for its medieval and Renaissance forms, see Mia Gerhardt, *Essai d'analyse littéraire de la pastorale* (Assen: Van

Gorcum, 1950); Renato Poggioli comments brilliantly on them in *The Oaten Flute* (Cambridge, Mass.: Harvard University Press, 1975); and Helen Cooper surveys them as recurrent characteristics of the European mind in *Pastoral: Medieval into Renaissance* (Totowa, N.J.: Rowman and Littlefield, 1977). In *Spenser, Marvell, and Renaissance Pastoral* (Cambridge, Mass.: Harvard University Press, 1970), Patrick Cullen distinguishes usefully between the Arcadian pastoral of Sannazaro and the moral pastoral of Mantuan, pp. 13–26.

CHAPTER 1

1. I have relied upon the best modern biography, Antonio Altamura, *Jacopo Sannazaro* (Naples: Silvio Viti, 1951) for most of the details that follow; see also the narrower accounts, Erasmo Pèrcopo, *La vita di Jacopo Sannazaro* (Naples: Società di Storia Patria, 1931) and Francesco Torraca, *Jacopo Sannazaro* (Naples: Vincenzo Morano, 1879).

2. For the historical context up to and after his birth, see Benedetto Croce, *A History of the Kingdom of Naples*, trans. Frances Frenaye (Chicago: University of Chicago Press, 1970).

3. For accounts of Panormita and other humanists in his circle, see Vittorio Rossi, *Il Quattrocento*, 5th ed. (Milan: Vallardi, 1953); Giuseppe Toffanin, *Storia dell'umanesimo*, 3 vols. (Bologna: N. Zanichelli, 1950), also in an abridged English translation by Elio Gianturco, *History of Humanism* (New York: Las Americas, 1954); Eugenio Garin, *Italian Humanism*, trans. Peter Munz (New York: Harper and Row, 1965); and Francesco Tateo, *L'umanesimo meridionale* (Bari: Laterza, 1972).

4. See Francesco Tateo, *Umanesimo etico di Giovanni Pontano* (Lecce: Milella, 1972).

5. For these Neapolitan humanists see Mario Emilio Cosenza, *A Biographical and Bibliographical Dictionary of the Italian Humanists*, 6 vols. (Boston: G. K. Hall, 1962), and Catherine B. Avery, *New Century Italian Renaissance Encyclopedia* (New York: Appleton-Century-Crofts, 1972).

6. For dating see Silvio Monti, "Ricerche sulla cronologia dei *Dialoghi* del Pontano," *Annali della Facolta di Lettere e Filosofia dell'Universita di Napoli* 10 (1962–63), 254–76.

7. Giovanni Pontano, *I Dialoghi*, ed. Carmelo Previtera (Florence: Sansoni, 1943), p. 85; all subsequent references in parentheses are to this edition. For illuminating commentary on *Antonius* and *Actius*, see Tateo, *Umanesimo etico*; on *Aegidius*, Giuseppe Toffanin, *Giovanni Pontano fra l'uomo e la natura* (Bologna: Zanichelli, 1938); and for a perceptive study of their place in the classical tradition and humanist innovation, David Marsh, *The Quattrocento Dialogue* (Cambridge, Mass.: Harvard University Press, 1980). A close reading of these humanist texts should warn us not to limit our concept of Renaissance rhetoric exclusively to the play of figures and tropes. That limitation derives from the later Ramistic emphasis on *elocutio*, but it still persists in the work of small armies of plodding scholiasts on the one hand and in the brute force of recent "deconstructionist" literary theoreticians on the other.

Among the modern scholiasts, Brian Vickers dogmatically reduces rhetoric to a sterile taxonomy of tropes with his frigid insistence that *elocutio* is the hinge of rhetorical theory; in his vapid criticism of current scholarship, "Rhetorical and Anti-Rhetorical Tropes," *Comparative Criticism* 3 (1981), 105–32, Vickers labels other approaches as "anti-rhetorical."

8. For rich historical background see George Hersey, *Alfonso II and the Artistic Renewal of Naples* (New Haven, Conn.: Yale University Press, 1969); see also Ernesto Pontieri, *Per la storia del regno di Ferrante I d'Aragona* (Naples: Edizione scientifiche italiane, 1969).

9. See Maria Corti, "Le tre redazioni della 'Pastorale' di P. J. De Jennaro," *Giornale Storico della Letteratura Italiana* 131 (1954), 305–51, especially pp. 342–51.

10. See Ludwig Pastor, *The History of the Popes*, trans. F. I. Antrobus, 36 vols., 5th ed. (London: Routledge and Kegan Paul, 1950), vols. 3–10 covering 1458–1534.

11. Collected in *Un divorzio ai tempi di Leone X da XL lettere inedite di Jacopo Sannazaro*, ed. Ettore Nunziante (Rome: Loreto Pasqualucci, 1887).

12. See *The Greek Bucolic Poets*, trans. J. M. Edmonds, Loeb Classical Library (London: Heinemann, 1912); and Gilbert Lawall, *Theocritus' Coan Pastorals* (Washington, D.C.: Center for Hellenic Studies, 1967).

13. See *Greek Bucolic Poets*, trans. Edmonds.

14. Virgil, *Works*, trans. H. Rushton Fairclough, Loeb Classical Library, 2 vols. (London: Heinemann, 1916–18). All subsequent quotations from Virgil refer to this edition. For various modern readings, see Bruno Snell, *The Discovery of Mind*, trans. Thomas Rosenmeyer (Oxford: Oxford University Press, 1953); Michael Putnam, *Virgil's Pastoral Art* (Princeton, N.J.: Princeton University Press, 1970); and Paul Alpers, *The Singer of the Eclogues* (Berkeley: University of California Press, 1979).

15. All references to Calpurnius and Nemesianus are to *Minor Latin Poets*, trans. J. Wight Duff, Loeb Classical Library (London: Heinemann, 1934).

16. All references to Dante are to *Opere*, ed. Michele Barbi et al. (Florence: Società Dantesca, 1960). For Neo-Latin pastoral in Italy see Enrico Carrara, *La poesia pastorale* (Milan: F. Vallardi, 1909); in Europe as a whole see W. Leonard Grant, *Neo-Latin Literature and the Pastoral* (Chapel Hill: University of North Carolina Press, 1965).

17. References to Francis Petrarch, *Bucolicum Carmen*, trans. Thomas Bergin (New Haven, Conn.: Yale University Press, 1974).

18. Longus, *Daphnis and Chloe*, trans. George Thornley, Loeb Classical Library (London: Heinemann, 1916).

19. See *Tutte le opere di Boccaccio*, ed. Vittore Branca et al; 17 vols. (Milan: Mondadori, 1964–76); the *Ameto* is available in the edition of Nicola Bruscoli (Bari: Laterza, 1940); for Sannazaro's debt to Boccaccio see Francesco Torraca, *La materia dell'Arcadia* (Città di Castello: S. Lapi, 1888).

20. For a brief overview of the Petrarchan tradition, see William J. Kennedy, *Rhetorical Norms in Renaissance Literature* (New Haven, Conn.: Yale University Press, 1978), pp. 20–78; for incisive commentary on Petrarch's

poetry and the model that it created see Mariann Regan, *Love Words: The Self and the Text in Medieval and Renaissance Poetry* (Ithaca, N.Y.: Cornell University Press, 1982), pp. 184–222, and Greene, *The Light in Troy*, pp. 81–146.

21. Petrarch, *Rime*, ed. F. Neri (Milan: Ricciardi, 1951).

22. Benedetto Gareth, il Cariteo, *Le Rime*, ed. Erasmo Pèrcopo (Naples: Accademia delle Scienze, 1892). For the background of fifteenth-century Neapolitan poetry by Cariteo, Caracciolo, and Aloisio, see Marco Santagata, *La lirica aragonese* (Padua: Antenore, 1979), pp. 296–341.

23. All quotations from Sannazaro's vernacular poetry refer to Iacobo Sannazaro, *Opere volgari*, ed. Alfredo Mauro (Bari: Laterza, 1961). In his notes to that superb edition Mauro records the variants that I cite. Because publication of the *Rime* was posthumous, it is difficult to determine whether the variants in subsequent editions owed to manuscript evidence or to the authority of Sannazaro's literary executors or to the intervention of editors and printers. The closest study of the problem is Pier Vincenzo Mengaldo, "La lirica volgare del Sannazaro," *Rassegna della Letteratura Italiana* 66 (1962), 436–82. Mengaldo argues that editors based their revisions on sound manuscript evidence; see especially pp. 473–74.

24. See below, pp. 99–100, 109–14.

25. In footnotes to his splendid edition of Sannazaro's Italian works, Alfredo Mauro asserts that Sannazaro collected, reworked, and even completely rewrote the lyrics of his youth after his return to Naples in 1504; see pp. 445–52. Mauro speculates that their division into two parts reflects Petrarch's division in reverse order: the first part laments the death of a young beloved, while the second part depicts a mature, more complex relationship with another woman, presumably Cassandra Marchese. The evidence is thin, however. A more detailed analysis of dating and structure is Carlo Dionisotti, "Appunti sulle rime del Sannazaro," *Giornale Storico della Letteratura Italiana* 140 (1963), 161–211. Dionisotti claims that "sestodecim'anno" of Sonnet XCVIII refers to the political catastrophe of 1494, and accordingly assigns the *Rime*'s composition to 1478–94. Their present arrangement in the form published after the poet's death in 1530 hardly reflects any consistent intention. Though the second part builds towards a political and religious climax, the first part remains without design. Dionisotti suggests that the first part may offer a sampler of Sannazaro's early work, while the second part sketches a dramatic narrative that Sannazaro never fully achieved; see pp. 173–75.

26. Propertius, *Elegies*, trans. H. E. Butler, Loeb Classical Library (London: Heineman, 1912).

27. Dionisotti speculates that Sannazaro composed the sestina later than the other *Rime* as an introduction to the sequence; see "Appunti sulle rime del Sannazaro," pp. 175–76.

28. All quotations from Sannazaro, *Opere volgari*, ed. Mauro. See also Francesco Torraca, *Studi di storia letteraria napoletana* (Livorno: F. Vigo, 1884), pp. 263–78, and G. M. Monti, "Tre farse," *Archivum Romanicum* 11 (1927), 177–209. For royal spectacles in England with relevance for continental forms, see Stephen Orgel, *The Illusion of Power* (Berkeley: University of California Press, 1975).

29. For the form, see Hoyt Hudson, *The Epigram in the English Renaissance* (Princeton, N.J.: Princeton University Press, 1947). For commentary on Renaissance Neo-Latin poetry see Paul Van Tieghem, *La Littérature latine de la Renaissance* (Paris: E. Droz, 1944); Leo Spitzer, "The Problem of Latin Renaissance Poetry," *Studies in the Renaissance* 2 (1955), 118–38; John Sparrow, "Latin Verse of the High Renaissance," in *Italian Renaissance Studies*, ed. Ernest Fraser Jacob (London: Faber and Faber, 1960), pp. 354–409; and Francesco Tateo, "La poesia latina del rinascimento," *Cultura e Scuola* 10 (1964), 13–21. For older views see Benedetto Croce, "La poesia latina," *Poesia popolare e poesia d'arte* (Bari: Laterza, 1967), pp. 442–90, and Augusto Sainati, *La lirica latina del Rinascimento* (Pisa: Spoerri, 1919); the last is most extravagant in its praise of Sannazaro as the most personal, interior, and imaginative Neo-Latin poet, pp. 163 ff. For indispensable aids, see Jozef Ijsewijn, *Companion to Neo-Latin Studies* (Amsterdam: North Holland, 1977). For the pioneering Renaissance epigrams of Panormita, see the modern anthologies of Florence Gragg, *Latin Writings of the Italian Humanists* (New York: Scribners, 1927); and Francesco Arnaldi et al., *Poeti latini del Quattrocento* (Milan: Ricciardi, 1964), with facing Italian translations. For accomplished Neo-Latin epigrams by Sannazaro's friend, Marullus, see the anthologies of Gragg and Arnaldi, as well as Alessandro Perosa and John Sparrow, *Renaissance Latin Verse* (Chapel Hill: University of North Carolina Press, 1979); and Fred J. Nichols, *An Anthology of Neo-Latin Poetry* (New Haven, Conn.: Yale University Press, 1979), with facing English translations. See also I. D. McFarlane, *Renaissance Latin Poetry* (Manchester: Manchester University Press, 1980).

30. *Opera Latina Scripta ex Secundis Curis Jani Broukhusii* (Amsterdam: Gerard Onder, 1728); I refer to it for those epigrams expurgated from all Italian editions since 1535.

31. *Le Opere volgari di M. J. Sannazaro* (Padua: Giuseppe Comino, 1723), p. 413.

32. For dating, see Antonio Altamura, *La tradizione manoscritta dei carmina del Sannazaro* (Naples: Silvio Viti, 1957).

33. Quotations from Jacopo Sannazaro, *Egloghe, elegie, odi, epigrammi*, ed. Giorgio Castello (Milan: Carlo Signorelli, 1928), supplemented by the Amsterdam edition of 1728. In numbering the epigrams, I give first the Amsterdam number, then the corresponding one in Castello thus: I.13 (Amsterdam)/11 (Castello).

34. For a survey of the ode see Carol Maddison, *Apollo and the Nine* (Baltimore, Md.: John Hopkins University Press, 1960), and for Horace, Michael O'Loughlin, *The Garlands of Repose* (Chicago: University of Chicago Press, 1978).

35. For metrical subtleties see James Halporn, Martin Ostwald, and Thomas Rosenmeyer, *The Meters of Greek and Latin Poetry* (Indianapolis, Ind.: Bobbs-Merrill, 1963).

36. Quotations from Sannazaro, *Egloghe, elegie, odi, epigrammi*, ed. Castello.

37. For a survey of the form see Georg Luck, *The Latin Love Elegy* (London: Methuen, 1959).

38. For selections from Pontano see Gragg, *Latin Writings*, Arnaldi et al.,

Poeti latini, Perosa and Sparrow, *Renaissance Latin Verse*, Nichols, *Anthology*, and McFarlane, *Renaissance Latin Poetry*. For criticism see Ettore Paratore, *La poesia di Giovanni Pontano* (Rome: Ateneo, 1967).

39. See Altamura, *La tradizione manoscritta*, p. 54.

40. Quotations from Sannazaro, *Egloghe, Elegie, odi, epigrammi*, ed. Castello.

41. See Altamura, *Jacopo Sannazaro*, pp. 137–39.

42. See M. M. Crump, *The Epyllion from Theocritus to Ovid* (Baltimore, Md.: Johns Hopkins University Press, 1931), and Clark Hulse, *Metamorphic Verse* (Princeton, N.J. Princeton University Press, 1981).

43. Quotations from Sannazaro, *Egloghe, Elegie, odi, epigrammi*, ed. Castello.

44. See Thomas M. Greene, "The Life and Death of Solitude," *Studies in Philology*, 70 (1973), 123–40.

CHAPTER 2

1. See Alfredo Mauro, "Le prime edizione dell'*Arcadia*," *Giornale Italiano di Filologia* 2 (1949), 341–51. An earlier edition, now lost, may have appeared in 1501.

2. See Maria Corti, "Le tre redazioni della '*Pastorale*' di P. J. De Jennaro," *Giornale Storico della Letteratura Italiana* 131 (1954), 305–51. For the complete *Arcadia*'s aesthetic unity see Eduardo Saccone, "Storia e delineamento d'una struttura" in his essays on *Il "soggetto" del Furioso e altri saggi* (Naples: Liguori, 1974).

3. See Corti, "Le tre redazioni," and Domenico De Robertis, "L'esperienza poetica del Quattrocento," in Emilio Cecchi and Natalino Sapegno, eds., *Storia della letteratura italiana*, 8 vols. (Milan: Garzanti, 1966), III, 357–784; De Robertis provides a succinct account of the textual history, pp. 728–32.

4. See Gianfranco Folena, *La crisi linguistica del quattrocento e l'Arcadia* (Florence: Olschki, 1952); and Maria Corti, "L'impasto linguistico dell'Arcadia," *Studi di Filologia Italiana* 22 (1964), 594–619. For sixteenth-century language see Cesare Segre, *Lingua, stile, e società* (Milan: Feltrinelli, 1963), pp. 355–82; Carlo Dionisotti, *Geografia e storia della letteratura* (Turin: Einaudi, 1967); and Bruno Migliorini, *The Italian Language*, trans. T. G. Griffith (New York: Barnes and Noble, 1966). Sara Sturm, *Lorenzo de'Medici* (New York: G. K. Hall, 1974), pp. 25–34, is also helpful.

5. All translations refer to Jacopo Sannazaro, *Arcadia and the Piscatorial Eclogues*, trans. Ralph Nash (Detroit, Mich.: Wayne State University Press, 1966); the original refers to Iacobo Sannazaro, *Opere volgari*, ed. Alfredo Mauro, (Bari: Laterza, 1961). For prose passages I indicate first Nash, then Mauro, thus: (29 [Nash] / 3 [Mauro]); for poetry passages I specify only the number of the eclogue and the line of verse thus: (I.10).

6. For the development of pastoral after Sannazaro, see Helen Cooper, *Pastoral: Medieval into Renaissance* (Totowa, N.J.: Rowman and Littlefield, 1977); Mia Gerhardt, *Essai d'analyse littéraire de la pastorale* (Assen: Van Gorcum, 1950); and Ellen Zetzel Lambert, *Placing Sorrow* (Chapel Hill: University of North Carolina Press, 1976). For Sannazaro's influence outside Italy, see

Francesco Torraca, *Gl'imitatori stranieri di Sannazaro* (Rome, Loescher, 1882). There are particularly illuminating comparative analyses in David Kalstone, *Sidney's Poetry* (Cambridge, Mass.: Harvard University Press, 1965), pp. 22–39, and Clay Hunt, *Lycidas and the Italian Critics* (New Haven, Conn.: Yale University Press, 1979), p. 28–40.

7. Quoted in Jacopo Sannazaro, *Arcadia* ed. Michele Scherillo (Turin: Ermanno Loescher, 1888), pp. cclxvi–cclxvii.

8. See the excellent stylistic studies by Domenico De Robertis, "L'esperienza poetica," pp. 732–40; Gianfranco Folena, *La crisi linguistica*, passim; and Fredi Chiappelli, "Sulla lingua di Sannazaro," *Vox romanica* 13 (1953), 40–50. For prose style, see Giorgio Petrocchi, *Sannazaro e la prosa narrativa del Quattrocento* (Rome: De Santis, 1966).

9. All references to the early text are to *Arcadia di Jacopo Sannazaro secondo i manoscritti e le prime stampe*, ed. Michele Scherillo (Turin: Ermanno Loescher 1888); based on the manuscript of 1489, this edition indicates revisions in the printings of 1502, 1504, and 1514, and notes sources and influences; for other good notes see *Opere di Jacopo Sannazaro*, ed. Enrico Carrara (Turin: UTET, 1952), based on Summonte's printing of 1504.

10. Reprinted in *Le opere volgari di M. J. Sannazaro* (Padua: Giuseppe Comino, 1723, p. 322.

11. All references to which these commentaries apply are to the Padua edition of 1723. I specify the commentator and the page of the reference thus: (Massarengo, p. 205). Translations are mine. For close readings of whole poems in the Renaissance see Lowry Nelson, Jr., "Renaissance Codes of Interpretation: The Lyric," *Actes du VIIIe Congrès de l'Association Internationale de Littérature Comparée* (Budapest: Akademiai Kiado, 1981), pp. 113–17.

12. For Sannazaro's achievements with late fifteenth-century forms, see two superb essays by Maria Corti, "Il codice bucolico" and "Rivoluzione e reazione stilistica nel Sannazaro" in her *Metodi e fantasmi* (Milan: Feltrinelli, 1969), pp. 281–323. For an older view that judges them less successful, see Attilio Momigliano, *Studi di poesia* (Bari: Laterza 1938), pp. 40–57. For a detailed analysis of Sannazaro's pastoral in the social and literary contexts of late fifteenth-century Naples, see Marco Santagata, *La lirica aragonese* (Padua: Antenore, 1979), pp. 342–74.

13. For Sannazaro's prose see Giorgia Petrocchi, *Sannazaro e la prosa narrative del Quattrocento* (Rome: De Santis, 1966).

14. For a good analysis, see Lambert, *Placing Sorrow*, pp. 89–98.

15. For a strained psychoanalytical approach to these motifs through Jungean myths, see Vittorio Gajetti, *Edipo in Arcadia* (Naples: Guida, 1977), pp. 75–90.

16. In a historical reading, the tree could stand for the royal house of Naples, recently uprooted by foreign invasions in 1495 and 1501; see the commentary in *Arcadia*, ed. Scherillo, pp. clxxvi–ccviii, and also Vittorio Rossi, *Il Quattrocento*, 5th ed. (Milan: Vallardi, 1953), pp. 507–8.

CHAPTER 3

1. See Antonio Altamura, *La tradizione manoscritta dei carmina del Sanna-zaro* (Naples: Silvio Viti, 1957), p. 54.

2. See Battista Spagnolo, *Eclogues*, trans. Lee Piepho (Binghamton, N.Y.: CMERS, 1983).

3. For the *Meliseus* see Fred J. Nichols, *An Anthology of Neo-Latin Poetry* (New Haven, Conn.: Yale University Press, 1979), pp. 128–41. For dirges see J. B. Trapp, "The Poet and the Monumental Impulse," Society for Renaissance Studies: Occasional Papers no. 6 (1980), 1–20.

4. See Francesco Arnaldi, *Poeti latini del Quattrocento* (Milan: Ricciardi, 1964), pp. 316–93.

5. For a fuller account see William J. Kennedy, "The Virgilian Legacies of Petrarch's *Bucolicum Carmen* and Spenser's *Shepheardes Calender*,: ACTA: Congress of Center for Medieval and Early Renaissance Studies (Albany, N.Y.: State University of New York Press, 1984).

6. This quotation refers to Cristoforo Landino, *Scritti critici e teorici*, ed. Roberto Cardini, 2 vols. (Rome: Bulzoni, 1974), I.222.

7. Quotations from Juan Luis Vives refer to *Opera*, reprint of the 1782 Monfort edition, 8 vols. (London: Gregg Press,1964), here quoted from II.32. For the Christianizing of pagan pastoral elegy see Ellen Zetzel Lambert, *Placing Sorrow* (Chapel Hill: University of North Carolina Press, 1976), pp. 52 ff.

8. Quotations from Landino's commentary refer to *Publii Vergilii Bucolica, Georgica, Aeneis*, with the commentaries of Servius, Donatus, Probus, and Cristoforo Landino (Venice: Bernardino Stagnin, 1507), here quoted from sig. Diiᵛ. This edition contains the first printing of Probus's commentary. For an exposition of Landino's "negative" method of commentary adumbrated in this passage, see Michael Murrin, *The Allegorical Epic* (Chicago: University of Chicago Press, 1980), pp. 27–50.

9. Quotations from Antonius Mancinellus refer to *Opera Virgiliana cum decem commentis*: Servius, Mancinellus, et al (Lyons: J. Crespin, 1529), here quoted from p. LVIII.

10. Quotations from Badius Ascensius are from the same Crespin edition, p. LVI.

11. References to Pierius Valerianus are to the same Crespin edition, p. LVII.

12. Petrarch's notations are reproduced in *Francisci Petrarcae Vergilianus Codex*, eds. Giovanni Galbiati and Achille Ratti (Milan: Hoepli, 1930), here quoted from Sig. 7ᵛ.

13. Quotations from Jacopo Sannazaro, *Piscatory Eclogues* , ed. Wilfred P. Mustard (Baltimore, Md.: John Hopkins University Press, 1914); translations from Jacopo Sannazaro, *Arcadia and the Piscatory Eclogues*, trans. Ralph Nash (Detroit, Mich.: Wayne State University Press, 1966).

14. Quoted in Mustard, ed., p. 80.

15. See A. Bartlett Giamatti, "Proteus Unbound," in *The Disciplines of*

Criticism, ed. Peter Demetz et al. (New Haven, Conn.: Yale University Press, 1968), pp. 437–76.

16. Quotations from *Opera di M. J. Sannazaro*, (Venice: Francesco de Franciscis, 1593); the poem has not been reprinted since 1768.

17. See Altamura, *La tradizione manoscritta*, p. 20.

18. The letters are printed in Sannazaro, *Opere Volgari*, ed. Mauro; for annotations see *Un divorzio ai tempi di Leone X da XL lettere inedite di Jacopo Sannazaro*, ed. Ettore Nunziante (Rome: Loreto Pasqualucci, 1887).

19. John Milton, *Complete Poetry and Selected Prose*, ed. Merritt Hughes (New York: Odyssey Press, 1957), p. 668.

20. Louis Martz, *Poet of Exile*, (New Haven, Conn.: Yale University Press, 1980), p. 254.

21. Marco Girolamo Vida, *Christiad*, trans. Gertrude C. Drake and Clarence Forbes (Carbondale: Southern Illinois University Press, 1978); see Mario Di Cesare, *Vida's "Christiad" and Virgilian Epic* (New York: Columbia University Press, 1964). For fine appreciation of Virgil's epic technique see Mario Di Cesare, *The Altar and the City* (New York: Columbia University Press, 1974).

22. For a thorough study of the midrashic tradition, see Raymond E. Brown, *The Birth of the Messiah* (Garden City, N.Y.: Doubleday, 1977).

23. Quotations from Jacopo Sannazaro, *De Partu Virginis*, ed. Antonio Altamura (Naples: Gaspare Casella, 1948).

24. See Thomas M. Greene, *The Descent from Heaven* (New Haven, Conn.: Yale University Press, 1963), pp. 144–70 for a superb reading of the passage.

25. See Giulia Calisti, *Saggio sul poema sacro nel Rinascimento* (Città di Castello: 1926.), for the influence of Mantuan's *Parthenice I* on the characterizations of Mary and Elizabeth.

26. References are to the *Novum Testamentum Graece et Latine*, ed. Eberhard Nestle (Stuttgart: Würtembergische Bibelanstalt, 1906).

27. For the influence of the dramatic "*sacre rappresentazioni*" on the iconography of the nativity scene, see Calisti, *Saggio sul poema sacro*, pp. 73–79.

28. For Virgilian echoes in Proteus's speech see Calisti, *Saggio sul poema sacro*, pp. 45–52. In "Sannazaro and Milton's Brief Epic," *Comparative Literature* 20 (1968), 116–32, Stewart A. Baker discusses the pastoral metaphors animating this and other key episodes in the poem.

29. Hans-Georg Gadamer, *Truth and Method* (New York: Seabury Press, 1975), pp. 267ff. (original German edition, 1960).

30. *Ciceronianus*, trans. Scott, New York: Columbia University Teachers College Press, 1908), p. 118.

Index